INTERPERSONAL BEHAVIOR

INTERPERSONAL BEHAVIOR

History and Practice of Personality Theory

ROBERT C. CARSON

ALDINETRANSACTION
A Division of Transaction Publishers
New Brunswick (U.S.A.) and London (U.K.)

Sixth paperback edition 2010
Originally published in 1969 by Robert C. Carson.

This book is printed on acid-free paper that meets the American National Standard for Permanence of Paper for Printed Library Materials.

Library of Congress Catalog Number: 2009036898
ISBN: 978-0-202-36325-7
Printed in the United States of America

Library of Congress Cataloging-in-Publication Data

Carson, Robert C., 1930-
Interpersonal behavior : history and practice of personality theory / Robert C. Carson.
p. cm.
Originally published: Interaction concepts of personality. Chicago : Aldine Pub. Co., [1969]
Includes bibliographical references and index.
ISBN 978-0-202-36325-7 (alk. paper)
1. Interpersonal relations. 2. Personality. I. Title.

HM1106.C373 2009
302--dc22

2009036898

Foreword

It is particularly gratifying to me that the first of a projected series of publications on contemporary personality theory should be Robert Carson's integration of transactional theories of human behavior. Theory in the social sciences in general and psychology in particular seems to move forward by means of an adversary procedure, which yields in time to a fruitful integration of two or more competing viewpoints. Carson's book effectively defines and persuasively defends a position that thus far has not received the attention it deserves. There are probably many advantages in this open and vigorous competition of ideas, for only a committed believer in a particular point of view can present it with conviction, defend it zealously, and yield his position only grudgingly in the face of compelling evidence. A less than devoted defense of a theory is conducive to a bland eclecticism that stultifies rather than stimulates rigorous analysis and productive research. If for example everyone had graciously acknowledged that nature and nurture are no doubt equally contributory to any given pattern of behavior, we would not have had the impressive yield of illuminating investigations from geneticists, ethologists, and laboratory experimentalists who have generated very strong partisan views on the issue.

The notion that significant individual behavioral characteristics are as much a product of particular social interactions as the expression of personality "types" is not altogether new. At the same time, it is a position that has not been vigorously and systematically advanced and defended in competition with other viewpoints. Our intuitive approach to concepts of personality dictates assigning durable characteristics to others for it is most important in the conduct of our daily activities to be able to count on relative stability of behavior from those on whom we depend. Life would be unbearably complicated if every encounter were uncertain and problematic. Hence it is more than a convenience, it is a necessity, to develop rough normative data on the behavior of significant others and then assume that there will be little departure from the mode. It is easier once our assessment is made to decide that A is always "irresponsible," B is always "serious and hardworking," C is generally "irritable," and D is uniformly "kind, cheerful, and helpful."

Since science, in its early stages at least, is merely a systematic examination of intuitively generated premises, it is not surprising that theories of personality have tended first to focus on the elucidation of those dependable characteristics that are found "inside" the individual.

Given our propensity for seeing others as having relatively immutable traits, it seems awkward and inconvenient to add a situational notation each time we make an attribution to them. Moreover, we lack not only an adequate formal taxonomy of demands inherent in social situations, but even an elaborated vocabulary in common use applicable to interpersonal transactions. Thousands of words describing personality traits can be found in the English language, yet those descriptive of commonplace social interactions are few indeed. It is difficult to believe that Berne could have created as much excitement as he did with his delineation of a limited number of interpersonal "games" were it not that he was focusing our attention on an aspect of our experience that is very real and poignant but simply ignored because we have lacked a convenient vocabulary and frame of reference to record it.

This book, then, is important because it forces our attention to the fact that attributions to others are incomplete without reference to the circumstances in which a particular behavior occurs. Moreover, Carson states clearly that while personality characteristics may not be ephemeral, any observed stability is necessarily the product of whatever propensities may be said with accuracy and confidence to be "inside" the person and the interpersonal situation in which they are expressed. Ordinarily we pay attention mainly to interpersonal events that confirm our stable expectations. Carson urges us to examine more carefully the effect of noncomplementarity on supposedly stable personality characteristics.

The author introduces us to the principal interpersonal theorists in a series of expository chapters that are both lucid and authoritative. In the concluding chapters, however, his long experience as a clinical psychologist enables him to make an unusually telling application of interaction concepts of personality to the field of mental and emotional "illness." Carson makes clear that while most of us have struggled along despite an incomplete understanding of the social parameters in behavior theory, many people designated as "mental patients" have suffered very real harm as a consequence of being perceived as having a "diseased" personality rather than as individuals who, under certain circumstances, behave deviantly.

He asserts, as others have, that institutions and treatments often seem designed to perpetuate deviant behavior rather than modify it. What Carson adds to this critique is a well-developed concept of treatment aimed at changing the social behavior—the interpersonal style—that has led to a psychiatric diagnosis. In propounding a psychotherapy that avoids the medical "disease model," he does not adopt a position that rules out, as some radical behaviorists would propose, significant internal processes. Rather, the author attempts to define a practice that demonstrates what he set out to do in the first place: to underline in detail the impossibility of separating the individual from his social matrix if we wish to comprehend and eventually modify human behavior.

Ralph W. Heine

ACKNOWLEDGMENTS

Most of this book was written during a sabbatical leave spent with the social psychology section of the Department of Psychology, University of North Carolina at Chapel Hill. I am deeply indebted to that department and university for the physical resources they provided me, and to my immediate colleagues during the year—Thomas D. Cook, Chester A. Insko, John Schopler, and John Thibaut—for the warm and stimulating work atmosphere they created. Whatever merit this book may possess is due in large measure to the extraordinary intellectual quality of the environment in which it was conceived and written. The year was supported in part by a United States Public Health Service Special Research Fellowship award to the author (#1-F3-MH-35, 994-01) through the agency of the National Institute of Mental Health. I am grateful for this material support of my efforts.

Various publishers graciously extended permission for me to reproduce copyrighted material. These include The William Alanson White Psychiatric Foundation, The American Psychiatric Association, the *American Journal of Psychotherapy,* The New York State Department of Mental Hygiene, Psychologists Interested in the Advancement of Psychotherapy, W. W. Norton & Co., The Ronald Press, The Williams & Wilkins Co., John Wiley & Sons, and the McGraw-Hill Book Company. I am grateful to all of these organizations and also to the American Psychological Association, whose liberal policy with respect to copyrighted material rendered unnecessary specific requests for permission to reproduce brief passages from certain of their publications.

Thomas D. Cook, Chester A. Insko, Charles Kronberg, Harold G. McCurdy, Terry G. Vance, and Mary Carson, my wife, each read and commented upon specific portions of the manuscript as it was being written. Their encouragement and help was invaluable. I owe a special debt of gratitude to Barbara S. Gold and John Thibaut, who read and made editorial suggestions on virtually the whole of the manuscript. It was thereby very materially improved in readability and semantic precision. I, of course, accept full responsibility for whatever shortcomings the final version may have.

I had not intended to write this or any other book at the outset of my academic leave. It owes its existence to the series editor, Ralph Heine, and to Alexander Morin of the Aldine Publishing Company. On the basis of an incredibly vague statement of what I thought I *might* do, these gentlemen offered prompt acceptance and strong encouragement, giving me a completely free hand to develop the book in whatever way I saw fit. I hope that their faith has been in some measure vindicated.

Finally, I extend thanks to my typists, Judy Edquist and Edna Bissette, for their alert and skillful production of the final copy.

R. C. C.

Contents

CHAPTER 1

Introduction

This book represents an excursion—or, to use a perhaps slightly more dignified term, an inquiry—into an area of human behavior at once fascinating and exasperating. Fascinating because it is a class of behavior that, while peculiarly resistant to cognitive analysis and clarification, is nevertheless for most of us the subjectively crucial issue throughout our lives. It is exasperating for the same reasons. It is with some humility, then, that I have attempted herein to analyze, describe, and to some extent explain the transactions that occur between persons. As will shortly become clear, I think that in so doing we can account for a great deal of what is ordinarily meant by the term *personality*. The analysis focuses upon the smallest possible unit of social interaction, the dyad, or two-person group, because to do otherwise would severely tax the author's—if not the reader's—capacity for scholarship and abstract thought. Insofar as any larger group of persons is reducible to dyadic units, the concepts examined here might have a greater range of applicability, but we will generally ignore these more extended implications.

The reader with some knowledge of personality theory will already know that the major intellectual forebear of this book is the eminent American psychiatrist and social scientist Harry Stack Sullivan (1892–1949), whose thinking we will have occasion to consider in some detail in Chapter 2. This is, however, only in small degree a book about Sullivan's theories. It is his fundamental conception of personality in terms of interpersonal processes, in the broadest sense, with which we are mainly concerned. Beyond that, an attempt will be made to reformulate Sullivanian conceptions into a more systematic framework, one more firmly tied to observable events, or at least to empirically testable hypotheses. This is a project, it might be noted, of which Sullivan himself would almost certainly have approved. It should be acknowledged at the outset, however, that, despite rapid advances in the social sciences in the past two decades, the goal is an exceedingly ambitious one and will necessarily fall considerably short of complete success. We are in an area of the most intimidating complexity, where empirically valid generalizations are not easily established or formulated, and where investigators are themselves a long way from the development of a commonly shared language and concept-system. To some extent, this book represents an integrative effort. It is an eclectic selection of concepts and relevant empirical findings that seem to provide a relatively systematic, although incomplete, account of socially significant personal conduct.

Sullivan was fundamentally a clinician, and so am I. It may be appropriate, therefore, to provide the reader with a brief example of the kind of observation of behavior—readily accessible to any clinician, and indeed to many who are not—that is likely to lead one to think of personality in interpersonal terms. The example will also serve as a useful reference point to illustrate concepts to be introduced later. I have chosen the example from Sullivan, whose inimitable style of clinical description surpasses anything that I could offer from my own experience. Sullivan is here introducing some comments about what he calls the "hysteric dynamism":

> Let us say that a man (call him Mr. X) with a strong hysterical predisposition has married, perhaps for money, and that his wife, thanks to his rather dramatic and exaggerated way of doing and saying things, cannot long remain in doubt

that there was a very practical consideration in this marriage and cannot completely blind herself to a certain lack of importance that she has in her husband's eyes. So she begins to get even. She may, for example, like someone I recently saw, develop a never-failing vaginismus, so that there is no more intercourse for him. And he will not ruminate on whether this vaginismus that is cutting off his satisfaction is directed against him, for the very simple reason that if you view interpersonal phenomena with that degree of objectivity, you can't use an hysterical process to get rid of your own troubles. So he won't consider that; but he will suffer terribly from privation and will go to rather extravagant lengths to overcome the vaginismus that is depriving him of satisfaction, the lengths being characterized by a certain rather theatrical attention to detail rather than deep scrutiny of his wife. But he fails again and again. Then one night, when he is worn out, and perhaps has had a precocious ejaculation in his newest adventure in practical psychotherapy, he has the idea, "My God, this thing is driving me crazy," and goes to sleep.

Now the idea, "This thing is driving me crazy," is the happy idea that I say the hysteric has. He wakes up at some early hour in the morning, probably at the time when his wife is notoriously most soundly asleep, and he has a frightful attack of some kind. It could be literally almost anything, but it will be very impressive to anyone around. His wife will be awakened, very much frightened, and will call the doctor. But before the doctor gets there, the husband, with a fine sense of dramatic values, will let her know in some indirect way that he's terribly afraid he is losing his mind. She is reduced to a really agitated state by that. So when the doctor comes, the wife is in enough distress—in part because of whatever led to her vaginismus—to wonder if she might lose her own mind, and the husband is showing a good many odd symptoms. And the doctor probably doesn't know anything about losing minds anyway, and so he begins to wonder if he is going to lose *his* mind. But presently things quiet down.

Now let us say that the doctor in this case is a high-grade

> but somewhat inexperienced psychiatrist and that he sets out to get the history of the immediate situation from which this business grew. He might get an awful lot of details—details about distressing situations in the office, the terrible strain that the husband has been under from the pressure of his work—all of them within the limits of ordinary human plausibility as a basis for a quite nervous condition. And, of course, he would learn how very useful the wife has been in sort of protecting the husband from these things and in giving him as much rest and quiet as possible. But there will be no comment about anything else—no faintest suspicion of anything the least bit out of the way in the sex life. Even if our somewhat inexperienced psychiatrist, suspecting that there is possibly something a little bit off in the sex life somewhere, pushes hard in that area, he won't get any very good leads. So he will probably prescribe sedatives and a rest or a change of scene or some other damn thing, and hope for the best. (Sullivan, 1956, pp. 204–206) [1]

What is going on here? With the benefit of Sullivan's notable abilities as a raconteur, the general outlines are fairly clear. We see a mutually punitive interaction, in which Mrs. X retaliates with satisfaction-deprivation for her husband's exploitative indifference to her, and is herself victimized by her husband in counter-retaliation. This entire transaction takes place on a level of communication where it is unnecessary, and perhaps impossible, for the parties involved to acknowledge their participation. Even a reasonably sophisticated third party, as Sullivan notes, might not be able to identify readily the particular interactional patterns of this marital situation. And this despite the fact that interpersonal difficulties of this order of magnitude are, generally speaking, relatively transparent.

The disorders of interpersonal relations that are likely to come to the attention of professional helpers are magnified, so to speak, and therefore more readily observable than the more subtle trans-

1. Reprinted from *Clinical Studies in Psychiatry* by Harry Stack Sullivan, M.D., by permission of W. W. Norton & Company, Inc. Copyright © 1956 by the William Alanson White Psychiatric Foundation.

actions that characterize all of our daily lives. It is probably for this reason that most of the major systems of personality theory, including the interpersonal, have had their origins in clinical practice. It is for this reason too that many of the illustrations provided in this book depict "clinical" phenomena. But the reader should be alert that illustrations of concepts, however dramatic, do not constitute proof of the utility or validity of those concepts, a point that has seldom been appreciated in the literature of personality theory. We shall have to be wary of the seductive but logically weak tendency to attribute validity to an idea on the basis of a seemingly compelling, and perhaps esoteric, anecdote from real life. Scientific rules of evidence are generally more stringent, and we shall strive here to approximate these more stringent requirements.

Where does this leave us in regard to the case of Mr. and Mrs. X, who are, after all, mythical persons? In fact, this particular example was chosen partly because it is fiction, albeit one whose essential features occur commonly enough in the real world. The example is manifestly *not* offered as proof of anything, either here or on the subsequent occasions when we will refer to it. You will recall, rather, that the case of Mr. and Mrs. X was introduced as an example of a type of phenomenon which contributed very greatly to the development of interactional conceptions in the study of personality. With these caveats in mind, then, let us return very briefly to a consideration of this unfortunate couple. There are just one or two more points to be made.

It would appear that the essential causes of Mr. and Mrs. X's current difficulties with one another antedate the situation itself, and very probably even their first premarital encounter. We are given to understand that Mr. X is a generally self-absorbed and opportunistic person, and Sullivan suggests that Mrs. X had some prior propensity to react to the situation in the specific manner in which she did—that is, by having an attack of vaginismus which would abruptly terminate Mr. X's sexual satisfaction with her. Can it be that the presumably long-standing personal characteristics of these two persons were such as to insure beforehand the occurrence of the particular events recorded here, and that the events themselves are merely the natural and logical outcome of a sustained relationship between two such people? An affirmative answer to this question would not be completely erroneous, but the question is itself a deceptively oversimplified one. One wishes to know, for example, how these two persons convinced themselves to arrange their lives together in the institutionalized form of marriage, or what it is that energizes and maintains Mr. X's generalized orientation toward exploitation of others, or why Mrs. X "chooses" the particular form of retaliation she does, or simply why it is that the two of them seem unable or unwilling to clarify consensually what is going on between them, a clarification that might lead to a more objectively satisfactory accord. This is the level of question to which this entire book is addressed. For the present, we will leave Mr. and Mrs. X behind in order to prepare the groundwork for a more comprehensive and systematic perspective from which to view them.

Orientation and Rationale

Because this book departs somewhat from traditional treatments of the subject matter of personality, it seems necessary to give a measure of explicit attention to the predilections and assumptions that constitute its conceptual substrate. This discussion will also serve to delimit the scope and the principal analytical foci of the field of investigation to which our attention will be directed in the following pages.

THE NATURE OF PSYCHOLOGY

The definition of an intellectual discipline at any point in time is almost necessarily presumptuous, and for this reason there will be no formal attempt to do so here. The reader, however, may harbor definitions of his own, and I am more than a little concerned that these may be unduly restrictive, in which case some of what I want to say may run a considerable risk of being regarded as something other than psychology. Contemporary definitions of psychology almost invariably assert, in one way or another, that it is the study of behavior. Now, this is a quite reasonable definition, and it is one to which, as a matter of fact, I subscribe. Difficulties often arise, however, in the elucidation of this definition. The founding fathers of modern psychology, among whom there were some truly outstanding men, have, because of their efforts to build an objective science, exerted an unwarranted determining influence upon contemporary psychology and psychologists. The imposition of a rigid behaviorism in accounting for how organisms come to do whatever they do seems to me to be epistemologically unnecessary, an anachronism that has long since served its function of sensitizing us to the intellectual perils of "subjectivity" and "mentalistic" concepts. Behaviorism in its purest and most radical form—*exclusive* concern with overt, observable events—seems to me to insure a psychology that is sterile, especially in regard to *human* behavior, which is of course the focus of our attention. Some readers will undoubtedly feel that the uncompromising behaviorism described here is no longer a consequential force in psychology, hence undeserving of my attack. It is indeed true that the qualifications for being identified as a behaviorist have been relaxed considerably in recent years. Nevertheless, it seems necessary for me to be clear at the outset that an individual's reflections about his and others' behavior are significant data. I find it essential to examine a person's behavior *in the light of* his constructs of the events impinging on him.

Having said this, it now becomes necessary to introduce a correction factor at the other end, so to speak. I do not believe that a science can be founded on subjective, private experience. Ultimately, we do need the anchor of objective, publicly observable behavioral events. This requirement, however, does not preclude our making inferences about the subjective experiences and other unobservable aspects of the persons whose behavior we study; and we shall especially wish to do so when such inferences are helpful in explaining and predicting behavioral phenomena. It will be well, however, to be especially cautious about inferences of this kind, recognizing the temptation to substitute our own private experiences for those of our subjects.

THE NATURE OF PERSONALITY

The concept subsumed by the term *personality* is an ancient one, probably as old as man, *qua* man, himself. To what kinds of observations does it refer? Quite simply it refers to the regularities or consistencies that characterize a given individual's behavioral repertoire; these regularities are believed somehow to distinguish the individual as a person and to render his behavior predictable. Now, there are several ways in which behavioral regularity, consistency, or predictability might plausibly be explained, and virtually all of them have at one time or another been advanced as a theory of what we call personality. Let us consider some of these. Insects exhibit marked regularities in behavior on the basis of inherited capacities for reaction patterns. Is it possible that this is analogous to personality at the human level? But insects of a given species all seem to be pretty much alike, whereas we tend to associate personality with some degree of distinctiveness and individuality. In order to account for personality as an inherited reaction pattern, we would need to postulate some indeterminate number of possible inheritable patterns. This strategy has in fact been tried quite a number of times in the history of human thinking about personality, never with any great success in predicting or accounting for the behavior of persons.

One of the difficulties of the more simple varieties of what might be called inherited disposition theories of the origins of personality is that they tend to suggest a permanent and static quality—a relatively invariant structural foundation—for such regularity as may exist in the behavior of a person. We know from experience, however, that persons change throughout their lives, and that quite dramatic alterations of characteristic behavior may be brought about by radical changes in the "stimulus" circumstances of the external environment, in prisoner-of-war camps, for example. Observations of this kind have so impressed some theorists, indeed, that they have championed an almost diametrically opposite viewpoint on the nature of personality. According to this conception, such regularities as may exist in an individual's behavior arise not from any internal characteristics he may possess, but rather from the tendency of a person's environment to make uniform or consistent demands upon him. One form of this point of view, a sociological one, asserts that personality is nothing more than the constellation of a person's social roles. This is an intriguing approach, and in one form or another it has led to a great deal of creative research. We may ask, however, if it will account in itself for the range of phenomena with which we are concerned. The answer seems to be that it will not. Individual differences in behavior typically remain salient in the face of quite powerful and uniform environmental demand characteristics—in the military service, for example, or in rigidly disciplined, controlled schools. Even rigorous control of the environment, such as occurs in many psychological experiments, does not "wash out" idiosyncratic reactions, although the experimenter—quite legitimately—may for his purposes dismiss them as experimental "error."

Is there a middle ground? Yes there is, and at the risk of being called an incorrigible middle-of-the-roader, it is where I think we should be standing. The facts seem to require that we attribute a portion of the regularities in individual behavior to some form of relatively persistent dispositional tendencies existing "within" persons. These dispositional tendencies, variously conceived as traits, habits, "needs," and so forth, are in the main acquired in the course of experience rather than being innately determined, and they are subject to alteration as a consequence of new experience. But we must also acknowledge the power of the immediate situation as an influence upon behavior. Even the most inveterate and irrepressible clown may be reduced to appropriate somberness at the funeral of his dear old grandmother, however unconcerned about her he may have been prior to her demise.

I think we can now state a general principle, one which represents a fundamental idea underlying the whole of this book. It was first formulated explicitly, I believe, by Kurt Lewin (1935). It is this: *a person's behavior in any situation is jointly determined by the characteristics of that situation, as he perceives them, and by the particular behavioral dispositions of which he is possessed at that time.* If this seems very simple and obvious to you—merely an elegantly stated cliché—you lack the proper set for reading this book critically. It is, indeed, a widely accepted notion that behavior is the resultant of intra-individual and environmental forces—in Lewin's terms, $B = f(P, E)$. However, the concrete elucidation of this seemingly simple formulation is extremely difficult; I hope to persuade the reader to empathize with my efforts to invest this long-standing abstraction with more meaning for the typical student of personality than it now has.

THE FIELD OF INQUIRY

Our goal is to understand, insofar as possible, the behavior of persons, and more particularly the behavior of persons in relation to other persons. We shall not be concerned with the fine details of this behavior, such as the form of particular muscle contractions or of autonomic nervous system responses, except to the extent that they may aid in an understanding of a given social transaction. We are dealing, then, with what Tolman (1932) has termed *molar* (as opposed to *molecular*) behavior, the significant activities of individuals as they go about the business of living. We shall also not be concerned with what individuals do when they are not engaged in interpersonal relations, although we shall argue that the mere physical absence of others does not preclude their having an influence on an actor. To insure that the reader is properly introduced to the author's perspective on several key problems with which we will be fairly persistently engaged, the remainder of this chapter is devoted to a brief introduction to these issues.

Some Fundamental Issues

Our goal, stated in somewhat different terms, is that of achieving an understanding of the regularities and redundancies in the pattern of an individual's relations with other persons. We have suggested that in order to do so we will find it necessary to take into account not only those dispositional tendencies of the person, but also the characteristics of the particular situation in which he finds himself. In many cases, of course, the most important of these situational characteristics will consist of the behaviors of the other person, which are themselves the product of *his* dispositional tendencies *and* the situation, including the behavior of the first person. If you are beginning to sense that you are being ineluctably drawn into something akin to a multidimensional chess game your intuition is correct. It is pointless to attempt to treat simply a process that is inherently complex; it *is* very complicated, and I am afraid it is going to get a bit worse before I can promise much improvement.

THE PROBLEM OF PERCEPTION

You may have noticed that the wording of the general principle stated on page 9 contains a qualifying phrase to the effect that the situational component of the determinants of behavior are operative only *as they are perceived* by the person. Organisms do not directly apprehend the external environment; the various forms of energy which impinge on the sensory receptor apparatus do not contain information in a form that is always immediately useful. Rather it is the case that we are all very elaborate, but very imperfect, computing devices when it comes to making "sense" out of the information provided to our senses by the so-called *objective* environment. This means that there is considerable possibility of slippage occurring between what is "out there" and our experience of it, as is readily demonstrated in visual illusions. It also means that our behavior, insofar as it is determined by the environment, is a product only of what we perceive the environment to be—not of what it *is*. If you surmise that the discrepancy between "real" reality and perceived reality has given psychologists a great deal of trouble because of the impossibility of controlling with certainty the experience of subjects whose behavior they wish to study, you are right.

On the other hand, the perceptual process has provided psychology with some of its most fascinating problems. At the human level, at least, it is clearly an extremely intricate mechanism which is subject to biasing from many sources, including the individual's values and needs and the character of his favored techniques for coping with stress. (See, for example, Secord and Backman, 1964, Chapter 1; Eriksen, 1966.) The extension of this work to the process of interpersonal impression formation, sometimes called person perception (Secord and Backman, 1964, Chapter 2; Tagiuri and Petrullo, 1958), is an area of very direct concern to us, and we shall have occasion to refer to it often in the pages that follow. For now it may be noted that we have already added an increment of complication to an already complicated model: the behavior of the two persons engaged in a typical dyadic interaction is determined by the dispositional tendencies inherent in each of them at the time and by their perceptions of their own and of each other's behavior, as well as their perceptions of other aspects of the situation—perceptions biased in turn by their dispositional tendencies. The accuracy of these perceptions, or perhaps we should call them interpretations, could, moreover, range from complete veridicality to virtually complete illusion. Fortunately, it will usually be possible for our purposes to render a coherent account of behavior without giving explicit attention to all of these possible contingencies, although it may help to keep us honest if we do not entirely suppress them. In any case, we have not yet put before you all of the stubbornly difficult problems which must be taken into account in construing behavior. Read on.

THE PROBLEM OF UNCONSCIOUS MENTATION

If the title of this section strikes you as paradoxical, you already have some appreciation of the difficulty. The idea that complex, nonrandom mental processes may occur outside of awareness antedates Freud by very many years, although he is usually credited as being the first to give comprehensive and systematic attention to this concept. It is basically something of a philosophical anomaly, although it has been very useful as a heuristic device in explaining various otherwise obscure peculiarities of behavior. However, it has been much overworked and has come to serve as a convenient device for a type of pseudo-explanation. In many cases a more fine-grained analysis of the situation in which it is invoked will prove it to have been an unnecessary and unwarranted assumption. I am not quite prepared to make remarks about the "last refuge of scoundrels," but I should like to adopt in what follows a high threshold for the admissibility of the unconscious mind as an explanatory construct.

But we must be careful here not to deprive ourselves of too much. We are told (Watzlawick, Beavin, and Jackson, 1967, p. 95) that something on the order of 10,000 discrete impressions per second impinge upon our sense receptors. Clearly we would all be reduced to quivering masses of disintegrated activity if we were required to process in awareness more than a miniscule fraction of this "information," and just as clearly we possess mechanisms for the control of awareness, some of them subject to voluntary setting or biasing and some—doubtless many more—not. Awareness is therefore a highly selective phenomenon, and we know from perceptual experimentation (Eriksen, 1966) that the selectivity can operate in both directions—that is, it can function to enhance the salience of relatively indistinct cues or to mitigate that of relatively distinct ones. The selection process itself, moreover, is presumably subject to the same sort of variation in the degree to which it may, under given conditions, enter into awareness.

These remarks are directly relevant to Sullivan's concept of *selective inattention,* and they also introduce its psychological opposite, which may be termed *selective enhancement*. The idea is that the cognitive representation of minimal cues from whatever source, internal or external, may, with or without awareness, be selectively enhanced or selectively diminished by the person as he processes information in the course of adapting to the situation in which he finds himself. There is a great deal more to be said about this process, but additional discussion is perhaps best postponed until we are in a position to be more concrete. One additional point may be clarified here concerning the relationship between the concepts of selective inattention and those of the Freudian unconscious and its close relative, repression. It has sometimes been suggested that the distinction is a purely nominal one, a consequence of Sullivan's alleged proclivities for coining new terms. That view represents an incorrect reading of Sullivan, and it would also misrepresent the present discussion. While selective inattention, as viewed here, is an involved process, it is an exceedingly modest one by comparison with repression and the unconscious, and would by no means be capable of mediating the extraordinary feats of integrated behavior of which the latter are said to be conjointly capable.

THE PROBLEM OF CIRCULARITY

Gregory Bateson (1958) has defined social psychology as "the study of the reactions of individuals to the reactions of other individuals" (p. 175). The proportion of social psychologists who would accept this definition of their field is unknown, but a rather vexing problem is posed for those who would, especially those who worry about what Brunswik (see Hammond, 1966) has termed the "ecological representativeness" of their experimental research. The traditional models of psychological research and theory are based upon a notion of causality which is linear and undirectional, and does not allow for feedback mechanisms whereby the "effect" may influence or alter the "cause." There is reason to believe that this may not be a very substantial problem in highly simplified situations in which one may be interested in the relations between circumscribed physical "stimuli" and organismic "responses" to them, although even here the question has been pointedly raised (Merleau-Ponty, 1963). Where the issue is one of the contingencies existing in the relations between persons, however, we are clearly faced with a difficult problem, if our purpose is one of causal analysis. Consider, for example, how we should go about locating the root "cause" of the difficulty in the highly mutually contingent interaction between our own Mr. X and his wife.

The problem of circular causality in person-environment relationships actually has two distinguishable aspects. The more obvious of these is the difficulty of establishing cause-effect relationships within a finite series of events which originate alternately in the person and in his environment. If the person and his environment are each reacting to the other, as is commonly the case in social interaction, where are our "causes" and our "effects"? One can, of course, seek to locate a "first cause," so to speak, of which all subsequent events in the series are in some sense the effect, but such a strategem will frequently entail an arbitrary choice as to primacy. We might designate this type of problem as one involving *alternating reactions*. The other form of circular causality is a more subtle one and operates at the level of a single event-reaction unit. If a person's reaction or "response" to an event is determined by his perception of that event, as we have proposed, and not by the objective event itself, it follows that the truly functional "stimulus" that evokes his response is in part determined by that response, in the sense that one of its component parts is his perceptual representation or "interpretation" of the stimulus. Thus the *functional* stimulus is determined by a component of the person's total response to it, and it may be altered by that response. Can we then hold that the stimulus "caused" the response, when in fact the converse would be an equally accurate characterization of the situation? We can, but it must be recognized that we do so largely as a matter of convenience. This second type of circular causality might be termed the *response-determined stimulus* effect.

Given these observations, the question of causal analysis in social interaction sequences assumes a most perplexing character. One is never quite sure that he has clearly identified what is actually going on in regard to the structure of contingencies obtaining among events in any series of events. In their very stimulating recent book on human communication, Watzlawick, Beavin, and Jackson (1967) argue that the "punctuation" of event sequences of the order of complexity involved in interpersonal transactions must always, in the final analysis, be arbitrary. By "punctuation" they mean the differentiation of an event sequence into smaller event sequences that have their own beginnings and ends. We can well imagine, for example, that Mr. and Mrs. X would continue to differ in locating the point of origin of their difficulties even if they were somehow capable of acknowledging and agreeing upon the real nature of those difficulties. The authors go on to note that such punctuation, however arbitrary it may be, is necessary for human beings because it *organizes* what would otherwise be a quite unmanageable confusion of behavioral transactions. Many of the rules of interactional punctuation, they observe, are culturally shared ones, as is the case in our conceptions of the reciprocal roles of "leader" and "follower."

What does this analysis mean in terms of the task at hand? It means that we are occasionally going to have to be arbitrary in order to make any progress. This is a limitation we necessarily share with very many dedicated and conscientious students of human interaction. By recognizing it, we may be able to avoid some common pitfalls.

THE PROBLEM OF VOLITION AND PURPOSE

Many years ago the distinguished psychologist E. C. Tolman wrote the following: "Behavior as behavior, that is, as molar, *is* purposive and *is* cognitive. . . . [It] reeks of purpose and of cognition" (1932, p. 12). He then went on to define in an extremely careful way what he meant by this, referring to certain characteristics of the behavior of white rats while running mazes. If you are relatively unfamiliar with the literature of psychology, you may well feel impelled to ask, "Why all the fuss?" I am slightly embarrassed to tell you that Tolman's statement was at the time, and to some extent still is, regarded by some psychologists as highly controversial. This is part of the legacy of behaviorism of which we had occasion to speak earlier. Recent research suggests that even the white rat may have a "mind of his own" about how to run a maze, and I find exclusively mechanical explanations of the behavior of persons to be quite simply incredible. Let us acknowledge frankly that we do not yet understand how mental or cognitive events are related to overt behavior, which is another way of saying that we do not understand the nature of "volition" or "will." This issue has very deep roots in the history of philosophy and of psychology, and we cannot hope to solve it here. However, the position taken in this book is that our lack of understanding of the nature of volition is an inadequate basis for considering it to be an inadmissible concept, given its power, generality, and intuitive validity in accounting for a variety of behavioral phenomena. We shall consider in Chapter 3 a model of behavior as involving inherent *planfulness* which, for our purposes at least, affords an apparently satisfactory and workable reinterpretation of this issue.

THE PROBLEM OF TEMPORAL FOCUS

It is possible to discriminate two plausible, polar approaches to the issue of temporal perspective in the study of an individual's relations with his environment, including of course that portion of it occupied by other persons. On the one hand, one might take a kind of general systems approach and deal exclusively with events as they are immediately observable, attempting only to understand the interplay of forces as they determine moment-to-moment changes in the state of the system. This approach, which is essentially ahistorical, is sometimes described as *field-theoretical,* and is perhaps best illustrated in the work of Lewin (1935). In its most extreme form it precludes any representation of remote causation either in the past or in the future, including any notion of extended purposefulness in behavior. Watzlawick, Beavin, and Jackson (1967), advocating what is in fact an extreme form of this position, suggest that we adopt the analogy of the "black box" as a way of characterizing the person who is engaged in interpersonal communication—that is that we attend only to input-output processes and ignore the structural and functional characteristics of anything enclosed within the person's skin. There is, admittedly, a certain appeal to this simplified approach.

At the opposite extreme may be identified a conception which emphasizes the internal structure of the person as a product of his constitutional predispositions and the entire range of his past experience. Advocates of such a conception believe that it is virtually impossible to understand fully the nature of any current person-environment transaction without viewing it in the context of the individual's past history and the current status of his internal psychological makeup; the extreme of this approach would be to treat such current events as being very nearly epiphenomenal. Certain aspects of classical Freudian theory, for example, appear to be based upon this implicit model.

Our approach has perhaps already been implied in the foregoing sections. Like Sullivan, we shall try to integrate aspects of both perspectives. It is interesting, however, that Sullivan considered himself to be a field theorist and on many occasions made quite acid comments about the shortcomings of concepts like "individual personality" and "inner psyche." It does indeed appear that he was uncharacteristically confused in his own thinking about the distinctions he was trying to make, for which he has been taken to task by Murphy and Cattell (1952), among others.

Information and Communication

The information sciences, although barely out of their infancy, have reached a stage of technical complexity that exceeds the author's capacity for total comprehension. What follows is therefore not to be taken as representative of the level of sophistication of this field, and apologies are offered to communications specialists, with whose language I have taken some liberties. To the extent that one person's behavior is contingent upon that of another—to the extent that interpersonal influence, however slight, has occurred—we will regard communication as having taken place between them. The content of communication is information, the unit of which we will term a *message*. Messages are composed of various signs and symbols which vary in the extent to which shared meanings can be assigned to them; these signs and symbols constitute the *language* in which the message is encoded. It is readily seen, therefore, that *consensually valid* communication between two persons requires that the language in which the constituent messages are encoded be a shared one; to the extent that it is not, misunderstanding will occur. The discussion that follows borrows heavily from Bateson and his colleagues (see, for example, Bateson, Jackson, Haley, and Weakland, 1956), and from Szasz (1961), to whom much credit is due for their clarification of these difficult philosophical issues in a form which renders them consumable by the behavioral sciences.

A HIERARCHY OF LANGUAGES

Let us take so-called ordinary conversational language as our point of departure. Logical analysis indicates that it is actually a complex mixture of several different levels of languages. The first or basic level is termed object language, the signs (words) of which denote physical objects such as a table, a chair, a typewriter, and so on. At the next highest level we may distinguish signs whose referents are the signs of the object language, such as word, sentence, phrase, etc.; these signs constitute the first-level *meta-*

language, in that they are a language about a language. Progressively higher orders of metalanguages—languages referring to languages at a lower level of logical classification—are obviously possible and are in fact regularly employed in everyday communication. This hierarchized aspect of conversational language is quite unobtrusive, in part because the same linguistic stock of signs is employed at differing levels of usage; thus, we are here employing conventional English signs to discuss conventional English signs.

The term *language* is usually reserved for the type of mediating process involved in ordinary conversation, in which the relations between signs, or words, and their referents are, by convention, systematically coordinated. We wish here to extend the meaning of "language" to include signs for which the referents are not so precisely and consensually defined. We are referring, in other words, to a level of language *below* that of the object language, as described above. What kind of a language would this be? Let us return for a moment to Mr. and Mrs. X. The latter's vaginismus was, perhaps among other things, a *communication* to her husband, as that term is used here. He failed to interpret (decode) the constituent message accurately, partly because it was encoded in a language which is less denotative than the powerful and precise language of everyday conversation. Szasz (1961) suggests the term *protolanguage* for this general class of sign-referent relations, which are at a lower level, so to speak, than the object language. Protolanguage includes all sorts of gestural, postural, and vocal paralinguistic cues which, although lacking a precise, consensual meaning, can function as signs and convey information in message form. It also includes the "body language" employed by Mrs. X in the form of her "symptom," a type of communication device which is rather more common than you may think.

The distinction between conversational language and protolanguage can be illustrated in another way, as suggested by Watzlawick, Beavin, and Jackson (1967). Modern electronic computers are of two general classes—the digital and the analogue variety—and they utilize two correspondingly different forms of message material in their operations. The performance characteristics of the digital computer, in which the message material has a precise and arbitrary (conventional) relationship to the data being processed, are vastly superior to those of the analogue computer in terms of accuracy and versatility. The relationship of message material to data in the analogue computer is essentially a matter of approximating or mirroring actual magnitudes (by analogue), thus involving a certain irreducible error factor. The digital computer has perfect precision as an arithmetic *and* logical machine; the analogue computer is arithmetically imperfect, and its logical capabilities are exceedingly primitive. Conversational language, then, predominantly has the characteristics of digital message material, whereas protolanguage approximates the characteristics of analogic message material. Watzlawick et al. (1967) thus suggest that human communication is of two basic varieties—*digital* and *analogic*—and we shall employ their terminology to refer to these two general ways in which information may be encoded.

LEVELS OF COMMUNICATION

Just as there can be language about language—metalanguage—so too can there be communication about communication—metacommunication. Much metacommunication is obviously just that and is encoded in digital terms, as is being attempted here. Less obviously, we are all rather constantly engaged in analogically coded metacommunication in our attempts to communicate with others. That is, we attempt to provide "extra" information, through gestures, facial expressions, tone and tempo of voice, the setting in which we choose to talk, and the like, in order to express our intentions about how what we say is to be "taken." As will become clear, this is an extremely important form of communication, especially for our purposes, in that many communicational transactions between persons contain subtle, analogically coded definitions of the nature of the relationship obtaining between the communicants. It may be noted in passing that the degree of correspondence or consistency between the messages contained in the digital and analogic "channels" of any communication is by no means of a fixed or predictable magnitude, and it *can* be the case that the information in one channel is such as to contradict that in the other.

Plan of the Book

As has been noted, Chapter 2 is devoted to an extended summary of Sullivan's principal ideas and theoretical formulations. In Chapter 3 we shall examine the problem of the acquisition and maintenance of characteristic patterns of interpersonal behavior in the light of contemporary psychological theory and available empirical knowledge. Chapter 4 is largely devoted to the search for a theoretically and empirically adequate taxonomy of interpersonal behavior, in order to provide a convenient means of focusing the material to be considered in subsequent chapters. Chapter 5 outlines a theoretical framework within which to account for the functional processes of interpersonal relations, their integration, maintenance, and dissolution. Chapter 6 undertakes an analysis of complex rules, norms, and implicit "contracts" which emerge in interpersonal relationships and give to them their sometimes game-like character. Chapter 7 is devoted to an attempt to extend the analysis into the area of so-called mental disorder. Finally, Chapter 8 attempts to formulate some general principles of therapeutically induced behavior change as derived from the analysis and perspective presented.

REFERENCES

BATESON, G. *Naven,* 2nd ed. Stanford, California: Stanford University Press, 1958.

BATESON, G., JACKSON, D. D., HALEY, J., and WEAKLAND, J. Toward a theory of schizophrenia. *Behavioral Science,* 1956, **1,** 251–64.

ERIKSEN, C. W. Cognitive responses to internally cued anxiety. In C. D. SPIELBERGER (Ed.), *Anxiety and behavior.* New York: Academic Press, 1966. Pp. 327–60.

HAMMOND, K. R. Probabilistic functionalism: Egon Brunswik's integration of the history, theory, and method of psychology. In K. R. HAMMOND (Ed.), *Egon Brunswik's psychology.* New York: Holt, Rinehart & Winston, 1966. Pp. 15–80.

LEWIN, K. *A dynamic theory of personality.* New York: McGraw-Hill, 1935.

MERLEAU-PONTY, M. *The structure of behavior.* Boston: Beacon Press 1963.

MURPHY, G., and CATTELL, E. Sullivan and field theory. In P. MULLAHY (Ed.), *The contributions of Harry Stack Sullivan.* New York: Hermitage House, 1952. Pp. 161–79.

SECORD, P. F., and BACKMAN, C. W. *Social psychology.* New York: McGraw-Hill, 1964.

SULLIVAN, H. S. *Clinical studies in psychiatry.* New York: W. W. Norton, 1956.

SZASZ, T. S. *The myth of mental illness.* New York: Hoeber-Harper, 1961.

TAGIURI, R., and PETRULLO, L. (Eds.). *Person perception and interpersonal behavior.* Stanford, California: Stanford University Press, 1958.

TOLMAN, E. C. *Purposive behavior in animals and men.* New York: Appleton-Century-Crofts, 1932.

WATZLAWICK, P., BEAVIN, J. H., and JACKSON, D. D. *Pragmatics of human communication.* New York: W. W. Norton, 1967.

CHAPTER 2

Sullivan's Conceptions: Beginnings of a System

Harry Stack Sullivan was born into a moderately poor, farming family in Norwich, New York, on February 21, 1892. Not a great deal is known about his early development, except that it was not especially auspicious or happy from his own retrospective point of view, as gleaned from infrequent references in his published works. He was evidently lonely and isolated through much of his youth. He received his M.D. degree in 1917, and for the next two decades he immersed himself in the practice of clinical psychiatry at various hospitals in the Washington-Baltimore area and, beginning in 1931, in private practice. Much of his work throughout this period was devoted to the study and treatment of patients described as schizophrenic and obsessionally neurotic, two classes of behavior disorder that especially interested him. His thinking was strongly influenced by Adolph Meyer, Sigmund Freud, George Herbert Mead, Edward Sapir, and William Alanson White, all of them original thinkers in their own right. But he apparently began to formulate systematically his own distinctive viewpoint during the latter part of this early period of intensive clinical practice.

Sullivan was one of the original sponsors of the William Alanson White Psychiatric Foundation, incorporated in 1933. From that time he became increasingly engaged in teaching and lecturing, much of which was conducted under the auspices of the Foundation and its principal training arm, the Washington School of Psychiatry. In 1937, the Foundation established the professional journal *Psychiatry,* with Sullivan as co-editor (and subsequently editor). He was a significant contributor to this publication throughout the remainder of his life. By 1939 his thinking was sufficiently systematized that he could be prevailed upon to expose it in some detail in a series of lectures given at the Washington School of Psychiatry. These lectures were subsequently published in somewhat revised form as an issue of *Psychiatry,* and were reprinted many times in book form in the years thereafter. This small book, *Conceptions of Modern Psychiatry* (1953a), was the only one Sullivan ever wrote; it had had an enormous impact long before subsequent revisions and expansions of his thinking began to appear in print posthumously.

Sullivan continued to refine and expand his point of view in various lecture series, one of the most important of which was delivered at the famous Chestnut Lodge Hospital in Rockville, Maryland, from 1942 through 1946. Prior to his untimely death, he became increasingly interested in applying the insights of psychiatry and the social sciences to problems of international relations. He died in Paris in 1949 while engaged in pursuing this goal. Fortunately, he left behind voluminous notes and transcriptions and an exceedingly dedicated group of colleagues, to whose persistence and editorial talents we are indebted for what we know of the later developments in his thinking. The product of their efforts appears in five volumes: *The Interpersonal Theory of Psychiatry* (1953b), *The Psychiatric Interview* (1954), *Clinical Studies in Psychiatry* (1956), *Schizophrenia as a Human Process* (1962), and *The Fusion of Psychiatry and Social Science* (1964), the last two being collections of articles previously published in various other sources.

The published works of Sullivan comprise some two thousand pages of densely packed and intricately structured text. There is no completely satisfactory substitute for his own colorful prose, but several general-purpose resumés are available. These include various interpretations offered by Patrick Mullahy (1948, Chapter 10; 1952a; 1953), an extended treatment by Dorothy Blitsten (1953), and two excellent summaries, a brief one by Hall and Lindzcy (1957, pp. 134–51) and a very thorough one by Ford and Urban (1963, Chapter 14). Pearce and Newton (1963) have provided what is essentially a considerable elaboration of Sullivanian theory, incorporating various elements of other viewpoints, including the classical Freudian; it is doubtful that this elaboration represents an improvement, and even more doubtful that Sullivan himself would have found it palatable. A series of more critical and evaluative essays concerning Sullivanian theory appears in a volume edited by Mullahy (1952b).

Quite obviously it will not be possible here to render a complete account of Sullivan's thinking on interpersonal processes. Moreover, it should be emphasized that, while I have consulted all of the above sources in the preparation of this chapter, what follows is my own interpretation of Sullivan's thought. What I hope to accomplish is to present an approximately faithful portrayal of the outlines of his system. This will provide a kind of baseline, and in subsequent chapters we shall try to build upon the system in the light of current knowledge and theory.

The Interpersonal Nature of Personality

According to Sullivan, "personality is the relatively enduring pattern of recurrent interpersonal situations which characterize a human life" (1953b, pp. 110–11). Elsewhere (1953b, p. 104) he defines "pattern," somewhat curiously, as "the envelope of insignificant particular differences." It should here be noted that an "interpersonal situation," as Sullivan uses the term, requires the participation of only one "real" person, in that any other "persons" in any particular instance may be wholly illusory—that is, products of the real person's imaginations or fantasies. Sullivan thus regards personality as inconceivable other than in the context of interpersonal relations, except perhaps as a mere "hypothetical entity" whose employment may occasionally be necessitated by the limitations of our language.[1] Strictly speaking, then, personality is nothing more (or less) than the patterned regularities that may be observed in an individual's relations with other persons, who may be real in the sense of actually being present, real but absent and hence "personified," or illusory. It will perhaps be less confusing, and not a complete distortion of Sullivan's views, if we here conceive of personality as *manifesting* itself only in interpersonal relationships, whether real or illusory. How does personality, conceived in this way, become formed and what, so to speak, are its operating characteristics? Let us try to capture the essentials.

Human Infancy

The human neonate, according to Sullivan, arrives in the world as an animal, albeit a remarkably gifted one in the sense of his potential for accomplishment. He becomes truly human, a person, only as a consequence of relations with his elders and peers. But he does arrive with some equipment, or at least with certain capacities which will predictably develop. The most important of these, for the present purpose, are certain innate *tensions* and capacities for *experiencing*.

INNATE TENSIONS

The infant human animal has a variety of tensions or needs, "organic irritations," which recur periodically as a necessary consequence of his organismic construction. These include needs for food, water, warmth, elimination and prompt removal of the products thereof from contact with his skin, and so forth. Sullivan also postulates an innate need for "contact," particularly with another human body, thus anticipating by some years the well-known work of Harlow (1959) and his colleagues on the heretofore

[1] This actually illustrates some of Sullivan's confusion, alluded to in Chapter 1, concerning his own formulation of field theory. "Personality," of course, always has the status of a hypothetical construct; it always refers to abstractions about observations, and not directly to observations themselves.

unappreciated contact-needs of infant monkeys. Quite clearly the relief or satisfaction of such needs in the infant requires the co-operation of another individual, the "mothering one." The infant's vocal and motor reactions to these need states are said to evoke in the mothering one a distinctive constellation of responses that are classed under the general rubric of "tenderness." Without being explicit about the processes involved, although they can be rather readily imagined in terms of association learning, Sullivan suggests that the infant *acquires a need for tenderness* very early in life as a consequence of these kinds of interactions with the mothering person. This tenderness-need will later differentiate into other closely related needs for love, intimacy, and so on.

A brief comment is required about two additional varieties of need which are, according to Sullivan, innately determined. The first is the relatively unimportant category of "zonal" needs. These relate to needs for, so to speak, nonfunctional stimulation of various areas of the body known as *zones of interaction* (with the environment), such as the oral, anal, visual, and auditory zones. For example, the infant is said to have a need for non-nutritive stimulation of the oral zone even in the absence of hunger, a proposition which does indeed seem to be confirmable by observation. The other—and very important—category of innate need is termed, somewhat unhappily, a need for *power*. The referent of this term, for Sullivan, is an hypothesized innate need to grow, exercise one's capacities, and develop maximally. As such, it seems practically indistinguishable from the self-actualization postulate of Rogers (1959) and Maslow (1954), and from White's (1959) effectance motive. The continuous functioning of this need throughout life is such that, in the absence of thwarting circumstances, the person will manifest tendencies toward an effective and uncomplicated existence with his fellows. It is extremely important for an understanding of Sullivan that this concept be distinguished from one bearing a similar name—the *power drive*. The latter is an inauspicious acquisition of certain persons in response to the frustration of their power *need* and the sense of helplessness thereby suffered. The *power operation* is an interpersonal manifestation of the power drive, involving gross manipulation and exploitation of others.

THE EXPERIENCE OF THE INFANT

For Sullivan, all experience is essentially symbolic. Raw events, as such, do not register as experience. The symbolization process intrinsic to experience occurs in three "modes," of which the most primitive and earliest is the *prototaxic*. The prototaxic mode of experience, the only one of which the very young infant is capable, is reminiscent of William James's famous characterization of the world of the infant as one of "blooming, buzzing confusion." Experience in this mode is undifferentiated with respect to time and space, relationships and patterns. It consists of a series of discrete, unrelated impressions which exhibit an absence of punctuation or other constraint. Needless to say, there is no distinction between self and environment, and no differential localization of the sources of the impressions received. We do not, of course, know a great deal about experience in this mode. This is not to suggest that adults cannot have it—they can approximate it under certain circumstances, such as severe mental disorder or (I would surmise) psychedelic drug intoxication—but such experience is not readily communicated in articulate form to other persons. It has a "cosmic" quality. Sullivan advances the interesting speculation that the prototaxic mode is "the rough basis of memory" (1953b, p. 29).

The young infant gradually acquires a rudimentary form of perception, termed "prehension," by means of which he develops a vague capacity for foresight—that is, he becomes capable of prehending aspects of the immediate future and the courses of action that may bring them about. For example, crying comes to be prehended as action which leads to the foreseen relief of distress, and an appreciation of the "magical potency" of vocal behavior has its beginnings in this experience. In addition, certain experiences come to operate as "signs" that other experiences are about to follow, such as those of relief or of increased distress. Thus the infant begins to prehend that the world contains two nipples—a good one that brings relief, and a bad one that brings additional distress. As will be seen, the latter is associated with an anxious state in the mothering person. With the development of such abilities to identify differences in prehended objects, the infant takes his first steps toward experiencing in the next most advanced mode, the *parataxic.*

Sullivan docs not suggest any sharp line of demarcation in the shift from the prototaxic to the parataxic modes of experiencing. One of the earliest manifestations of the latter, however, is the capacity for complex experiences, in the sense that they are integrated out of data provided by more than one of the zones of interaction, for example visual *and* auditory. The essential characteristic of the parataxic mode of experience, however, is a more or less clear appreciation of relationships among experiences—not *logical, causal* relationships, but relationships of coincidence and concomitance, of similarity and difference. This is said to be the primordial form of knowing, and it makes its appearance within the first year of life. The chief importance of this mode of experience, as well as the prototaxic, is that it may influence and color subsequent cognitive functioning and remains operative as a possibility through adulthood. One of the key ideas in Sullivan's thought, in fact, is that cognition is always influenced by precedents from the past. As we shall see, this idea, in contemporary form, has some robust empirical support.

PERSONIFICATIONS

The idea that current perceptions and cognitions consist, in part, of remnants from past experience has no more important application than in Sullivan's concept of *personification.* The concept of personification refers to a complex, organized cognitive template or pattern—a mental image, if you will—of a particular person, not necessarily a real one. It is constructed out of experiences, largely in the parataxic mode, deriving from interaction with other persons. The relationship between the characteristics of any "real" person and those of the relevant internalized personification is inevitably a very complicated one, partly because of the inherent deficiencies of the parataxic mode of experience in mediating logical relations. If you are beginning to perceive some relationship between this discussion and our preceding one concerning analogic processes (in Chapter 1), you are on the right track, and you are probably experiencing in the parataxic mode.

Two classes of personifications which make their appearance in infancy are regarded by Sullivan as especially important—those relating to the mothering person, and those relating to the self. The child originally develops two separate and distinct personifications of the mothering person in the course of his interactions with the maternal object. One of these, the Good Mother, is constructed out of experiences of relief, satisfaction, and pleasure enjoyed in the presence of the mothering person. The other, the Bad Mother, is a cognitive construction arising from the experience of anxiety undergone in the presence of the mothering person. The infant at this stage does not perceive that the two "Mothers" relate to the same real person.

Gradually, the emergent patterning of the infant's experience begins to yield a differentiation of the somewhat special object, "me," and with the further elaboration of experience involving "me" this special object comes to have certain distinctive attributes. These attributes consist, most importantly, of *reflected appraisals* from the environment, originally experienced largely in the parataxic mode. To put it another way, the infant begins to develop a rudimentary sense of his *self,* based upon his experience of the environment's reactions to his activities. In short, he develops a personification of himself. More specifically, since his cognitive apparatus is still very limited, he develops separate personifications of himself for each of the major states of the appraising environment he is able to discriminate, of which there are three in number. One experienced state of the appraising environment is characterized chiefly by tenderness, giving rise to feelings of relative euphoria and contributing to the development of the personification "Good Me." Another is characterized chiefly by increasing tenseness and increasingly forbidding gestures, inducing anxiety in the infant and contributing to the development of the personification "Bad Me." The third rudimentary self-personification, which develops very gradually, is that of the "Not Me," an extremely important, but not very easily described, structure. Experiences that contribute to the Not Me personification are colored by very severe anxiety, by what Sullivan calls *uncanny emotion*. An example may help to clarify. Let us imagine that the mothering one is a person whose own experience with sexuality has involved very heavy doses of concomitant anxiety and that, as a result, her tolerance is very low for any displays of what she might regard as sexual interest in her offspring. And let us further suppose that her infant son has discovered that very interesting sensations can be provoked by the simple expedient of manipulating his penis. Upon mother's discovery of her child's enthusiasm for this pastime, we might expect that she would experience very severe anxiety and distress, accompanied by various overt behavioral manifestations. The latter would be prehended by the child in the form of uncanny emotion, in a manner to be described shortly, and this uncanny emotion would become associated, under these circumstances, with his own genitals. In the course of replicated experiences of this type, the child, it is said, will develop a vaguely structured self-personification whose content includes the genitals and any other attributes that have been associated with uncanny emotion. Such contents are specifically excluded as aspects of either Good or Bad Me. This is the Not Me personification, and, as may be surmised, it can be very troublesome in later life.

ANXIETY

We have already had considerable occasion to employ the term *anxiety*, and we should now try to give some attention to its definition. Anxiety is basically one of the tensions which the human infant comes into the world equipped to experience. Its prototypic emergence as an experience is occasioned by a type of empathic communication, an emotional contagion, transmitted from an anxious mother to her infant. It is characterized as a pronounced drop in euphoria, or feeling of well-being, and it is one of the most unpleasant of the experiences human beings are capable of having. As the experiencing capacities of the child mature, the precipitating circumstances of anxiety come to be associated with the disapproval of significant others, at first chiefly the parents. Beyond infancy the experience of anxiety, which occurs mainly in the parataxic mode, has the character of a drop in self-esteem or an increase in felt *insecurity,* and it always has an interpersonal referent. One of the most important aspects of anxiety occurring at any time in life is its pre-emptive quality—that is, it tends to occupy so much of the total content of awareness that other, concurrent events are not likely to be registered as experience. Needless to say, the emergence of anxiety severely restricts any learning which might occur in connection with particular circumstances. The most severe form of anxiety, that associated with the contents of the Not Me personification, is experienced as uncanny emotion, as awesome. The quality of this feeling state is suggested by the terms dread, loathing, and horror.

Later Developments and Acquisitions

Sullivan, in common with many other personality theorists, conceived of personality development in terms of various stages or "eras," the first of which is Infancy. He was careful to note that his own conception of stages had almost nothing to do with chronological age. Rather, he suggested, stages of personality development are best seen as transitions in which there is an identifiable and distinctive alteration in the character of the individual's relationships with others. The particular change involved in the transition from Infancy to the next stage, Childhood, is associated with the appearance of articulate verbal behavior. Sullivan, to a greater degree than any other major personality theorist, emphasized the crucial significance of language in personality development. The reasons for this emphasis may become clear in what follows.

LANGUAGE DEVELOPMENT

Not long after birth the child begins to be perceived by his parents as an educable organism, a fact that impinges upon their sense of parental responsibility as transmitters of the culture. We shall have more to say presently about Sullivan's notions of how the child learns, but for now let us simply note that parents generally show great enthusiasm for such linguistic skill as the infant may demonstrate, and that they very commonly expend a great deal of time and effort in training the child to form and to use words correctly—that is, according to the cultural prescriptions of their particular language community. Eventually, of course, these efforts nearly always achieve some measure of success: the Infant becomes a Child, that is, he becomes capable of consensually valid verbal communication. His verbal skills, however, do not suddenly emerge full-blown. On the contrary, he is likely to have put in something on the order of three rather harassing years of at least partial failure before coming up to standard in this regard. For Sullivan, these early "failures" are of considerable moment.

From the very first, the infant is exposed continuously to the linguistic signs and symbols of his language community—experienced, of course, in the prototaxic and parataxic modes. As observation will readily demonstrate, his response to such experience is generally an active one, not one of passive receptivity; the child *responds* with his own versions of linguistic virtuosity. Moreover, in addition to those utterances he actually produces for us to hear, it is assumed that a great deal of such "rehearsal" is carried on subvocally. The latter is an instance of a general class of behavior which Sullivan refers to as *covert processes,* which also include various nonverbal mental processes, such as images. Now, it is rather easily assumed that the original meanings attached by the infant to the various linguistic signs he begins to discriminate are something less than impressively congruent with the meanings of those same signs shared by his parents and other linguistically socialized persons in his environment. In other words, the infant develops out of his parataxic experience an essentially personal language system. The technical term for this is *autistic* language, which represents, if you will, the linguistic aspect of experience in the parataxic mode. What we have here then, I trust you will see, is a postulated vehicle of communication which has the interesting characteristic that it appears to be digitally coded when it is in fact analogically coded (see page 20). As is the case with parataxic processes generally, it is assumed that autistic meanings, once acquired, may persist into adulthood and may under certain circumstances become manifest. Indeed, Sullivan asserts, access to the autistic is required for success in certain fields, such as poetry.

Parents being what they are, however, the autistic performances of the infant, insofar as they become overt, are extremely likely to be frowned upon; and if that is the case, the infant is going to experience anxiety promptly following any public display of his linguistic eccentricities. So he learns to suppress any such public display, although he might still, of course, go on to develop further his peculiar ways by means of covert processes. In any case, what he does display overtly in the area of vocal performance continues to be very assiduously shaped up by his parents and others, such that he attains a passable skill in what we are here calling digital communication and enters into Childhood. Now, the attainment of a digitally coded language system is of momentous significance for further development. There are several reasons for this, and I shall try here merely to suggest the most important of these. In the first place, the child is now provided with a most efficient vehicle for checking out his experience of the world with that of others—in other words he has a first-rate mechanism for *consensual validation* in regard to the nature of reality, including that portion of it which constitutes himself. Second, all that the child will need subsequently to learn will be learned enormously more efficiently with the aid of a digital language, and some of the things he might wish to learn as he grows older are simply not learnable without it. Finally, the development of language is said to play a crucial role in the fusion of infantile personifications. Thus Good Me and Bad Me become just "me," and Good Mother and Bad Mother become just "mother," in each case, of course, with vestiges of the earlier personifications remaining. (Not Me, as will be seen, retains an independent existence.) Digital language provides the child with the wherewithal for experience in the *syntaxic mode,* the final and most powerful of the ways in which experience may be symbolized.

MODES OF LEARNING

No existing theory of personality has an entirely adequate account of how an individual acquires the characteristics that give him distinctiveness as a person, or, to put it another way, none has an adequate theory of learning. The reason for this is that we do not yet have a very clear understanding of distinctively human learning processes—the kind of learning that, for example, must be involved in the child's acquisition of the grammatical structure of his language (Brown, 1965, Chapters 6–7). Sullivan, in contrast to some other personality theorists, was acutely aware of this knowledge deficit and recognized it as one of the great unsolved problems of personality development. He suggested several processes that might account in part for the shaping and modification of the child's behavior toward the achievement of distinctive personhood. He describes them as follows:

Learning by anxiety. As has already been suggested, the occurrence of anxiety, by virtue of its effects upon awareness, generally tends to impede learning. Anxiety which is less than severe, can however, produce some learning of an inhibitory nature in the sense that its occurrence in contiguity with another experience may render less retrievable the memory trace of that experience. This is said to occur in connection with the transfer of attributes of the self-personification to the realm of the Not Me. A more important kind of learning mediated by anxiety is one in which variations in the level of anxiety function in the manner of a signal. Sullivan employs here the concept of an *anxiety gradient,* and hypothesizes that, quite early in life, the child acquires the capacity to discriminate increasing from diminishing levels of anxiety, learning to alter his behavior in a direction which is associated with the latter experience. He regards this as an extremely important form of learning, particularly in regard to the socialization of innate need tensions.

Learning by trial and success. This form of learning is said to be especially relevant in the acquisition of techniques for the *relief* of need tensions in early infancy. The infant experiences a need tension of some sort—let us say an oral zone tension—and engages in random manipulative activities until such time as he happens to place his thumb in his mouth. Success! The consequent relief of tension tends to "stamp in" as a "habit" the placing of the thumb in the mouth. The process described here is, of course, identical to the one psychologists call operant or instrumental learning.

Learning by rewards and punishments. Sullivan does not make very clear the distinction he intends between this form of learning and those previously mentioned, but it seems to be one based on the notion that reward and punishment learning occurs through the deliberate intervention of another person—the one who administers the reward or punishment. This kind of learning is said to become important in late infancy and to remain an important determinant of behavior modification throughout life.

Trial-and-error learning by human example. This type of learning, in which the individual deliberately strives to reproduce as accurately as possible the behavior of a model, was believed by Sullivan to be especially important in the learning of facial expressions, speech, and language. We now know, from the work of Bandura and Walters (1963), and others, that it can indeed be an important process in the modification of various kinds of behavior in children.

Learning by eduction of relations. Sullivan borrowed this concept from the eminent psychologist Charles Spearman, whose work on basic intellectual processes he admired. The concept refers to an obviously rather complex capacity of higher organisms to be able to appreciate relationships at some order of abstraction. Sullivan believed that much modification of human behavior was predicated upon changing conceptions of relations between events as they occur in nature, and that this process therefore qualifies as a kind of learning. Of course, the notion of cognitive learning is by no means strange to psychology, and it appears that Sullivan was here espousing merely one of its conceivable forms.

Thus, we see that Sullivan recognized a number of kinds of learning of which he believed human beings to be capable. He believed in fact that all of these processes were within the capabilities of the child prior to his attainment of articulate speech. The criticism sometimes advanced (Ford and Urban, 1963) that he did not have a theory of learning is therefore not quite justified—he had several, and *none* of those he entertained is inconceivable in the light of contemporary research and theory concerned with learning processes. We shall have more to say about the latter in the following chapter. For now, let us continue with Sullivan to discover some of the additional consequences of the individual's ability to learn, as he postulated them.

THE SELF DYNAMISM

Sullivan's concept of *dynamism* is a peculiarly elusive one. He defines it as a "relatively enduring pattern of energy transformations which recurrently characterize the organism in its duration as a living organism" (1953b, p. 103). "Pattern," as Sullivan uses the term, has already been defined (page 25). If we here take some slight liberty and read "energy transformation" simply as "behavior," we will not be far off the mark. Thus, *dynamism* refers to a class of behavior that is recurrent and is identifiable by virtue of the "insignificant particular differences" that characterize it from occasion to occasion. As such, it turns out to be very similar, as Hall and Lindzey (1957) note, to the psychologist's concept of *habit.* Now, Sullivan applied this term dynamism to all sorts of things in a rather confusing manner, which is the main reason why I am trying to limit its use here. It does not seem appropriate, however, to suppress the term entirely, and so I am allowing it this one exposure in a context in which it seems to fit singularly well—in relation to the extraordinarily important concept of the Self.

We have already had occasion to introduce the self dynamism in its rudimentary form in connection with the self-personifications of the infant, and to note that it is constructed out of reflected appraisals. But that is only part of the story. The function of the self dynamism, the basis of its gradual formation, relates to the recurrent experience of anxiety in encounters with significant others. The self dynamism develops as a means of controlling anxiety. The content of the self dynamism, which is provided by the interpersonal environment *as experienced* by the individual in the form of reflected appraisal, is the whole of what he can perceive as aspects of himself. The developing self dynamism, functioning as it develops, carries out its role of controlling anxiety through the control of awareness. It performs in such a manner that experiences associated with severe anxiety, uncanny emotion, simply do not register as being relevant to the *self,* which is that portion of the total personality of which one can be conscious and aware. Events of this type either are not noticed or are relegated to the Not Me, provided that the self dynamism is functionally intact. Thus, only reflected appraisals unaccompanied by severe anxiety can be utilized by the self dynamism in its further growth and expansion. A corollary observation is that the self dynamism has a self-perpetuating character; "new" data can be admitted to it only to the extent that they are consistent with the data already there. Experiences of reflected appraisal containing information about the self which is *inconsistent* with its current contents tend to arouse anxiety and to become suitable targets for selective inattention. Parenthetically, it might be noted that the person whose reactions provide reflected appraisal need not be real or actually present; he can be illusory or wholly imaginary, a product of covert process—in short, a personification. Readers who are familiar with the personality theory of Carl Rogers (1959) will note much that is similar in Sullivan's views of the self and its functioning.

The self dynamism—or what is sometimes called the *self system*—therefore constitutes the individual's developing personification of himself. Its importance in Sullivan's thinking cannot be overstated. It is the repository of all that the person "knows" about himself, good and bad, and it is the mechanism *par excellence* responsible for maintaining a linear course in the further development of his personality. Its major favorable influence is this integrative one, but it should be emphasized that it is also the chief deterrent to positive personality change resulting from new experience.

RESIDUAL ASPECTS OF THE PERSONALITY

In the assessment of total personality required in clinical practice Sullivan adopted what he called a tripartite perspective in order to organize his thinking and his investigative efforts. One of his three areas of concern was the contents and operations of the self system, the other two being the "rest" of the personality and sleep. The former consists essentially of all attributes of the individual's personality that are *unrepresented* in the self system; it is roughly co-extensive, in other words, with the Not Me personification. But how can this be? How can an individual long remain unaware of characteristics he in fact possesses? Sullivan here introduces a concept which is essentially identical to the Freudian notions of the unconscious and repression. He calls it *dissociation.* "Systems in dissociation" are those aspects of the personality, chiefly needs, that are more or less forcibly denied access to awareness, although they continue to be operative, to grow, and to develop. They are often expressed in unwitting behavior and in sleep—that is, in dreams—in disguised, parataxic (analogic) form.

There is good reason to believe that Sullivan was not very happy with this concept of dissociation; he felt he had sometimes given it "undue importance as an explanatory principle" (1953a, p. ix). He apparently found it essential, however, for he retained it throughout the period of his active theorizing. Presumably he found it difficult to extend the range of application of *selective inattention* as an explanation for all of the phenomena of unaware behavior with which he was acquainted, and I would suspect that this may have been due in part to his considerable familiarity with the sometimes bizarre and exotic phenomena of the very severe personality disorders.

INTEGRATING TENDENCIES

We are now in a fair position to do some summing up, to begin to demonstrate how this business of interpersonal relations "works," as Sullivan saw it. We have seen that the infant arrives in the world with certain biologically determined need tensions, and that his experience with significant others in the course of meeting these biological needs provides him with certain other things, among them the *interpersonal* need for tenderness and its later-developing derivatives, such as intimacy. It also provides him with developing psychological structures which render certain kinds of experiences anxiety-provoking, notably experiences of disapproval from real or fancied others. His need to avoid this anxiety is termed a need for *security;* his need to relieve biologically derived tensions is termed a need for *satisfaction*. These two kinds of needs, for satisfaction and for security, are the great driving forces, the motors, of human behavior.

The goals or end-states of these needs, as anticipated, are what bring persons together in "integrated situations," and they, in the final analysis, determine the nature and duration of such situations. Integrated situations (between persons) do not exist independent of these needs. Indeed, Sullivan suggests a converse relationship: the needs do not exist independent of an (at least anticipated or fantasied) integrated situation. This proposition is a product of Sullivan's field-theoretical persuasions. In any case, the goal of a person who is integrated with another may be said to be the achievement of satisfaction under conditions in which security is maintained or enhanced. In relatively uncomplicated interpersonal relationships, both parties are able to work this out in a smooth way; in relatively complicated ones, those in which one or both of the parties has some degree of "mental disorder," some frustration of satisfaction or security needs or both inevitably occurs. This is because needs for satisfaction and for security have become mutually oppositional for at least one of the parties in relation to that particular integrated situation. And if that is the case for one of the parties, his behavior is likely to make it extremely difficult for the other one to have a fully satisfactory *and* secure experience. This will doubtless become clearer as we move along, but the reader might profit some at this point by taking time out to consider once again the situation of Mr. and Mrs. X (pages 2–4) in the light of the concepts introduced to this point.

THE THEOREM OF RECIPROCAL EMOTION

Sullivan summarized his thoughts on interpersonal integration in terms of a "theorem" of reciprocal emotion: "Integration in an interpersonal situation is a reciprocal process in which (1) complementary needs are resolved, or aggravated; (2) reciprocal patterns of activity are developed, or disintegrated; and (3) foresight of satisfaction, or rebuff, of similar needs is facilitated" (1953b, p. 198). By "complementary needs" Sullivan refers to a situation in which a need of one person articulates with that of another person in such a way that the behavior relevant to these two needs tends to produce satisfaction (that is, "resolution") for both persons. The needs for dominance and submission, for example, would be complementary in this sense, as would shared needs for tenderness. If the reciprocal patterns of activity relevant to complementary needs are for some reason blocked from development—if, for example, they produce insecurity for one or both persons—then the integration of the two persons breaks down. Finally, an interpersonal integration is a learning experience, in the sense that the persons involved acquire foresight as to how to satisfy each other in relation to the particular needs in question, or they learn that the proffering of a similar integration in the future will lead to rejection and therefore experienced insecurity.

The Developmental Eras

Let us now return to the discussion of personality development with which we began the chapter. The principal features of the era of Infancy have already been presented, and we have also, in passing, touched upon many of the more important aspects of Childhood, such as digital language development and the fusion of infantile self-personifications into a syntaxically experienced concept of selfhood. The Childhood era extends from the time of appearance of articulate speech to that of the development of a need for interaction with compeers, other individuals having the same age and status characteristics as the child himself.

In many ways, the chief importance of the Childhood era for later personality development derives from the fact that it represents a time of intensive socialization efforts on the part of the parents, who now see the child as a very suitable—indeed a singularly appropriate—recipient of educational experience. Generally speaking, punishment makes its first significant appearance as part of the educational media during this period, and the manner of its introduction and use may have substantial implications. One of these concerns the opportunities afforded the child to acquire techniques for avoiding punishment when he has done something the parents consider "wrong." Possibly the most important of these techniques is the class of *verbalisms* children may inadvertently be taught to employ as a means of reducing or eliminating threats of punishment. Perhaps the best example is the gratuitously offered, "I'm sorry." In some families even the most outrageous crimes against person and property are magically erased by the mouthing of such phrases, accompanied, of course, by suitable reinforcing gestures. It was not Sullivan's intent in pointing out these matters to deny the functional and human significance of politeness and respect for others; quite the opposite. It is rather the misuse of such verbalisms in a magical and autistic way, and in fact the positive danger of such practices for healthy development, to which he wished to call attention. It *was* his contention that the initial training in the use of verbalisms of this type occurs in Childhood. Another related set of techniques of punishment-avoidance often learned during this period is concerned with concealment and deceit, a class of behaviors which Sullivan calls "as-if" performances. All children engage in as-if performances in the form of dramatization (for example, playing at being someone else) and various fantasy-like preoccupations. It is only when these come to be used extensively in the service of avoiding punishment through deception and concealment that they become problematic as possible long-standing adjustment devices.

Infants are, of course, capable of anger-like behaviors in the form of rage. The basic pattern for this behavior seems to be built in, a biological given. Anger becomes significant in personality development, however, only in the Childhood years, as punishment comes into frequent use as a parental training device. Anger, according to Sullivan, is rooted in the experience of anxiety. Sullivan speculates that its first appearance is occasioned by an instance of *unjust* punishment, duly recognized as such by the child. Heretofore, the child's characteristic response to punishment, as to any other indication of parental disapproval, has been one of insecurity, anxiety. Now, however, an element enters the response which has not been there before—the element of anger. Now anger, unpleasant though it is, is incomparably more pleasant than anxiety as an experience, and so it tends to "take over." Note what Sullivan is suggesting here. He is suggesting that the child learns under certain circumstances to "convert" anxiety to anger. And he adds to this the suggestion that, once learned, this conversion may become ingrained as an extremely useful operation for warding off insecurity. He recommends, in fact, that we look for the source of insecurity if we wish to understand *any* instance of anger in children or adults.

Needless to say, parents do not generally respond with enthusiasm to displays of anger in their children, particularly if they are themselves within its target range. In fact, even otherwise very liberal parents may be expected to have a specific intolerance for angry, aggressive behavior in their offspring. As a result, the child learns that it is frequently the better part of valor *not* to give vent to his angry feelings. But the anger remains, and in its suppressed form it is known generally as resentment, a feeling state not very facilitative of rewarding and growth-producing interpersonal relations. As early as the Childhood years, therefore, some children acquire pronounced impediments to further development by virtue of their frequent retreat to the particular type of covert process called resentment.

There is one more outcome—a particularly grave one—attributable to experiences in the Childhood era to which we should direct some attention. This is the so-called *malevolent transformation* of the need for tenderness. It happens that the parents of some unfortunate children, for one reason or another, are unwilling or unable to respond to and satisfy the child's need for tenderness. This may be due to factors inherent in the parents' personalities, or it may be due to various "reality" considerations that impose severe restrictions on the amount of time available to the parents for interacting with the child. Under such circumstances, the child's reaching-out for tender responses may run a considerable risk of being rebuffed, producing marked insecurity in the child. Repeated transactions of this type, according to Sullivan, cause the child to develop a protective maneuver to effectively prevent the painful sequence from running its course. The maneuver consists of "transforming" the need for tenderness so that its anticipated emergence becomes a specific signal to engage in malevolent behavior—to be hateful, attacking, and destructive. As can readily be seen, any start in this direction creates a vicious circle, and any possibility of tenderness is rapidly obliterated. This process, once ingrained in a person, tends to be extremely persistent and limiting of the possibilities of future relationships.

It can be seen, then, that many issues of extraordinary importance for future development acquire their initial definition and direction in the course of experience in the Childhood era. It would probably not be an exaggeration to regard it as the most crucial of the several eras, provided we do not lose sight of the fact that personality is a constantly growing, changing organization, and that any notion of irreversible trends is not a useful or accurate way to think about it. In any case, our discussion of the remaining developmental eras will be somewhat less extended.

THE JUVENILE ERA

The Juvenile era begins with the appearance of a strong need for interaction with age-mates. Its distinguishing characteristic, perhaps, is the reality shock provided by the unprecedented crudeness of interpersonal relations within the group of compeers and, to some extent, with nonparental authorities such as teachers. Among other things, this latter class of persons has the temerity to evaluate one's worth publicly in the form of letter grades and brisk notations scribbled upon one's cherished personal productions. Shocking as that is, however, it is gentle in comparison with the ridicule and ostracism one may suffer at the hands of one's age-mates. The latter are too busy protecting their own security and self-esteem to worry a great deal about the fine points of human relations, and interaction thus becomes altogether a rather trying situation wherein one's prestige is fairly constantly in danger of evaporating.

In brief, the name of the game in the Juvenile era is Competition and Compromise, and its functional significance in acquainting the child with "reality" and in providing training for coping with it is quite obvious. Children who are not severely handicapped by unfortunate earlier development learn how to "handle" themselves in order to retain a modicum of security, often by becoming very good at some particular activity which is valued among their peers, such as baseball, and emphasizing that as their claim to fame. A child with pronounced residual deficiencies from an earlier time, however—for example, one whose attempts at digital communication manifest a large autistic component—is likely to have a very bad time of it and to suffer the cruelty of disparagement and ridicule on a scale of which only Juveniles seem to be capable. It can also be the case that this training in competition and compromise miscarries in the direction of excessive effectiveness. Particular children may take to it with such great enthusiasm as a means of propping up a none-too-secure selfhood that the lesson is overlearned. Indeed, our own culture is markedly supportive of this form of security maintenance, an observation which caused Sullivan on many occasions to refer to American society as "prevailingly juvenile."

Sullivan expressed the view that, "with any good fortune," one might attain by the end of the Juvenile era an adequate *orientation in living,* a concept whose definition could well serve as a good definition of a mentally healthy state. It runs like this:

> One is oriented in living to the extent to which one has formulated, or can easily be led to formulate (or has insight into), data of the following types: the integrating tendencies (needs) which customarily characterize one's interpersonal relations; the circumstances appropriate to their satisfaction and relatively anxiety-free discharge; and the more or less remote goals for the approximation of which one will forego intercurrent opportunities for satisfaction or the enhancement of one's prestige." (1953b, p. 243)

THE PREADOLESCENT ERA

The beginning of the preadolescent era is marked, most outstandingly, by the first emergence of the capacity to *love*. Love, in Sullivan's terms, is a state of affairs in which the maintenance and enhancement of the satisfaction and security of *another person* is as important to one as is one's own satisfaction and security.

Sullivan believed that nothing remotely like this could occur in the younger child, parental illusions notwithstanding. This development in preadolescence is manifested in a kind of pairing process which characterizes preadolescent society, such that each child who has made it through to this point without major disaster selects a partner, a "chum," on whom to bestow this special kind of favor, the favor of intimacy. Usually this is someone of the same sex, but Sullivan is not referring here to the so-called "homosexual phase" of which the Freudians are fond of speaking. Sexuality does not come into the picture, in general, except as an instrumentality to further intimacy, as in the sharing of various sexual "secrets."

As in the case of all other eras, preadolescence has functional significance in personality development. One of its more important aspects is the opportunity provided for further very intensive mutual exploration of the nature of reality and of values within the two-group of the preadolescent dyad. In addition, various heretofore private aspects of the self are more or less openly revealed to the chum, who may then render judgments and opinions about them, based on his own experience. In a word, preadolescence provides a marvelously functional means of gaining a consensually valid outlook on the world and one's proper relationship to it—at a deeper level than has been possible to this time. The child who is incapable of entering preadolescence with his age-mates—by virtue, for example, of malevolent transformation or some other previously acquired impediment—is thus deprived of a crucial set of experiences, which is not readily compensated for in later life. In addition, of course, he will miss the sheer experience of intimacy, the practice and familiarization with its vicissitudes, which will become such an important issue shortly in relations with the opposite sex. The experience of loneliness, whose singular painfulness is equalled only by that of anxiety and jealousy, is said to first become a possibility in Preadolescence.

EARLY ADOLESCENCE

The era of Early Adolescence is brought to its rather dramatic opening with the maturation of the genital apparatus and the first appearance of a distinctly sexual need. Assuming that all has gone reasonably well to this point, the tension of sexual need will shortly be manifesting itself in somewhat awkward and misdirected approaches to members of the opposite sex, and in various covert processes having a frankly sexual content. The gang—that is, the system of chumships in which the boy or girl has been integrated —will begin to lose some of its overriding attractiveness, but will continue to function as an information network and validating mechanism for checking out what is real and reasonable, especially perhaps as regards the proper means of disposing of these new and powerful tensions. The major developmental task of the era may be said to be the accomplishment of the culturally expected shift in the direction of the intimacy need from a same-sexed to an opposite-sexed object, thus making possible a coordination of the separate needs for intimacy and sexual satisfaction in a heterosexual context. This is by no means always accomplished smoothly, even for individuals who do not have major blockages in their background. The key problem of Early Adolescence—and it is a very difficult one for very many youngsters—relates to the various collisions which are possible among three dominant need systems: the intimacy need, the sexual need, and the need to maintain security. Sullivan, never an enthusiast about the rationality of American culture, felt that in the specific area of softening the transition from childhood to adulthood, Americans have managed to be especially, extravagantly deficient. He tended to regard it as a minor miracle that *anyone* should be able, under the conditions of American life, to achieve a heterosexual integration providing simultaneous satisfaction of his sexual, intimacy, and security needs. The search for this is what Early Adolescence is all about. Needless to say, there are several ways in which the search may fail, and I shall leave it to the reader to fill in the picture from his own knowledge and experience.

LATE ADOLESCENCE

Late Adolescence is Sullivan's final developmental era. He describes it as follows: "Late adolescence extends from the patterning of preferred genital activity through unnumbered educative and eductive steps to the establishment of a fully human or mature repertory of interpersonal relations, as permitted by available opportunity, personal and cultural" (1953b, p. 297). The implicit meaning of this statement is that the attainment of true adulthood —the more or less successful negotiation of the various prior stages—leaves one free to explore and grow further in relationships with others, unimpeded by the warps and distortions arising from inappropriate personifications of self and others, anxiety-driven parataxic intrusions into experience, and the like. One has *power* to make the most of the opportunities which present themselves.

Distortions of Interpersonal Relations

Being primarily a clinician, a psychiatrist, Sullivan had a great deal to say about so-called mental disorder, which he regarded as nothing more or less than the distortion and complication of an individual's interpersonal relationships. Mental disorders, he urged, do not exist "inside" of persons. Moreover, there is nothing rare or extraordinary about them, and one cannot find a single characteristic of a mentally disordered person that is not widely shared by his more fortunate fellow humans. "We are all much more simply human than otherwise" (1953a, p. 16), he was fond of saying. Sullivan's thoughts on mental disorder are widely scattered throughout his published works, but are perhaps best summarized in *Clinical Studies in Psychiatry* (1956). We shall be able here to do no more than sample these thoughts in order to illustrate his approach and perspective on the general problem of behavior disorder.

MECHANISMS OF DEFENSE

Sullivan did not like the term *mechanism of defense,* but he did make extensive use of the concept to which the term refers—a mental device or strategy employed for the purpose of warding off anxiety. He believed, in fact, that one of the ways in which a mentally disordered person can be accurately characterized is in terms of his excessive and relatively exclusive reliance upon a single, particular defense mechanism or "security operation." Sullivan recognized four defense mechanisms as the primary ones: sublimation, obsessionalism, selective inattention, and dissociation, the last two of which we have referred to earlier. Let us take a closer look at these processes. *Sublimation* is defined as "the unwitting substitution, for a behavior pattern which encounters anxiety or collides with the self-system, of a socially more acceptable activity pattern which satisfies part of the motivational system that caused trouble" (1953b, p. 193). This is, then, essentially the Freudian notion of sublimation. According to Sullivan, sublimatory processes have their beginning quite early in life, certainly before the acquisition of language, and they occur at this point chiefly in connection with infantile satisfactions that arouse anxiety in the mothering one. The mothering one may, in fact, encourage sublimation, as when she removes the infant's hand from his penis and places a toy in his grasp. Once learned—and all of us learn it to some extent—sublimation operates in an exceedingly suave and automatic way in the partial resolution of various tensions which, if directly expressed, would lead to insecurity. Such residual tension as is not dischargeable in sublimated behavior is said to be relieved at night in dreaming. Sublimation is an important mechanism in life generally, and it usually functions without notable imperfection. It can be overloaded, however, as when a chronologically adult person channels his sexual needs entirely into sublimatory activities. Such a person is apt to have very nervous and sleepless nights, and eventually may require more drastic means to resolve his problems.

Obsessionalism. The defense mechanism of obsessionalism develops out of the child's earliest experiments with language, which, as you recall, carry a rather heavy freight of parataxis and autism. Verbalisms that seem to have magical potency in the reduction of anxiety (such as, "I'm sorry") are frequently actively taught to him. A good number of anxious children—especially in America, according to Sullivan—learn to preoccupy themselves, when anxious, with comforting verbal operations of an obscure and autistic variety. These may sound harmless and reasonable enough to an adult observer, who is perhaps not listening very attentively anyway, but they actually constitute a ritualistic, magical performance whose purpose it is to avoid *other* experience which would produce anxiety. The child's preoccupation blocks off all other channels of input to his experience. But can this persist into adulthood? Yes it can, and one may see it in rather dramatic form in so-called obsessional neurotics and in certain schizophrenic persons. It also occurs from time to time in many adults who do not otherwise appear severely mentally disordered. I have occasionally, for example, in periods of personal stress, delivered lectures to my somewhat mystified students that I am sure contained rather large amounts of obscure references of essentially autistic origin.

Selective inattention. Selective inattention is said to become important as a defense mechanism in the Juvenile era, in the trials and tribulations associated with the maintenance of prestige and self-esteem, the hallmarks of that era. As has been seen, selective inattention is a necessary part of the equipment of all of us in our dealings in everyday life. It becomes troublesome only when it is used too extensively in the service of security maintenance. To put it another way, "The thing that determines whether this [the use of selective inattention] is done well or ill, from the standpoint of long-range results for the person, is how smoothly the control of awareness excludes the irrelevant and includes the relevant" (Sullivan, 1956, pp. 42–43). Clearly, the person who must, for example, fail to notice huge portions of the information about himself coming to him by way of feedback from others is going to have very severe limitations on his effectiveness in social situations.

Dissociation. As we have seen, Sullivan was not entirely pleased with the concept of dissociation. He apparently felt that its retention was necessitated by certain fairly dramatic phenomena, such as behavioral automatisms like tics, and the sometimes very sudden emergence of frankly psychotic behavior in persons who did not show previous sign of gross personal deterioration, suggesting that some hitherto dormant process had erupted, "broken through," to gain control of the person's behavior. Sullivan believed that this mechanism of defense was a peculiarly dangerous one from the standpoint of mental health, partly because of the drastic disruption of personality which would necessarily attend any emergence into awareness of the contents of dissociated systems (that is, of the Not Me). Indeed, any such emergence into awareness would be tantamount to a basic change in personality. This, it might be noted, is what is done very gradually in skillfully conducted psychotherapy with the severely disturbed.

AN EXAMPLE OF "MILD" MENTAL DISORDER: JEALOUSY

I should like now, more by way of illustration than anything else, to examine very briefly certain clinical "syndromes" in the manner suggested by Sullivan's interpersonal concepts. The first of these syndromes is jealousy, an extremely unpleasant feeling state that is always related to a particular kind of interpersonal situation involving three individuals. The unpleasant feeling itself is occasioned in one of these persons by covert processes—fantasies and the like—whose content is concerned with intimate exchanges occurring between the other two persons, a content which often enough has a substantial basis in reality as provided by prior direct observation of at least suggestive behavior.[2] The most excruciating form of jealousy occurs when the person experiencing it has been on terms of *relative* intimacy with both of the others, but it also occurs where he has been seriously involved with only one of them. Now, the person who is capable of having a really full-blown attack of jealousy will be found to have also a specific deficiency in security in the area of his capacity to love—that is, in this aspect of his personification of himself. Moreover, according to Sullivan, this self-personification is more likely than not an accurate one, in the sense that the jealous person will usually be someone who has not yet made it to the Preadolescent stage of personality development, regardless of his current chronological age. He is a person whose security is readily threatened by demon-

[2] The question arises as to why a person would seemingly torment himself with unpleasant fantasies, apparently a specific failure of selective inattention. Sullivan does not address himself explicitly to this issue. The phenomenon is so common that it would seem indisputable, however, and may represent an instance of selective enhancement of anxiety cues, known to occur habitually in certain persons (Eriksen, 1966). No entirely adequate explanation of this paradoxical behavior is as yet available.

strations of his own relative failing in matters of intimacy. In addition, since he may still be working on problems of the Juvenile era, the painfulness of the experience is increased by the salient competitive element which enters in. The special painfulness of the situation in which the jealous person has been involved with both of the others derives from the additive effect thereby created—*both* are better with each other than he can be with either. The chief importance of jealousy to the professional clinician is that it not infrequently leads to elaborate rationalizing (obsessional) processes which may become frankly delusional in nature.

AN EXAMPLE OF MORE SERIOUS MENTAL DISORDER: HYSTERIA

We are fortunate in already having on record, as it were, an illustration of hysterical disorder. Mr. X, of Chapter 1, would be said to suffer from hysteria, and indeed a good case could be made that Mrs. X did too. You may recall that Sullivan referred to the hysteric's "happy thought." He describes it like this: "The hysteric might be said in principle to be a person who has a happy thought as to a way by which he can be respectable even though not living up to his standards. That way of describing the hysteric, however, is very misleading, for of course the hysteric never does have that thought. At least it is practically impossible to prove that he has had that thought" (1956, p. 203). Sullivan suggests, in other words, that the hysterical "symptom," which may be anything from an apparent disabling physical disorder to an attack of "nerves," is essentially a type of covert power operation that is *more or less* outside of the awareness of the individual who is engaging in it. He achieves satisfaction of an unacceptable need in a way which exempts him from blame, even by himself, for having that need. In Mr. X's case, the unacceptable need was presumably to retaliate for his wife's (also covert) rejection of him.

The hysterical predisposition, according to Sullivan, is characterized by marked interpersonal immaturity and self-absorption, which are in turn products of parental self-absorption. The parents of hysterically disposed people are said to be incapable of showing any fundamental respect or warmth toward their children, who tend to be treated as mere toys or baubles whose *raison d'être* is that of providing pleasure and entertainment for the parents. *Dramatizing* processes are therefore encouraged, and the child learns in this atmosphere that the principal value of other persons (an aspect of his personifications of them) is that they constitute an audience for his dramaturgical virtuosity. Needless to say, with this kind of training in interpersonal relations, the child is quite unlikely to make it beyond the Juvenile level of personality development, and his subsequent adult relationships are consequently badly marred by various immaturities, especially in the areas of intimacy and sexuality. Despite his self-absorption, therefore, he is likely to encounter many adult interpersonal demands which he simply does not have the equipment to handle; his response to these, characteristically enough, is often one which employs the dramatization techniques acquired in Childhood.

AN EXAMPLE OF SEVERE MENTAL DISORDER: SCHIZOPHRENIA

In Sullivan's view the schizophrenic disorder represents a failure of the self dynamism to maintain in dissociation the contents of the Not Me personification. As a consequence it loses control of awareness and admits to consciousness the chaotic and obscure referential processes of Infancy and early Childhood—the prototaxic and parataxic remnants of very early experience. The emergence of the Not Me in a setting of uncanny motion and chaotic modes of experiencing gives the onset of schizophrenia its distinctive coloration. The person is panic-stricken, perplexed, and confused, and what he says and does makes, at best, very little sense to persons whose self-systems are still intact. Gradually, however, there is in most instances a measure of control imposed by the person upon his rampant mental processes, and the form of this control will determine the particular "phenomena" of his disorder. He may, for example, obsessionally reconstruct his recent experience so as to impose some meaning upon it, thereby reducing somewhat the disturbing perplexity of it all. The problem with this solution is that it is usually very strikingly influenced by parataxic thinking and the necessity to deny responsibility for those "inhuman" aspects of himself of which the schizophrenic was so recently apprised by his self-system's failure. And so what he comes up with may be rather fantastic, as in the case of a young man I recently saw who attributed his problems to the purportedly outrageously seductive gestures of a young lady clerk—a young lady, who, as a matter of fact, had hardly noted his existence.

The major issue in schizophrenia, then, according to Sullivan, is the extensive employment of dissociation as a defense and the corollary fact of the existence in dissociation of substantial portions of the personality. As we have noted, this is regarded as a very dangerous state of affairs, and it is especially likely to lead to serious difficulty when a need as powerful as that of sexuality—and certainly this is one way in which *my* patient's difficulty may profitably be viewed—is subjected to the dissociative process. It is believed that the onset of acute schizophrenic psychosis in late adolescence or early adulthood is precipitated by some current interpersonal experience which happens to overload the dissociative defense.

Conclusion

We have seen in the foregoing something of the manner in which Sullivan conceived of interpersonal processes, and I trust that the general framework of his system of thought, as a system, has been adequately communicated. There is much food for thought here, and not a few of Sullivan's observations on the nature of the human condition have proved to be strikingly prophetic in terms of more recently acquired empirical knowledge. But there are some serious weaknesses too, especially perhaps in the area of explicitly stated systematic relationships. In a sense, the remainder of this book may appropriately be viewed as an attempt to repair these weaknesses and to build upon what seem to be the enduring strengths of Sullivan's conceptions. The following chapter undertakes to provide a more adequate foundation in respect to the basic processes of learning, perception, and cognition.

REFERENCES

BANDURA, A., and WALTERS, R. H. *Social learning and personality development.* New York: Holt, Rinehart & Winston, 1963.

BLITSTEN, DOROTHY R. *The social theories of Harry Stack Sullivan.* New York: William-Frederick Press, 1953.

BROWN, R. *Social psychology.* New York: Free Press, 1965.

ERIKSEN, C. W. Cognitive responses to internally cued anxiety. In C. D. SPIELBERGER (Ed.), *Anxiety and behavior.* New York: Academic Press, 1966. Pp. 327–60.

FORD, D. H., and URBAN, H. B. *Systems of psychotherapy.* New York: Wiley, 1963.

HALL, C. S., and LINDZEY, G. *Theories of personality.* New York: Wiley, 1957.

HARLOW, H. F. Love in infant monkeys. *Scientific American,* 1959, **200,** 68–74.

MASLOW, A. H. *Motivation and personality.* New York: Harper & Row, 1954.

MULLAHY, P. *Oedipus: Myth and complex.* New York: Hermitage House, 1948.

MULLAHY, P. The theories of H. S. Sullivan. In P. MULLAHY (Ed.), *The contributions of Harry Stack Sullivan.* New York: Hermitage House, 1952(a). Pp. 1–60.

MULLAHY, P. (Ed.), *The contributions of Harry Stack Sullivan.* New York: Hermitage House, 1952(b).

MULLAHY, P. A theory of interpersonal relations and the evolution of personality. In H. S. SULLIVAN, *Conceptions of modern psychiatry.* New York: W. W. Norton, 1953. Pp. 239–94.

PEARCE, J., and NEWTON, S. *The conditions of human growth.* New York: Citadel Press, 1963.

ROGERS, C. R. A theory of therapy, personality, and interpersonal relationships as developed in the client-centered framework. In S. KOCH (Ed.), *Psychology: A study of a science,* Vol. 3. New York: McGraw-Hill, 1959. Pp. 184–256.

SULLIVAN, H. S. *Conceptions of modern psychiatry.* New York: W. W. Norton, 1953(a).

SULLIVAN, H. S. *The interpersonal theory of psychiatry.* New York: W. W. Norton, 1953(b).

SULLIVAN, H. S. *The psychiatric interview.* New York: W. W. Norton, 1954.

SULLIVAN, H. S. *Clinical studies in psychiatry.* New York: W. W. Norton, 1956.

SULLIVAN, H. S. *Schizophrenia as a human process.* New York: W. W. Norton, 1962.

SULLIVAN, H. S. *The fusion of psychiatry and social science.* New York: W. W. Norton, 1964.

WHITE, R. W. Motivation reconsidered: The concept of competence. *Psychological Review,* 1959, **66**, 297–333.

CHAPTER 3

Learning Interpersonal Behavior

At breakfast on a recent morning my wife and I were observing the behavior of one of the several squirrels who frequent our back yard. This particular squirrel was busily engaged in a rather interesting bit of behavior. He was taking pieces of the bread we had thrown out (for the birds), removing them from the snow-covered ground, and depositing them on a portion of the branch of a nearby pine tree, some feet above the ground and in a spot that was well concealed by pine needles. He made repeated round trips. The behavior was objectively adaptive from at least two standpoints: (1) The ground was rather slushy, and the bread was becoming quite soggy from water absorption as it lay there. (2) The removal of the bread to a concealed location prevented its being eaten by the birds and by other squirrels, of whom there were several in the vicinity. When our squirrel could find no more bread, he repaired to his depository in the tree and proceeded to feast upon his cache. Altogether a quite impressive performance. Now, it happens that through the years my wife has learned not to ask me questions of a psychological nature, and I must presume that this is because my answers have usually not been very satisfactory. On this occasion, however, she took me by surprise and asked me how it was that a squirrel could do that! I stammered for a moment, and then made some none-too-intelligible remarks about well-known hoarding instincts of certain animals, the preprograming of astonishingly complex behaviors in the genetic materials, the possibilities of chained operant reinforcement learning, and so on. I think she realized before I did that I didn't really have much faith in any of these answers. The fact is that I do not have any strong conviction that I know how the squirrel comes to do what he does.

In dealing with a question of this kind, one can avoid a great many problems by not getting preoccupied about what might be going on in the mental life, such as it is, of the squirrel. In fact, it is possible to accomplish a tour de force by asserting, without evidence of course, that the squirrel has no mental life. Instead, one can adopt the position that the behavior of the squirrel is under the control of various stimuli impinging upon his central nervous system, and that the whole complex sequence of behavior runs off more or less automatically, without the participation of the squirrel, except insofar as he is an elaborate physico-chemical machine having the capacity to convert stimuli into responses. A certain credence (not proof) attaches to this view by virtue of the fact that any reasonably patient reinforcement psychologist worth his salt could arrange stimulus events in such a way as to teach some other squirrel to do what my squirrel did—and more! He could do so, moreover, without ever concerning himself in the slightest with how this all seemed to the squirrel. In fact, he would be very likely to take this perspective because it is extremely fashionable in psychology to assume that animals have no "minds," as that term is used in everyday life. Now, I think you can see the strategic advantages of such a perspective: one does not have to get involved in the messy business of the squirrel's private experience, if he has any. Of course, he might have some, in which case the assumption, although convenient, would be wrong.

The reason that my wife's question stumped me, momentarily

at least, is that, like many other respectable psychologists, I have developed the habit of thinking of animals in very simple stimulus-response terms. This is strange, because I do not really believe that the particular behavior in question was "instinctive"; nor am I at all convinced that a simple stimulus-response-reinforcement learning model—even one incorporating such quasi-cognitive constructs as "implicit" S-R associations—is capable of explaining that squirrel's behavior, without the most intuitively improbable contortions. In fact, there is some fairly impressive evidence (Breger and McGaugh, 1965; Lawrence and Festinger, 1962) that many behavioral capabilities of standard laboratory animals cannot be adequately explained within the framework of simple S-R models.

The point of all this, of course, is not to champion the mental capacities of squirrels, or of any other lower animals. Rather, my purpose is to dissuade you from any prior expectations that *human* learning is a completely straightforward matter, readily understood on the basis of allegedly firmly established empirical "laws." A case in point is the human's unique (so far as we know) capacity for digital language, a capacity that enormously complicates the processes involved in all but the most simple and—from our point of view—trivial of his behaviors. There is very good reason to believe (Chomsky, 1959; Fodor, 1965, 1966) that the so-called *laws of learning,* derived chiefly from animal research, are insufficient *in principle* even to account for the acquisition of language, to say nothing of the ways in which language may function in mediating other behaviors. This is not to suggest that we are completely without explanatory concepts to guide our discussion of how interpersonal behavior may be acquired or modified. Quite the contrary. It *is* true, however, that we will need to employ certain concepts that may now be unfamiliar to you. The danger of confusing you seems to me less likely than the danger of misleading you by oversimplification.

In this chapter, then, I shall try to lay a foundation for understanding the basic processes which, from the standpoint of contemporary theory and research concerned with human learning, are most likely to be involved in the acquisition, maintenance, and modification of socially significant behavior. As will become clear, the framework to be developed is one in which active, cognitive processes are strongly emphasized, an emphasis which is in keeping with modern trends of thought in psychology. Even my squirrel's behavior, I would venture to say, becomes more understandable if we attribute to him a certain amount of cognitive activity; in the case of the social behavior of persons, various kinds of cognitive operations must be assumed to play a dominant role.

Basic Processes in Human Learning

One of the more difficult tasks in a book of this kind is to organize the material in such a way that some order is imposed upon a subject that is not itself ordered or organized in a manner that suits the author's purpose. All such ordering and organizing is in the final analysis somewhat arbitrary, and one worries about obscuring important relationships or rendering unimportant ones unduly salient. Be that as it may, I have undertaken here to classify the field of human learning into two broad categories—*action learning* and *cognitive learning*—and to further subdivide these categories in terms that seem to me heuristically justifiable. I do not think that there is any intrinsic merit in the scheme I propose to use here; it merely suits my pedagogical predilections.

ACTION LEARNING

By *action learning* I mean relatively persistent alterations of observable behavior which are a product of experience. There are three principal categories of action learning with which we shall be concerned in this book: (1) cued behavior, (2) instrumental behavior, and (3) prompted behavior. These three categories are intended to be very general ones, but I do not suggest that they are necessarily exhaustive of the class of action learning here defined.

Cued behavior. This is essentially the kind of learning involved in classical or Pavlovian conditioning, in which a previously neutral "cue" comes to elicit, by contiguous pairing with another cue, a response that is similar to the response regularly elicited by the latter ("unconditioned") cue. This kind of learning is therefore dependent upon the existence of a prior cue-response contingency, which may be "reflexive" in nature or may be the the consequence of previous learning experience. Contiguity or association learning is believed to be especially important in regard to the "involuntary" behavior mediated by the autonomic nervous system, such as the arousal and recession of emotional and drive states, and it is this area that chiefly interests us. It is important to note that in this context the term *response* is used very loosely to refer to what is in all probability an extremely complex array of nervous system events. Thus, you may recall from Chapter 2 the speculation that the development of the Sullivanian need for tenderness in infants was a product of the pairing of the cues emanating from mother with those associated with biological satisfaction, such that the former cues come to have, in themselves, satisfying properties. Similarly, it is believed that the "response" of arousal of various emotional states (such as anxiety) may become attached to previously neutral cues through their occurrence in contiguity with cues already having the capacity to elicit the response in question. For example, the cues emanating from mother's presence may themselves acquire the property of eliciting anxiety responses if they have occurred sufficiently often in contiguity with cues (such as rough handling) that already have that property. While Sullivan did not explicitly use this learning model in his theoretical system, it can readily be seen as a plausible mechanism that may be involved in certain of his postulated psychic structures, such as the Good and Bad Mother.

Two of the more important characteristics of association learning, from our point of view, are that it is subject to *extinction* under certain circumstances, and that the cues which come to elicit any action exhibit *generalization* along dimensions of similarity. Extinction refers to a process whereby repeated presentations of the previously neutral (but now functional) cue, in the absence of further pairing with the originally critical, effective cue, results in weakening and eventual disappearance of the more recently acquired cue-response contingency. The extinguishing of the response under these conditions seems to be the general rule, but there may be a specific exception in the case of the conditioned anxiety response, which often shows remarkable persistence. This is due in part to the fact that avoidance behavior is generated by anxiety, and such behavior, becoming anticipatory, effectively removes the individual from contact with the cues eliciting anxiety; thus, extinction of the anxiety response cannot occur because the cues eliciting it are, in effect, prevented from occurring in any fully developed way. One important implication of these ideas concerns the role of the so-called defense mechanisms (such as selective inattention), which may properly be regarded as avoidance behaviors, in the perpetuation of conditioned anxiety responses.

By and large, any action elicited by a particular cue can also be elicited by other cues that are in one way or another similar to it. This is the phenomenon of cue (or stimulus) generalization; it appears to be an analogically mediated process. In other words, the particular relationship of similarity in cue generalization need not be—and in the case of generalized emotional behavior probably is usually *not*—logical or digital in nature. If a particular emotional response comes to be elicited by a given cue constellation, it may also be elicited by other, analogically related cues, and this process occurs without the intervention of conscious evaluation or judgment. Converted to Sullivanian terms, cue generalization, as conceived of here, is largely a parataxically mediated process. Extending this thinking somewhat further, certain effects postulated by Sullivan in regard to the determining influence of early experience upon later interpersonal relations can be explained thus: The parataxic distortions that sometimes emerge in given relationships might be due, in part, to the eliciting of emotional responses acquired at an earlier time by some analogical relation existing between the cues emanating from the other person in the contemporary relationship and those associated with an earlier significant other, or with a personification of him. For example, anxiety responses originally learned to cues emanating from an authoritarian father might generalize to contemporary relationships in which the other person emanates authority cues.

Association learning is generally regarded as the simplest form of learning of which organisms are capable. It is evidently a quite primitive process, and it is probably as close as human beings ever get to learning entirely "automatically"—that is, without the involvement of consciousness and the so-called higher mental processes. Even in the case of association learning, however, recent research has indicated that, in humans at least, it is rather markedly subject to certain kinds of cognitive influence. A case in point is provided in a recent study by Feather (1967). Working with the salivary response, which has traditionally been viewed as autonomically mediated, she found that subjects were able to inhibit or enhance conditioned salivation "on demand"; the magnitude of the conditioned response could be readily manipulated by the "instructions" given to the subjects. This finding, and other similar ones, suggest quite strongly that simple cued behavior may be a more complex process in humans than has heretofore been suspected, and that cognitive processes may definitely intervene to influence conditioned responses of even the so-called vegetative or autonomic variety.

As has already been suggested, our principal concern with cued behavior or association learning relates to the cueing of emotional arousal or its dissipation, including the arousal and dissipation (satisfaction) of drives. The terms *secondary drive* and *secondary reward,* respectively, are often employed with reference to the latter processes. The "responses" involved in such cueing are mainly physiological ones. Now, the cognitive identification of many of these kinds of responses by the person experiencing them often cannot be accomplished with precision merely by attending to his internal state. In other words, the phenomenal experience of many of these kinds of physiological events, taken by itself, may not be sufficient to inform the person adequately of the specific type of feeling he is having! As a result, the person must rely upon other, contextual information in order to "decide" what it is that he is feeling, be it anger, joy, sadness, or whatever. The influence of contextual information in the identification of personally experienced emotional states has been impressively demonstrated by Schachter and Singer (1962). Briefly, these investigators produced physiological arousal artificially by injecting their (unknowing) subjects with adrenalin. By manipulating contextual cues, they found that they could readily produce in these persons subjective feelings of anger, euphoria, or of no particular emotional arousal. Additional work on this problem has essentially confirmed these earlier findings. What does this mean in terms of cued emotionality in interpersonal relations? The most important implication would seem to be that the person's own cognitive interpretation of his cue-produced emotional state will often depend in part upon the context in which it occurs, including the behavior of other persons present in the situation. It might be noted in passing that Sullivan's somewhat vague suggestion that anger represents converted anxiety might be at least partially explained along these lines.

Very generally, then, the kind of learning mechanism involved in cued behavior must be seen as playing a most important role in interpersonal relations, where the cues supplied by one person may have substantial effects upon the emotional experience of the other. Moreover, this cueing process can occur "automatically" and outside of awareness. We will do well, however, to remain alert to the possible influence of cognitive processes in determining the manner in which any cued behavior actually affects the course of particular interpersonal integrations.

Instrumental behavior. The prototype of instrumental (or operant learning) behavior is the white rat learning to press a lever in the Skinner Box apparatus. The basic procedure involves an arrangement whereby a press of the lever delivers some "reward" (such as food or water) to the animal in the box; under these conditions the animal (if he is hungry or thirsty) rapidly learns to spend a goodly portion of his time in the box dutifully pressing the lever. Now, it happens that this observation, appropriately expanded, has very great generality across situations and species of organisms. By and large, organisms learn to do things that are followed by pleasant experiences for them, and they learn to avoid doing things that are followed by unpleasant experiences for them. Elimination of the "reward" or "punishment" usually results in eventual "extinction" of the behavior in question. This fundamentally hedonistic characteristic of organisms has attained the status of a "law" in psychology; it is called the *empirical law of effect,* and, so far as I know, there are no psychologists who would dispute the generality of the observations to which it refers. It is basically a law relating to *performance,* and not to the nature of the learning process. There are some minor problems in defining pleasantness and unpleasantness, because this has a tendency to invite an annoying circularity (pleasantness is anything the organism will work to produce, and vice versa); but there have been some ingenious solutions to the impasse, the details of which need not concern us. To return for a moment to my squirrel, I have no doubt that his extraordinary performance was brought off through the operation of the empirical law of effect. If you will think about that for a second, you will see that I am merely asserting that he engaged in his complicated activities because these activities have had pleasant consequences for him in similar situations in the past, or because he could in some way "foresee" that they would have pleasant consequences in this situation.

There is another, less generally accepted, form of the law of effect which states that stimulus-response connections immediately preceding a "reinforcing event" are *automatically strengthened,* such that the probability of recurrence of the response in the same or similar circumstances is increased by some order of magnitude. This is a statement of the *theoretical law of effect,* and it is advanced by its proponents as a general law of learning. It asserts a conception of learning as a mechanical strengthening of stimulus-response associations by the occurrence of "reinforcement." Now, the notion of *reinforcement,* as it applies to the theoretical law of effect, has been rather constantly troublesome, and its precise definition continues to be a matter of controversy. We cannot explore these conceptual problems in any detail here, but interested readers will find them well summarized in a recent paper by Pribram (1963). As a practical matter, a reinforcing event usually turns out to be about the same thing as a pleasant experience. (In the case of escape and avoidance learning, the reinforcement is the termination of an *unpleasant* experience.) The other controversial aspect of the theoretical law of effect, the notion that learning consists of the automatic strengthening (by reinforcement) of S-R associations, has been no less troublesome, partly because of the obvious difficulty of devising a means of experimental verification which would be independent of the operation of the noncontroversial empirical law of effect.

But there are, in addition, more substantive difficulties with the assertion that what is called instrumental learning necessarily occurs according to the theoretical law of effect, and Breger and McGaugh (1965) have recently provided an excellent summary of these. We have already had occasion to mention that the learning of language seems clearly to involve processes that exceed the explanatory power of S-R reinforcement theory. Moreover, there are even less complex "emitted" behaviors that seem to be learned in ways other than that suggested by the theoretical law of effect. Examples are numerous, and they include studies of so-called latent learning (Tolman and Honzik, 1930; Thistlethwaite, 1951), resistance to extinction (Lawrence and Festinger, 1962), imitation (Herbert and Harsh, 1944; Bandura and Walters, 1963), perceptual learning (Hebb, 1949), discrimination reversal (Goodwin and Lawrence, 1955; Mackintosh, 1963), and imprinting (Moltz, 1960). Even at the level of gross description, the behavior of animals (and persons) engaged in instrumental learning performances does not appear to conform to the theoretical law of effect, which suggests that what is learned are specific and increasingly stereotyped "responses." As anyone who has run animals in learning experiments (as I have) knows, this is not what happens. What happens is that the animal learns, in general, how to achieve a particular effect, and he may develop several grossly different methods for doing so. As Breger and McGaugh (1965) point out, this is what Tolman meant by "purposive behavior." The implications of purposiveness for achieving an understanding of interpersonal relations are of the greatest importance, and we shall return to this point presently and expand upon it in some detail.

In recent years, one of the most active areas of psychological research on human subjects has been that of so-called *verbal conditioning,* which in the large majority of cases is probably a misnomer. This field was opened by Greenspoon's (1955) discovery that he could manipulate the verbal output of subjects (that is, he could get them to increase their production of plural nouns) by dispensing social approval (for example, "Uh-huh") whenever they uttered, in the course of conversation, a word which fit some pre-established criterion. This and hundreds of subsequent findings of a similar kind were interpreted as instances of automatic instrumental or operant reinforcement learning. Some force was lent to this interpretation by virtue of the fact that subjects who had "learned" frequently denied during subsequent interrogation that they had been "aware" of the influence of the "reinforcement." More recent research (Dulany, 1962; Spielberger, 1962; Spielberger and DeNike, 1966), however, suggests that most of these earlier (and many more recent) experiments are most parsimoniously explained as simply not involving the kind of learning they were supposed to demonstrate. Rather, it seems to be the case that subjects routinely see this type of experimental situation as an exercise in problem-solving, the problem being to discover what the experimenter wants! The typical subject is extremely active cognitively during the experiment, trying out various "hypotheses" and the like, and he is at least partially "aware," even though he may deny this in a cursory interrogation. The implication is that a good deal of what is billed as a demonstration of human operant conditioning is nothing more than a trivial illustration of the fact that a human subject will frequently do what the experimenter wishes, if he can figure out what that is, and if he wants to please the experimenter. The experimenter's utterances and gestures in these situations are perhaps best considered as a special case of "prompting" (see below) rather than as "reinforcement."

How generally applicable is this form of interpretation of phenomena said to represent human instrumental learning? We can only speculate, but I would place my bet on the side of its being very general indeed. To put it another way, I suspect that much of what is commonly regarded as "reinforcement" is, at the human level at least, merely "information," which the subject uses in order to guide his behavior in pursuit of desired experience. This is an old idea whose origins may be found in Tolman (1932). Granting this (which many psychologists would probably resist doing), is *anything* in human behavior learned on the basis of straightforward automatic reinforcement principles? I think that probably a good deal is, or at least these principles are currently the best explanatory devices we have for accounting for certain kinds of behavior change. *Some* of the verbal conditioning studies, for example, do seem to involve this sort of effect. Two recent doctoral dissertations completed by students of mine (Stein, 1967; Riddle, 1968) have shown powerful evidence of verbal conditioning *without* awareness of reinforcement contingencies; in the latter case, in fact, awareness seems to have impeded learning performance. The point that I am trying to make, once again, is that human performances are exceedingly complicated, and that active cognitive processes of a purposive, foresightful, hypothesizing variety are the rule rather than the exception in determining all of human behavior, and certainly in that portion of it which interests us—namely, interpersonal behavior.

The importance of instrumental learning in the acquisition or modfication of characteristic interpersonal behavior can be fairly summarized in the following way. We must acknowledge the power of the empirical law of effect in determining behavior. With few (and possibly no) exceptions, behavior tends in the direction of maximizing pleasure and minimizing pain or displeasure, although we should expect to find, of course, many individual variations as to what constitutes pleasure and pain. Sullivan emphasized the empirical law of effect in his *learning by anxiety, learning by trial and success,* and *learning by rewards and punishments* (pages 35–36). The hedonic element, then, is critical in instrumental behavior. But does it operate directly and "automatically" to strengthen given responses? Possibly so in certain cases, but this will not suffice as a general formulation of learning, especially in regard to complex behavior. Much of the instrumental behavior of persons (and for that matter of animals) involves complicated cognitive and purposive elements which are quite unmanageable within the framework of a peripheral S-R reinforcement theory. The most significant instrumental behaviors of persons do not seem to be learned "responses," but rather learned *strategies* for achieving certain hedonically relevant events. This idea will be given more explicit attention later, but I think my squirrel was employing such a strategy in concealing the bread.

Prompted behavior. Many of the actions humans learn to perform are learned on the basis of prompting or information provided by the environment—that is, on the basis of pre-response *guidance* rather than post-response reinforcement. One need only consider the process of acquiring skill with a golf club to appreciate the difference, although I would not deny that finally getting off a good hit is a tremendously pleasant experience, the anticipation of which is presumably one of the reasons for trying to acquire the skill. A great deal of cognitive learning is achieved by prompting, as will be seen, but for the moment let us focus upon prompted action learning. The modes of prompting are legion. They include all forms of observational learning such as attempted imitation of models, or what Sullivan referred to as *trial and error learning by human example.* They also include such processes as active instruction and advice, as exemplified in the functions of the golf pro. Less obviously, much of what is called practice or rehearsal, either overt or covert, seems to be a type of self-prompting which utilizes feedback information from attempted performances to guide future performances. Undoubtedly, in everyday life we all use many subtle signs and signals, often without awareness, which have the character of prompts to others, such that their behavior toward us is modified in personally pleasing directions. Some persons, for example, develop considerable expertise in prompting compliments and other flattering behavior, while others become expert in the subtle instigation of rage through prompting operations; the "target" persons in these instances may thus be induced to modify their characteristic social behavior, at least in relation to the person who is doing the prompting.

As has been suggested above, much of what would ordinarily be called instrumental behavior would seem to be very similar in principle to prompted behavior, the only distinguishing feature being the temporal one: whether the information used as a guide for action occurs before or after (or possibly *during*) the initial occurrences of the behavior in question. Thus, in the "verbal conditioning" situation, the experimenter *could* simply inform the subjects beforehand that he approved of their using, let us say, plural nouns. Other things being equal (for example, motivation to please the experimenter), one would expect this to be a more efficient device for increasing plural noun production than the experimenter's post-response "Uh-huh," simply because the latter is less informative than the direct prior instructions. Of course, this brings up the question of the permanence and generalizability of the response to new situations—you will recall that the term *learning* implies a relatively permanent alteration in behavior. As a matter of empirical fact, however, the case for the permanence or generalizability of verbal responses conditioned in the standard way (that is, by using "uh-huh" or some similar social "reinforcement") is, with a few notable exceptions, most unimpressive. It is conceivable, in any event, that instructional prompting which implied that it is generally a good thing, or that it generally pleases others, to say plural nouns (or what have you)—as might be the case with many kinds of more subtle social reinforcement—could well result in some more or less persistent behavior change. This would qualify as learning, and it is not far removed in principle from a very common (and presumably generally effective) instructional technique employed by parents and other trainers—namely, pointing out or otherwise making salient the conditions and contingencies for maintaining social approval.

Action learning and interpersonal behavior. The three kinds of action learning described in this section jointly provide a useful means of accounting for much of what can be observed in the area of interpersonal behavior. We assume that the child begins to develop his own characteristic style of interpersonal behavior in consequence of the operation of these processes in the course of his early experience, and we also assume that any notable changes in interpersonal behavior occurring later in life must involve these same processes. The fact that persons can cue, reinforce, and prompt each others' behavior has enormous significance for interpersonal behavior modification and for an understanding of interpersonal relations, as will be shown in the pages that follow. Throughout this section, however, we have emphasized the degree to which cognitive and informational processes may influence and modulate almost every aspect of action learning. We now turn to the cognitive processes themselves in order to gain a clearer understanding of their nature and of the manner in which their influence manifests itself.

COGNITIVE LEARNING

As has already been suggested, the distinction between action and cognition is, in some ways at least, an arbitrary one, and it is important that you not be misled by this instance of the sometimes almost accidental categorizing habits of psychologists, which I share. It was pointed out in Chapter 1 that organisms do not, by and large, have direct commerce with the world of objective "reality." To the extent that action of any sort is determined by this reality, the causal relation is mediated by perceptual and other cognitive processes; the organism does not respond to the real world but rather to his perception of it. This fact in itself would justify our attention to the manner in which cognitions and perceptions are formed and to their mode of operation. Beyond that, however, persons, and possibly other higher organisms, exhibit an extraordinarily strong need to maintain consistent relationships between their actions and their cognitions such that, in the course of a given action sequence, either may be modified in order to bring it into accord with the other. This fact, whose recognition contributed to the development of Festinger's (1957; Brehm and Cohen, 1962) well-known theory of cognitive dissonance, underscores the essential futility of attempting to understand human behavior in any complete way without attending to both its action and its cognitive aspects, and to the manner in which they interact.

As might be expected, the interdependence of action and cognition frequently complicates efforts at causal analysis of the behavior of persons. It also complicates our efforts to understand how actions and cognitions are learned, because complex interrelations between action and cognition are likely to be involved in nearly all significant learning experiences, at least at the human level. The general field of verbal learning, including verbal operant conditioning, is an exemplary case in point (Mandler, 1967). Despite the evident interdependencies, however, it seems necessary to deal with cognitive learning as a separate process if we are to retain a reasonable semblance of pedagogical orderliness. In this section, then, we shall try to identify and analyze the more important aspects of cognitive learning, under which rubric are included all of those processes involved in the modification of an individual's *knowing* or *understanding.* One large class of the cognitive processes, that of perception, involves the mental operations of an interpretive character performed upon incoming sensory information, and we shall have occasion to consider this particular class of cognition at some length.

Information needs. We make the assumption that the individual guides his behavior in the direction of perceived maximization of hedonic reward. The latter may be associated with various "primary" satisfactions such as the alleviation of hunger or sexual gratification, with minimization of acquired anxieties and insecurities, or with the realization of more abstract, symbolic "values" associated with the cue properties of certain kinds of events the individual may strive to bring about or avoid. We also assume that past action learning will usually have provided the individual with a hierarchy of favored actions for any given situation—that is, that he will tend to select, from among the actions he perceives as possible in a given situation, those actions which have been most successful in the past in maximizing relative pleasure. Now, obviously he will often be confronted with new situations, situations that are different in important respects from anything he has encountered in the past. Even if his environment is relatively stable, *he* changes over time, if only by virtue of biological maturation, and this will usually entail at least modest change in the goals of his interactions with the environment. In short, the individual, under normal circumstances, learns that being a creature of habit has distinct limitations (as well as undeniable advantages) in terms of maximizing hedonic outcomes. He also presumably learns that the probability of his being able to act in a way which maximizes these outcomes is directly proportional to the adequacy of his knowledge about the relevant conditions, and to his ability to predict the consequences of the actions he might take in a given set of circumstances. The advantages of having an adequate "cognitive map" (Tolman, 1948) of the environment must become obvious to even very young children.

At least one psychologist, George Kelly (1963), has developed an entire theory of personality around the central notion that the organization and direction of behavior is determined by the manner in which the individual cognizes or conceptualizes (construes) his experience. One of the cardinal principles in Kelly's theory is that the individual actively seeks throughout life to extend and refine his concept system by making behavioral choices which accomplish that end—that is, he is motivated to engage in behaviors which enhance his ability to anticipate events by refining the "personal constructs" by means of which he organizes the information provided by the consequences of those behaviors. This information-seeking tendency of persons is more than an interesting hypothesis. Both White (1959) and Berlyne (1960) have reviewed an impressive array of empirical studies which suggest that all of the higher animals share strong tendencies to engage in information-seeking behavior of various kinds. Whether innate or acquired, such needs are of obvious functional significance for adaptation, and we may assume that their existence is practically universal in the human species. We also assume that the ultimate motivation supporting much exploratory behavior in humans is extrinsic in nature—that the knowledge is desired for its instrumental significance in achieving various collateral goals. One needs to know the lay of the land in order to be able to mine it effectively. This is not to deny, however, that knowledge and "mastery" may, in themselves, have rewarding properties.

Uncertainty and its reduction. The intimate relationship between the adequacy of one's conceptions of reality and one's ability to have his needs met suggests that uncertainty about personally significant matters will be experienced as an unpleasant state of affairs—something to be avoided. In fact, persons do exhibit strong tendencies to avoid uncertainty and confusion as they contemplate immediate action choices, sometimes even at the cost of selectively inattending to available, relevant (but conflicting) information. Jones and Gerard (1967) integrate a large number of empirical observations on this and related phenomena in terms of their concept of *unequivocal behavior orientation,* a postulated state toward which the individual in a decision situation is said to strive.

The reduction of subjective uncertainty by avoiding information, however, has obvious limitations in the long run. It is probably a special case of uncertainty reduction employed routinely only by persons for whom uncertainty has somehow become a cue for relatively severe anxiety, and employed by most of the rest of us only, as Jones and Gerard suggest, after a "decision" has been made, where it operates to facilitate action. In the more general case, in which the reduction of uncertainty, while desired, is not urgently required, it may be surmised that the individual maintains open channels for the reception of information, and that he actively seeks it out in those areas of his life in which he anticipates the possible occurrence of hedonically relevant events. Quite obviously, a very great amount of this information transmission is socially mediated, especially for the child, whose direct experience with the world beyond his immediate home surroundings is necessarily limited. Jones and Gerard list the more important modes of information transmission as follows (pp. 128–31):

Descriptive instruction, which involves the offering of symbolically (usually verbally) coded interpretations of events and relations among events. It is in this manner, presumably, that most of us acquire the greater part of the information we have about the natural or real world, the way things are, and how they function. The content of descriptive instruction is concerned with the nature of objective reality, and it may be correct or incorrect.

Advice and consultation is not directly concerned with the nature of objective reality, but rather with issues of "appropriate" behavior under given conditions. It goes beyond a mere description of what the world is like in one or another of its aspects and is directed to questions of the adequacy or propriety of alternative courses of action. Its content may thus be either tactical or essentially moral in nature.

Social comparison refers to a process in which information, particularly information relating to oneself, is extracted from observations of the behavior of others. The concept of social comparison was first advanced by Festinger (1954), chiefly as a means of integrating certain observations of the behavior of persons in small groups in regard to the achievement of consensus in matters of attitude and belief. Attitudes and beliefs, by their very nature, are frequently not confirmable through observation of objective "reality." They are confirmable, however, in the realm of *social reality* provided only that some standards of evaluation may be derived from observations of the behavior of persons whom one likes or respects. Interest in social comparison processes in recent years has tended to focus upon the manner in which they function in the definition of one's own beliefs and in the assessment of one's own abilities and traits. Jones and Gerard (1967) note that social comparison may be analyzed into two separate and distinct processes, *comparative appraisal* and (here they use a term with which we are already familiar) *reflected appraisal.* The former of these refers to the use of observations of the performances of others in respect to given activities or tasks in order to determine the adequacy or standing of one's own performance. The implicit question is, "How good am I at this?" or, "How do I measure up relative to these other folks?" Reflected appraisal, on the other hand, involves an estimation or inference about another person's evaluation of some aspect of ourselves, based upon his behavior *toward us;* the behavior itself, of course, is usually only implicitly evaluative in nature. Thus, the individual, by attending to the behavior of others, may learn a great deal about himself in quite subtle ways. It is evident that the empirical investigation of social comparison processes, which is currently developing at a quickening pace (Latané, 1966), holds great promise in increasing our understanding of the manner in which the *self* is formed and modified, a promise which Sullivan would doubtless have applauded.

Observational learning refers to the congeries of learning experience whereby persons derive information through direct observation, other than social comparison, of events occurring around them. The latter include, of course, the behavior of other persons and its consequences, from which a great deal of knowledge of social norms and social role expectations may be acquired. We also learn by observation to anticipate the effects of our actions in relation to particular other persons, and to modify them accordingly—a process which Sullivan recognized in his "theorem of reciprocal emotions" (see page 40).

Empathic cognizance is a process in which information about the feelings of others and their probable reactions in given circumstances is gained by a kind of direct intuition, by immediate inference. Nearly everyone claims to have employed this type of knowing in his own experience, but it has proved to be extremely difficult to define and measure it adequately for purposes of controlled empirical research (Cronbach, 1955), partly because the transmitted messages are undoubtedly coded in largely analogical terms. Our reliable knowledge about such empathic processes is therefore exceedingly limited, despite their generally acknowledged ubiquity.

Descriptive instruction, advice and consultation, social comparison, observational learning, and empathic cognizance, then, appear to be the principal modes of transmission available to the individual in acquiring cognitive information from his surroundings. It may be noted in passing that these modes are roughly ordered along a continuum of decreasing explicitness, and that the coding of the constituent information seems correspondingly dimensionalized between strongly digital and strongly analogical poles. One implication of this observation, in Sullivanian terms, is that, in general, the *consensual validity* of the information obtained will be relatively high in the case of descriptive instruction and relatively low in the case of empathic cognizance, the other modes being intermediate in this respect.

Perceptual learning. In dealing with the modes of transmission of cognitive knowledge or understanding in the above section, we have in a sense put the cart before the horse, an arrangement which should now be corrected. As has been repeatedly emphasized, information does not proceed from events in the real world directly into one's brain. Information from the environment in its functional form is actually a product of a greater or lesser degree of "processing" of sensory data. There is therefore at least one step between an event "out there" (for example, the provision by another person of a unit of descriptive instruction) and the formation of an enduring cognitive unit regarding that event. In Kelly's (1963) terms, one "construes" experience, and part of this construing takes place immediately as the experience is registered. This process is ordinarily termed *perception,* and we might well ask whether there is such a thing as perceptual learning—whether the processing mechanism itself might be subject to relatively persistent alteration based on experience. The fairly obvious answer is yes, and there is a great deal of empirical evidence which may be interpreted to support such an assertion. Bruner (1957) has provided a theoretical framework that effectively integrates much of the available knowledge in this area, and we shall follow his thinking in our discussion.

Bruner's analysis is organized around the concept of *perceptual readiness,* which refers to the likelihood of arousal or evocation of a given percept in response to a particular pattern of sensory stimulation. The relations between patterns of sensory stimulation and perceptual "interpretations" of them are considered to be probabilistic in nature, the probabilities being determined, in part, by past experience. For example, if a particular object, say an apple, is presented to you for your inspection, your perceiving it as an "apple" is by no means absolutely assured. The likelihood of your doing so is dependent upon numerous conditions, including the degree of exposure of the apple to your inspection, and—more basically—upon whether or not the category "apple," with its associated defining characteristics, is a part of your prior cognitive equipment.

A perceptual "category," according to Bruner, can be conceived as a set of specifications or rules which determine what events impinging upon the sensory apparatus will be experienced as equivalent. The category "apple," for example, would presumably involve specifications as to general size, shape, color, and surface texture—limits by means of which any particular object could be judged as either equivalent or not equivalent to the class of objects represented by the category. Perception is therefore a type of decision process in which inferences are made about the nature of impinging events, objects, or attributes of objects on the basis of previously existing discriminatory specifications; the latter may or may not be consciously recognized and subject to verbalization by the perceiver. Bruner goes on to note that categories vary in their degree of *accessibility*—the readiness with which they intrude themselves in the perceptual process under given conditions. Certain of a person's categories are routinely accessible, while others come into operation only very rarely. This characteristic of categories is said to serve two functions: (1) It minimizes the degree to which the environment presents surprises. (2) It maximizes the likelihood of attainment of desired objects and events owing to the enhancing effects of adient motivation upon category accessibility. The accessibility of the category "apple," for example, would be relatively great for the person who has a current, specific hunger for apples, so much so, in fact, that he might occasionally mistake some other object for an apple. The latter is an instance of the interesting phenomenon of motivationally determined misperception, which Bruner conceptualizes in terms of category accessibility. A more general statement of this idea is that, under conditions of less than optimal observation or objective stimulus definition, perception will be veridical (that is, "correct" or leading to accurate prediction) in proportion to the degree that the accessibility of the person's categories accurately reflects the frequency with which events are actually encountered. Should motivational factors (either facilitative or inhibitory) distort category accessibility, perceptual errors will occur whose content is determined by the character of these distortions.

This general approach to the problem of perception affords us an analytical tool of very considerable power and versatility. Individual differences in perception and various perceptual idiosyncracies and biases are readily accounted for within a framework whose empirical foundations are exceptionally well developed. Limitations in perceptual veridicality, by and large, may be assumed to be due to one or the other of two types of causal agent. The most fundamental of these would be the person's failing to have learned the most appropriate categories and event expectancies for effective differentiation of his environment. Various of his categories, for example, may have limits which are too broad or too narrow for the manner in which the environment is in fact structured, as in the case of the politically reactionary individual whose excessively broad "communist" category may include a substantial array of stimuli that would not be categorized as "communist" by most other persons. Inadequate or inappropriate category learning is presumably the result of (1) limitations or peculiarities in the nature of the perceptual training experiences to which the individual has been exposed, (2) distortions introduced by attitudinal or motivational predispositions, or (3) biological impediments such as mental deficiency.

The other principal causal agent operating to reduce perceptual veridicality is concerned with the accessibility of the categories that have been learned. It seems likely that in many cases it would be difficult, as a practical matter, to distinguish this kind of problem from one involving category learning, but the distinction should be clear conceptually. The difficulty here is that a more accessible category may operate to mask or prevent the use of a less accessible, but more veridically representative, one. Category accessibility is related to the expectancy of appearance of the relevant stimuli, to the motivational state of the individual (which may instigate a searching orientation), and to the breadth of the acceptance limits of the category in question. In general, categories with very narrow acceptance limits are relatively inaccessible. Bruner (1957) advances the interesting speculation that the phenomena encompassed by the Freudian concept of "repression" represent the establishment of very narrow category limits, such that the critical ("repressed") category remains unactivated by any and all stimulus inputs which fail to make an extremely precise criterial match.

The power of this conceptual framework may be briefly illustrated with reference to Sullivan's thinking (Chapter 2), which, while less systematic, strongly emphasizes perceptual processes. We might think of various of Sullivan's mental structures in perceptual category terms. Particularly relevant are those designated as *personifications,* including Good Mother, Bad Mother, Good Me, Bad Me, and even Not Me—a category that remains inaccessible under normal circumstances. The Sullivanian *self system* is readily conceived as a complex system of more or less accessible attribute categories, and its self-perpetuating character may be partly accounted for in terms of an organization of categories whose limits become increasingly well defined and resistant to experience-induced change throughout early life. It is conceivable, in short, that input stimuli relating to the self, and those relating to other persons, are "processed" through previously established cognitive category systems which share many of the characteristics of Sullivan's notion of personifications. An obvious corollary is that we have here a suggested mechanism for at least certain instances of *selective inattention* and *dissociation,* in terms of the absence or inaccessibility of maximally appropriate categories relevant to particular, personally significant stimulus inputs. *Parataxic distortions,* in their *cognitive* as differentiated from their *emotional* (see page 62) aspect, may be viewed as the result of inappropriate uses of unduly accessible or excessively broad categories in the formation of impressions of others (person perception) from stimuli provided by them. Finally, it may be noted that *consensually valid* communication can occur between persons only to the extent that they encode and decode transmitted information in terms of a shared cognitive category system; *autistic* language is encoded in terms of relatively eccentric or idiosyncratic categories.

Thinking and problem-solving. A great deal of behavior, especially at the human level, is mediated by various symbolic manipulations of information which has already been processed perceptually and subsequently stored in memory. Relatively immediate and direct responses to perceived stimuli are probably atypical in the total behavioral output of persons. If we exclude from consideration "undirected" thinking, such as reverie, fantasy, and the like, and concentrate upon the more important class of directed thinking or problem-solving, we find a kind of self-generated learning of considerable importance. Sullivan's *eduction of relations* learning and all manner of so-called *insight* learning, of which, by the way, higher animals having the relevant experiential background (information) seem capable (Harlow, 1949), represent situations in which new behavioral strategies for the attainment of goals are evolved wholly at the cognitive level. This "freedom from immediacy" is enormously aided by the development of (digital) language as a medium for encoding, storing, and in various ways symbolically transforming experience, as Bruner (1964), among others, has pointed out.

We cannot afford here to delve deeply into the immensely complicated topics of cognitive problem-solving and insight learning. It may suffice to note that these processes are continuous with more strictly perceptual ones, and that the theoretical model presented in the preceding section will also serve to integrate much of what we know about directed thinking. It too is a decision-making, inferential process which operates upon previously acquired cognitive elements as well as those currently being formulated from incoming sensory data. It is also in large part a matter of categorizing various cognitive elements on the basis of comparative matching with established, but modifiable, criterial specifications. Human beings are capable of imagining the state of affairs they desire to bring about, working back from there to determine the intermediate states of affairs that will be required for goal attainment, and formulating and discarding proposed actions on the basis of their meeting or failing to meet criterial specifications of probable effectiveness. As in the case of perception, we may assume that the adequacy or "veridicality" of an individual's problem-solving efforts will be a function of the adequacy of his categories (concepts) for the task at hand, and of their current accessibility in the given situation.

Plans and Strategies: An Integration

To reiterate, this chapter aims to provide a basic conceptual framework for understanding the processes involved in the acquisition and modification of interpersonal behavior. This is a problem of learning, and I believe that we have in the foregoing touched upon all of the basic forms of learning with which we need to be concerned in rendering an adequate account of the processes whereby persons learn to adapt to each other. The discussion, however, has necessarily been rather abstract and piecemeal, lacking in both specific referents and in overall integration. The former deficiency cannot be rectified here; subsequent chapters will undertake to do so. In the remainder of this chapter I should like to provide some greater conceptual integration of the ideas presented here. The theoretical model I shall employ borrows heavily from the thinking of Miller, Galanter, and Pribram (1960), which is in turn strongly influenced by the functional and design properties inherent in modern information-processing technology. The basic ideas are very similar to those advanced by Campbell (1966) in a more recent analysis.

THE ORGANIZATION OF BEHAVIOR

The foregoing discussion has dealt rather disdainfully with traditional formulations of learning as they apply to human behavior, and particularly with those associated with the S-R reinforcement position. That position has been attacked because the model of learning postulated by it does not seem capable of handling the range of phenomena with which we hope to concern ourselves. This is not to say that it could not possibly be made to do so if we will allow for some considerable stretching and straining. The argument for making such allowances is not completely without merit, for these conceptions continue to prove somewhat fruitful in highly simplified learning situations. On the other hand, I do not find this a sufficiently compelling reason to retain the model in areas where its limits are clearly surpassed and its usefulness severely compromised. Ideally, we should like to have a model capable of incorporating the essential features of S-R reinforcement notions as relevant to a certain class of simple learning phenomena, but one also able to extend beyond this level of phenomena without necessitating drastic shifts in the concepts employed. Is such a model feasible? It would seem so.

Our discussion to this point has strongly emphasized the role of information and the cognitive processes in determining human behavior. It pictures man as an information-processing, planful, decision-making animal. It has even been suggested that man is not the only animal who engages in such activities, although I shall be satisfied if I have convinced you that they are abundantly and very crucially involved in any moderately complex human performance. This is hardly a startling insight, even for a psychologist. Yet it has proven surprisingly difficult until recently to construct general behavior theories that could comfortably accommodate this insight and at the same time avoid certain empirical, logical, or philosophical pitfalls. A detailed recounting of the latter issues would take us rather far afield and will not be attempted here. Suffice it to say that the main outlines of a solution have begun to appear, and that they involve a much greater appreciation of the complexity of structure and events which must be postulated in order to account adequately for *any* behavior, including "simple" reflexes. In short, behavior—and especially complex human behavior such as speaking an articulate English sentence—has been discovered to require a very intricately structured and organized series of underlying events, in which information-processing and feedback mechanisms play a critical role. Within this changing perspective on the structure of behavior it becomes possible to integrate readily, without strain, the kind of cognitive and purposive elements whose inclusion would appear to be dictated by the implications of our own analysis.

The Image. Behavior, according to Miller, Galanter, and Pribram (1960), is an intrinsic aspect of the life of organisms; it is *always* occurring as long as the organism is alive. The content of behavior, its specific forms, is determined by the organism's *Image* and his *Plans.* The concept of Image refers to everything that the organism has heretofore learned. The Image, then, includes all knowledge of the world, correct or incorrect, that the particular organism—let us say the person—possesses. It also includes all of the "values" the person has acquired—that is, the affective significance, on a scale of desirability versus undesirability, which he attaches to any particular state of affairs. Such states of affairs may represent objects, events, ideas, persons, or literally any experience the individual may have. The Image may be thought of as the individual's comprehensive "cognitive map" or "schema" of the structure and functioning of the universe, and it includes the particular "value" he places upon its diverse aspects. The Image is, of course, not a fixed entity, but rather changes constantly with new experience.

Plans. The exploitation of the Image is accomplished by means of Plans, which are themselves usually represented in the Image. Plans are analogous to computer programs in that they are hierarchically ordered processes that control the order in which a sequence of operations (behaviors) is to be performed. Plans constitute an intrinsic aspect of behavior, and therefore of living. Like computer programs, Plans incorporate feedback loops whereby the consequences of given operations are matched or compared with some standard in order to generate decisions as to what future operations will be performed. The unit of analysis used by Miller, Galanter, and Pribram is such a feedback loop, called a TOTE (for Test-Operate-Test-Exit) unit. TOTE units *can,* by the way, be conceived in "reinforcement" terms. Plans are of varying degrees of complexity and hierarchical organization, and may involve any number of intricately layered and nested TOTE units, each having its own Test and Operate phases. The Operate phase of a higher-order TOTE may consist of another TOTE unit, or a series of them. The "nesting" of TOTEs, as well as other features of this conceptual approach, is illustrated with reference to a Plan for hammering a nail until its head is flush with a surface. The latter is an aspect of the Image, involving elements of both knowledge and "value" (assuming one wants the nailhead to be flush), and it constitutes the Test phase of the overall, highest order TOTE. This Test, in other words, involves the question, Is the nailhead flush? If the answer is "yes," an Exit message is effected and the execution of the Plan terminates. If, however, the answer is "no," an Operate message is effected. The Operate phase of the overall TOTE consists of two interrelated sub-TOTES having a common Test phase. The latter Test concerns the current position of the hammer. If it is Down, the Operate message is "lift;" if it is Up, the Operate message is "strike," following which the flushness-of-the-nail Test is again performed—and so on. It is readily seen that this Plan, which is basically similar to the flow charts used in the programing of computers, will indeed result in a flush nailhead. Miller, Galanter, and Pribram argue strongly, on the basis of behavioral as well as neurophysiological evidence, that an adequate account of behavior requires the adoption of a theoretical model having the general hierarchized, structural, and feedback characteristics suggested by this brief example. Their argument, whose manifold details are beyond the scope of the present volume, is a powerful and convincing one, although further research will almost undoubtedly require revisions in the particulars of the approach they advocate. In any event, I am eager only that you appreciate the general outline of these ideas.

As is perhaps obvious, not all Plans are consciously and deliberately formulated and executed. Many learned Plans appear to become routinized and automatized, as in the case of motor skills. In animals, instinctive behaviors represent the execution of inherited, stereotyped, involuntary Plans. Certain Plans at the human level are so broad and encompassing as to constitute a kind of life style, as may be the case, for example, in respect to the individual's meta-Plans—his Plans for formulating Plans. Even in the case of a very deliberately formulated Plan, it is likely that at any point in time only those parts of it which are currently being executed are in focal awareness, and even those may quite conceivably escape attention. When we speak of Plans, then, we are not necessarily referring to deliberate, conscious processes. On the other hand, we should not lose sight of the fact that many Plans, perhaps especially those involving significant interpersonal events, have substantial elements of deliberateness, at least in their initial formulation.

TACTICS AND STRATEGY OF BEHAVIOR

Behavior is directed toward the achievement of valued states of affairs according to the means dictated by the individual's "knowledge" of the structural and functional characteristics of the universe. It is mediated by Plans that incorporate the relevant values and "information." Plans vary in their degree of generality or specificity, and in the number of lower-order Plans ("Subroutines") they subsume. It seems appropriate, therefore, to consider very abstract, general plans as being *strategical* in nature, and lower-order ones as being essentially *tactical*. This conception, as it applies to personality, permits us to think in terms of very high-order Plans that may determine an individual's general "style of life," and also in terms of lower-order ones that operate at the level of day-to-day adaptation to specific situations. It is conceivable that values at the tactical level will occasionally be renounced in favor of achieving strategical objectives in terms of an overall "master" Plan. This conception, which has an obvious relationship to notions of personal maturity (such as the ability to delay immediate gratification), also implies some interesting possibilities in regard to "disturbed" interpersonal behavior, as will be shown in subsequent chapters.

Motives. A "motive," according to Miller, Galanter, and Pribram, comprises two independent parts: value and intention.

Value, as we have seen, is an aspect of the Image in which some state of affairs is vested with affective significance. An "intention" refers to a Plan for realizing the value, and especially to the uncompleted parts of a Plan whose execution is already in process. Motives, as the term is used here, may of course function outside of awareness.

Problem-solving. Behaviors required for the realization of valued states of affairs—that is, Plans for achieving them—emerge from the execution of search-and-solve Plans. The latter consist, in part, of Test phases involving an Image of the desired end state and any intermediate states believed to be prerequisite. Search-and-solve Plans, in a sense, start at the end in this fashion and proceed backward toward the construction of an ordered sequence of events that will produce the desired end state. Often, the TOTE units involved in search-and-solve Plans call for Operating phases in which overt behavioral "Tests" are performed in order to provide further information to aspects of the Image from which the problem-solution Plan must evolve. The solution of any given problem might predominantly involve the construction of a better Image or the elaboration of an effective Plan to exploit it. Miller, Galanter, and Pribram suggest that the phenomenological (that is, the self-perceived) aspects of problem-solving are more often associated with the construction of alternative Images as to the nature of the problem than with alternative Plans relating to a particular Image. It should be noted that "the construction of an alternative Image" is tantamount to the refinement or extension of a "category" or "construct" system in the language employed, respectively, by Bruner (1957) and by Kelly (1963).

ANXIETY AND CONFLICT

The present analysis suggests two forms of personal "conflict" to which individuals may become subject. One of these is the commonly recognized conflict of motives, where two or more mutually incompatible values become salient simultaneously. The second type of conflict, which is considerably less obvious, is a conflict of currently functioning Plans, such that they require mutually incompatible operations. As Miller, Galanter, and Pribram point out, the individual will almost necessarily be unaware of a conflict of this type (since any recognized incompatibility would compel re-Planning), in contrast to the frequently very obtrusive nature of conflicts involving incompatible desires. The discovery by the person that two or more of his Plans are incompatible would seem to entail a more or less drastic revision of his Image in respect to the areas of his life that are involved. If a conflict of Plans cannot be resolved through abandonment of one or more of them, "neurotic" behavior is said to be the result.

Enforced abandonment of Plans, especially those of a strategical order, is believed to induce intensified emotionality, which may manifest itself as *anxiety* if it cannot be contained by the provision of a focus for it in the Image (for example, by cognitive elucidation in the manner suggested by the work of Schachter and Singer [1962], as described above) or in ongoing action. The advent of anxiety necessitates the formulation and execution of Plans for coping with it, such as defense mechanisms. This view of anxiety provides an alternative to viewing it exclusively as a learned (cued) fear response, and there is some sound empirical support for the hypothesis that anxiety *can* result from the interruption of planned sequences of behavior. Mandler and Watson (1966), for example, have recently reviewed evidence from a number of human and animal experiments which appears to confirm this point. A good deal of what is known about the interpersonal induction of anxiety in human subjects (for example, by disconfirming their social role expectancies [Grinker, 1966]) can also be interpreted in this light.

Overview

Consider the situation of a person about to undergo his initial encounter with another person. What he brings to that situation is an enormously complex system of "knowledge" and cognitive apparatus for processing new information, a variety of potential emotional reactions which might be cued off by particular events, a set of "values" that represent his immediate and long-range objectives, and a rich store of behavioral Plans that constitute his established strategies and tactics for maximizing his hedonic outcomes. The situation, as represented in his Image, will have various characteristics which are only partly determined by the "objective" state of affairs, since the latter will have been processed in terms of the nature and accessibility of the constructs or categories available to the person at that time. His initial "cognitive map" may or may not be relatively veridical. Should such a condition of contingency or unpredictability be represented in the Image, we might suppose that a search-and-solve Plan is activated at the outset whose function will be to test the veridicality of the initial cognitive map. The execution of such a Plan will presumably involve various tentative gestures toward the other person, whose reactions can then be matched to the Test phase of the search-and-solve TOTE. If the match is poor, the Image regarding the nature of the situation will require revision. This revision, of course, can be accomplished only within the limits set by the constructs currently available to the person.

As the interaction gets under way, there is continuous, perceptually mediated monitoring of events and, if necessary, revising of the Image. Plans are executed in accord with the moment-to-moment cognitive representation of the situation, and in accord with the person's momentary and long-range motivational objectives. Many of these Plans, including various subroutines, will be well-established ones which have been rehearsed many times in past encounters whose perceived characteristics belonged to the same categories as those evoked in the present situation. These Plans may run their courses with a minimum of conscious attention to their execution. The other person, however, has his own Plans and may present relatively novel or unanticipated stimulus configurations. He may prompt behaviors for which no ready-made Plan exists; he may withhold expected "reinforcements"; he may engage in behavior that does not reciprocate the behavior offered; or he may cue various emotional reactions and in this way induce disruptive alterations in the motivational and cognitive aspects of the first person's Image. In short, he may do any number of things that force the first person into an essentially problem-solving orientation, leading to revision of Image, Plans, or both. Presumably, any such occurrence will normally occupy some of the attention of the temporarily stymied person, and we would expect to find elements of the process represented in consciousness. We would also expect that the experience, since it involves an interruption in the execution of Plans, will be accompanied by a certain amount of anxiety.

As the interaction continues, the person accrues information from and about the other person which is duly processed and stored for future reference in the Image. He may also acquire new information about himself and new elaborations of his Plans, and these too become part of the experience record stored in the Image. This would suggest that, in all but the most stereotyped or role-limited interactions, the actors change to some degree as they interact. In relatively persisting or repeated interactions between the same persons, moreover, one would surmise that the overall direction of change tends toward increased mutuality and reciprocity, and a good deal of empirical evidence can be marshalled in support of this surmise. Be that as it may, we know too that many potentially persistent interactions never seem to get off of the ground and are peremptorily terminated by the actions of one or both parties. In these situations we must assume that the hedonic outcomes of one or both parties to the interaction have been insufficiently rewarding (or excessively "costly"), and that it has proven impossible for them to effect a mutually satisfactory behavioral articulation. There is, of course, also a kind of middle ground in which a relationship may be both persistent *and* relatively unsatisfactory. In the pages that follow we will endeavor to explore in greater detail the conditions affecting these diverse trends in dyadic relationships, and to illustrate the centrality of the processes involved to what is commonly regarded as "personality."

INTERPERSONAL BEHAVIOR AND THE HABITS OF SQUIRRELS

Having come to the end of this somewhat widely ranging chapter, I cannot forego one more reference to the hero of its opening pages, whose remarkable talents (or at least those of his kin) have continued to enliven my breakfasts throughout this period of writing. The point of the squirrel story was that he seemed to have a Plan, a strategy for determining events—not only immediate ones, but also those that constituted potentialities for his future satisfaction, or the lack of it. He was engaged in purposive behavior. The behavior of persons in relation to other persons exhibits this same characteristic.

REFERENCES

BANDURA, A., and WALTERS, R. H. *Social learning and personality development.* New York: Holt, Rinehart & Winston, 1963.

BERLYNE, D. E. *Conflict, arousal and curiosity.* New York: McGraw-Hill, 1960.

BREGER, L., and MCGAUGH, J. L. Critique and reformulation of "learning theory" approaches to psychotherapy and neurosis. *Psychological Bulletin,* 1965, **63,** 338–58.

BREHM, J. W., and COHEN, A. R. *Explorations in cognitive dissonance.* New York: Wiley, 1962.

BRUNER, J. S. On perceptual readiness. *Psychological Review,* 1957, **64,** 123–57.

BRUNER, J. S. The course of cognitive growth. *American Psychologist,* 1964, **19,** 1–15.

CAMPBELL, D. T. Pattern matching as an essential in distal knowing. In K. R. HAMMOND (Ed.), *Egon Brunswick's psychology.* New York: Holt, Rinehart & Winston, 1966. Pp. 81–106.

CHOMSKY, N. Review of B. F. Skinner, "Verbal Behavior." *Language,* 1959, **35,** 26–58.

CRONBACH, L. J. Processes affecting scores on "understanding of others" and "assumed similarity." *Psychological Bulletin,* 1955, **52,** 177–94.

DULANY, D. E., JR. The place of hypotheses and intentions: An analysis of verbal control in verbal conditioning. In C. W. ERIKSEN (Ed.), *Behavior and awareness.* Durham, N.C.: Duke University Press, 1962. Pp. 102–29.

FEATHER, SARA. The effect of facilitatory and inhibitory instructions upon salivary conditioning. Unpublished doctoral dissertation, Duke University, 1967.

FESTINGER, L. A theory of social comparison processes. *Human Relations,* 1954, **7,** 117–40.

FESTINGER, L. *A theory of cognitive dissonance.* Evanston, Ill.: Row, Peterson, 1957.

FODOR, J. Could meaning be an r_m? *Journal of Verbal Learning and Verbal Behavior,* 1965, **4,** 73–81.

FODOR, J. More about mediators: A reply to Berlyne and Osgood. *Journal of Verbal Learning and Verbal Behavior,* 1966, **5,** 412–15.

GOODWIN, W. R., and LAWRENCE, D. H. The functional independence of two discrimination habits associated with a constant stimulus situation. *Journal of Comparative and Physiological Psychology,* 1955, **48,** 437–43.

GREENSPOON, J. The reinforcing effect of two spoken sounds on the frequency of two responses. *American Journal of Psychology,* 1955, **68,** 409–16.

GRINKER, R. R., SR. The psychosomatic aspects of anxiety. In C. D. SPIELBERGER (Ed.), *Anxiety and behavior.* New York: Academic Press, 1966. Pp. 129–42.

HARLOW, H. F. The formation of learning sets. *Psychological Review,* 1949, **56,** 51–65.

HEBB, D. O. *The organization of behavior: A neurophysiological theory.* New York: Wiley, 1949.

HERBERT, M. J., and HARSH, C. M. Observational learning by cats. *Journal of Comparative Psychology,* 1944, **37,** 81–95.

JONES, E. E., and GERARD, H. B. *Foundations of social psychology.* New York: Wiley, 1967.

KELLY, G. A. *A theory of personality.* New York: W. W. Norton, 1963.

LATANÉ, B. (Ed.). *Studies in social comparison.* Supplement No. 1, *Journal of Experimental Social Psychology.* New York: Academic Press, 1966.

LAWRENCE, D. H., and FESTINGER, L. *Deterrents and reinforcement: The psychology of insufficient reward.* Stanford, Calif.: Stanford University Press, 1962.

MACKINTOSH, N. J. Extinction of a discrimination habit as a function of overtraining. *Journal of Comparative and Physiological Psychology,* 1963, **56,** 842–47.

MANDLER, G. Verbal learning. In *New directions in psychology,* Vol. III. New York: Holt, Rinehart & Winston, 1967. Pp. 1–50.

MANDLER, G., and WATSON, D. L. Anxiety and the interruption of behavior. In C. D. SPIELBERGER (Ed.), *Anxiety and behavior.* New York: Academic Press, 1966. Pp. 263–88.

MILLER, G. A., GALANTER, E., and PRIBRAM, K. H. *Plans and the structure of behavior.* New York: Holt, Rinehart & Winston, 1960.

MOLTZ, H. Imprinting, empirical basis, and theoretical significance. *Psychological Bulletin,* 1960, **57,** 291–314.

PRIBRAM, K. H. Reinforcement revisited: A structural view. In M. R. JONES (Ed.), *Nebraska symposium on motivation, 1963.* Lincoln, Neb.: University of Nebraska Press, 1963. Pp. 113–59.

RIDDLE, DOROTHY I. The effect of verbal conditioning on self-esteem. Unpublished doctoral dissertation, Duke University, 1968.

SCHACHTER, S., and SINGER, J. E. Cognitive, social, and physiological determinants of emotional state. *Psychological Review,* 1962, **69,** 379–99.

SPIELBERGER, C. D. The role of awareness in verbal conditioning. In C .W. ERIKSEN (Ed.), *Behavior and awareness.* Durham, N.C.: Duke University Press, 1962. Pp. 73–101.

SPIELBERGER, C. D. and DENIKE, L. D. Descriptive behaviorism versus cognitive theory in verbal operant conditioning. *Psychological Review,* 1966, **73,** 306–26.

STEIN, L. S. The conditioning of self-esteem as a function of need for approval. Unpublished doctoral dissertation, Duke University, 1967.

THISTLETHWAITE, D. A critical review of latent learning and related experiments. *Psychological Bulletin,* 1951, **48,** 97–129.

TOLMAN, E. C. *Purposive behavior in animals and men.* New York: Appleton-Century-Crofts, 1932.

TOLMAN, E. C. Cognitive maps in rats and men. *Psychological Review,* 1948, **55,** 189–208.

TOLMAN, E. C., and HONZIK, C. H. Introduction and removal of reward and maze performance in rats. *University of California Publications in Psychology,* 1930, **4,** 257–75.

WHITE, R. W. Motivation reconsidered: The concept of competence. *Psychological Review,* 1959, **66,** 297–334.

CHAPTER 4

Varieties of Interpersonal Behavior

In the main, the last three chapters have been concerned with behavioral processes in general, and not with the specifics of interpersonal behavior. We have come now to a point in our discussion where it would be increasingly difficult to proceed at this level of abstraction. We need now to develop a language for the description of actual behavior in interpersonal situations so that we can focus down upon the concrete events of interpersonal transactions. We have seen something of how interpersonal behavior can be acquired and modified; the task now is to decide what behaviors should occupy our attention. The domain of interpersonal behavior is an exceedingly vast one whose natural ordering or principles of organization—if it has any—are not immediately apparent. As a matter of fact this domain does appear to have some order, and we are going to have to tease it out from the not-inconsiderable research literature at our disposal. How shall we proceed?

A Taxonomy of Interpersonal Behavior

Clearly, we need some means of breaking down interpersonal behavior into a functional system of classes or categories. The differentiation should be sufficiently fine to permit discussion of behavior in reasonably precise terms, but not so fine that the categorization represents little improvement in economy over a description of discrete behavioral events. The categories should be meaningful ones, in the sense that they form conceptual unities whose empirical referents can be clearly specified. They should also, in the aggregate, be sufficiently general and exhaustive that few instances of interpersonal behavior—including "abnormal" interpersonal behavior—will be discovered to be unclassifiable. A final criterion is that our categories should, if possible, be related to each other in some formal and conceptually consistent way. If we can impose upon the phenomena of interpersonal behavior an organizational schema which has these characteristics, we will have moved a considerable distance toward our ultimate objectives. Before we proceed, however, let us detour briefly into certain technical and methodological considerations so that you can understand the nature of the research that we shall have to depend on for guidance.

A TECHNICAL ORIENTATION

Any principle of categorization involves rules for grouping entities on the basis of some common or shared attributes. Now, if you think of behavioral acts as entities, you will see that our conversational language involves many such categorizations. Thus, interpersonal behavioral entities such as A *strikes* B, A *insults* B, A *threatens* B, and A *blocks* B's progress, may all be categorized as "aggressive" behaviors, and it may be said that A in these examples has exhibited the *trait* of aggressiveness. But would it not also be proper to say that A exhibited dominance, or offensiveness, or insolence, or cruelty, or any number of other such traits? The problem with our common linguistic categorizations of behavioral acts is that we quite literally have an embarrassment of riches. Many years ago, Allport and Odbert (1936) were able to identify approximately 18,000 distinctive English words representing particular categorizations of human behavior, and the list has undoubtedly grown considerably since that time. Even assuming that we could get substantial agreement among persons as to the meaning and limits of these categories in behavioral terms—an assumption which deserves no great credence —we would still be faced with an impossibly huge and confused array of markedly overlapping classes for sorting behavioral acts.

Linguistic redundancy can be reduced by a rather simple expedient: we can toss out all but one of any group of terms having identical, or nearly identical, category limits in regard to their behavioral referent. Conceivably this could be accomplished with no greater instrumentation than a good dictionary. This would help somewhat, but I am afraid that we would still have a rather overwhelming residue. The number of discriminable shades of differences of interpersonal behavior as it occurs in nature *is,* after all, enormous, even though it may not be as large as our available verbal labels would suggest. Psychologists have developed a technology for reducing large behavioral domains of this sort to manageable limits, and we shall have to turn to this technology for a solution. The basic assumption it rests upon may be stated somewhat as follows: To the extent that a given class of behavior, x, *covaries* with another class of behavior, y, the two classes of behavior share common elements and may be regarded as psychologically equivalent. The basic operation employed in the estimation of such behavioral covariation is the well-known coefficient of correlation. Thus, if instances of two classes of behavior are observed to covary to the extent that the correlation between them approaches 1.00 (with the sign of the coefficient being *either* positive or negative), the two classes of behavior are assumed to be psychologically equivalent and may therefore be "collapsed" into a single class. (In the case of a near-perfect *negative* correlation we would have an instance in which a single behavioral dimension had been obscured by obverse class labels— for example, "friendliness" versus "unfriendliness.")

It is actually fairly rare for behavioral classes to correlate with each other at a near-perfect level. Lesser—but still quite substantial—correlations, however, are extremely common in various behavioral domains, including the interpersonal. In other words, many classes of behavior appear to share common elements, although retaining their own distinctiveness. We can therefore speak meaningfully of behavioral "clusters," which consist of classes of behavior exhibiting a high order of intercorrelation, and which presumably have a common core of psychological meaning or significance. Let us suppose, for example, that we are able to observe a small group of persons engaged in discussion about some problem. Let us also suppose that, as observers, we are able to agree on the behavioral referents of various classes of behavior, such as dominance, friendliness, and talkativeness, and that these three behaviors show covariation within the members of the group. That is, members who rate high on talkativeness also tend to rate high, let us say, on the other two variables, and members who rate low on any one of the three also tend to rate low on the other two. We would thereby have identified an interpersonal behavioral cluster consisting of dominant, friendly, talkative behavior. If we wish, we might even assign a general label to this cluster, such as "leadership."

This describes in essence the logic of the technique of *factor analysis*—a rather complicated mathematical procedure by means of which a matrix of intercorrelated variables can be reduced to the minimum number of clusters necessary to account for the principal relationships existing among the variables. It is a mathematically precise way of discovering and purifying the fundamental nature of the overlap in any group of intercorrelated variables or classes of behavior. Properly utilized, it is an excellent device for the reduction of complex domains of behavior to their principal dimensions or components. For this reason, it has an obvious application to our search for meaningful categories of interpersonal behavior, and we shall presently consider some relevant research in which the technique has been employed.

Interpersonal behavior exhibits a most interesting property, one that deserves special comment and explanation. Although this property is conceptually rather simple and easy to understand, its technical features are somewhat difficult to communicate.

In brief, a great deal of interpersonal behavior exhibits a circular —technically a *circumplex*—ordering. This means that categories of behavior within this domain are intercorrelated in such a way that they may be systematically ordered in terms of the magnitudes of the correlations existing between any two of them, and that the form of this ordering is circular, that is, without beginning or end. Consider the following example. Let us say that we are able to identify sixteen meaningful categories of interpersonal behavior (such as dominating, boastful, aggressive, submissive, friendly, etc.) and to establish a reliable coefficient of correlation for every possible pairing of these sixteen "variables." We should then have an index of the degree of covariation, expressed in terms of correlation, of each variable with every other variable (total $= [N^2 - N] / 2 = 120$ correlations). A circumplex ordering of these sixteen variables would mean that the variables could be arranged in an endless sequential (circular) order such that the size of the correlations of any particular variable with the other fifteen would first decrease monotonically (without directional change) to a certain point and then increase monotonically, as a function of the magnitude of the separation of the variables within the sequence. An arrangement of this kind would therefore place psychologically similar variables in proximity to each other around the circumference of an imaginary circle, and would give maximum sequential separation between variables having maximum psychological dissimilarity. In general, variables at either end of any diameter of such a circle would be maximally dissimilar (perhaps "opposite") psychologically, whereas immediately adjacent variables, having relatively high intercorrelations, would be maximally similar in the sense in which that term is used here. Circumplex orderings of this type have been found with striking regularity and contentual consistency in studies of interpersonal behavior, and we shall have a look at some of these results presently.

The techniques of correlational analysis, particularly the derivatives of factor analysis and the circumplex model, provide us with powerful conceptual and operational tools for reducing the domain of interpersonal behavior to a manageable size and for imposing upon it an empirically justifiable systematization. If we can identify the principal dimensions or factors of this domain, these will serve as useful orienting guides to its basic organizational structure, thus permitting the development of categories that realistically reflect that structure. This would seem to be within the realm of possibility. In addition, we have the happy circumstance that a factorially valid category system which also exhibits the systematic characteristics of a circumplex may be highly feasible. The discovery of such an aesthetically and conceptually pleasing order in a behavioral domain is somewhat surprising. Let us review the evidence.

EMPIRICAL STUDIES: FACTORIAL

Roger Brown (1965), in his celebrated textbook on social psychology, has conducted a careful conceptual analysis in search of basic "dimensions of interpersonal relationship." His approach is a rather broad and sweeping one, utilizing evidence from many sources within the social sciences; factorial studies are generally not included. This impressive analysis of the formal characteristics of human interaction concludes that two major dimensions are practically universal in such interaction. They are *status* and *solidarity*. Human beings organize their social relations according to a vertical hierarchy which involves elements of dominance-submission, respect, and presumed relative personal worth. Cross-cutting the latter dimension is one that involves solidarity, friendship, esteem, and affection, or their absence. Brown notes that all manner of interpersonal behavior, including forms of personal address, reflects the implicit operation of these fundamental organizing principles, and the evidence and illustrations he adduces in support of this assertion are most intriguing and intuitively compelling. Here, then, is a good lead for us. Let us see whether or not it will hold up under more precise scrutiny in the area of direct person-to-person interaction.

Carter (1954), in an early review of factorial studies of interpersonal behavior in small groups, analyzed the results of five separate research efforts in this area. The data collected in these studies consisted of (1) ratings of the behavior of small groups of college men engaged in three different group tasks; (2)

ratings of the behavior of trainees made by the assessment staff in the famous World War II Office of Strategic Services program; (3) ratings of leaders made by members of various groups; (4) ratings of U.S. Army officers made by their immediate subordinates; and (5) sociometric peer ratings gathered from members of rifle squads on frontline combat duty. After examining and comparing the results of the factor analyses carried out on these varied data, Carter concluded that three factors could account for a major portion of the behavior variance in all of the studies. He named these factors as follows: (1) Individual Prominence and Achievement, (2) Aiding Attainment by the Group, and (3) Sociability (establishment of cordial and satisfying relationships). Factor 1, as he describes it, seems to have much in common with a dominance-subordination dimension, while Factor 3 is similar to a solidarity or affiliation-disaffiliation dimension. Factor 2 seems to relate to a kind of task-oriented cooperativeness, and may be specific to a task-group situation. This review, therefore, provides partial support for the view that interpersonal behavior can be structured according to at least the two dimensions Brown has suggested.

A series of factor analytic studies by Borgatta and his colleagues provide further support. In the first of these, Borgatta, Cottrell, and Mann (1958) factor analyzed the rankings made by graduate students meeting in small discussion groups. Each member of each group was ranked by his peers on sixteen personality traits and twenty-four categories of manifested behavior. These rankings were subjected to a factor analysis, from which there emerged two factors that accounted for major portions of the variance and three additional ones of relatively minor significance. The two major factors were individual assertiveness and sociability. Following up on this, Borgatta (1960) carried out a similar study upon rankings provided by 238 college men and women who met together for discussion in brief, newly formed, small groups. The data analyzed were the average rankings for each individual on each of 36 trait and behavior variables, and the entire procedure was carried out twice for samples of subjects of each sex. The factor structure was similar for both sexes with the exception that the first factor—individual assertiveness—was unusually salient for the males, and the replication provided a generally good fit to the initial analysis. The second factor was, once again, sociability, followed in order by manifest intelligence, manifest emotionality, task interest, and (tentatively) volatility. The percentages of variance accounted for by the various factors are not given, but it may be assumed that their magnitudes decrease with each successive factor. The final study in this series (Borgatta, 1964) was carried out on five-person, nonoverlapping groups of sorority (N = 315) and fraternity (N = 144) members. Group members were well known to each other, and each member was ranked by the other four on 34 descriptive characteristics. The results were subjected to factor analysis separately by sex, but the same factor structure emerged for both sexes. It is as follows: (1) assertiveness, (2) likability, (3) emotionality, (4) intelligence, and (5) responsibility. The first two factors again appear to relate directly to the dominance-subordination and affiliation-disaffiliation dimensions, but the proportion of variance they account for is again not reported.

Not even the behavior of a mother toward her child seems free of these apparently ubiquitous components. Schaefer (1959) reanalyzed several sets of data previously reported by himself and others relating to maternal behavior. His analysis is directed particularly toward data obtained from the following sources: ratings made by trained observers of the behavior of 56 mothers whose interactions with their children during testing sessions were noted and recorded; ratings made from written notes based on home interviews with 34 mothers; and intercorrelations among eight behavioral traits derived from ratings of "parental press" variables in 48 families. In addition, Schaefer reanalyzed previously reported intercorrelations among the 19 variables of the Fels Parent Behavior Rating Scales. Factor analysis of the first three sets of data yielded two factors, with very small residual variance. These factors are labeled control-autonomy and love-hostility. There were less clear-cut results on the Fels Scales, but they were generally confirmatory. In a later paper, Schaefer (1961) also reviewed studies of child behavior from the same perspective, and concluded that there are also two major factors operative here. One of them, love-hostility, is familiar. He labels the other one extraversion-introversion, but it is clear from the context that other terms such as assertiveness-submissiveness would have been equally appropriate. Becker et al. (1962) and Becker and Krug (1964), using data from sources described below, provide additional confirmatory evidence on the factorial structure of maternal behavior, and their results also suggest that the behavior of fathers toward their children may be similar in terms of the principal dimensions of "Negative Emotionality-Warmth" and "Strictness-Permissiveness." Finally, Slater (1962), in a study based on reports of parent behavior provided by 138 male college freshmen, was able to identify by cluster analysis two correlationally independent dimensions around which the behavior of both parents, as reported, appeared to center: emotional supportiveness and warmth (warmth vs. coldness), and inhibitory demands and discipline (strictness vs. permissiveness).

Becker and Krug (1964) offer additional relevant evidence in the area of child behavior. These authors reanalyze the data from the earlier (1962) Becker et al. study in which 71 five-year-olds were evaluated on 72 behavior rating scales by two kindergarten teachers and by each of their parents. This was an extensive study in which mothers and fathers were interviewed and were themselves rated by trained observers. The ratings of child behavior were intercorrelated and factor analyzed. The emergent factor structure was somewhat complex, but the first two centroid factors of the initial factorization were described as Introversion-Extraversion and Emotional Stability-Instability. Inspection of the scales that load maximally on these factors reveals that Introversion-Extraversion has a quite substantial submission-dominance component, and that Emotional Stability-Instability is strongly weighted with a nonhostile-hostile dimension. The main intent of the authors in this paper is to describe a circumplex model of child behavior based on a five-factor solution of the behavior rating intercorrelations. We shall consider this model presently, but it is appropriate to note here that two of their five bipolar factors are labeled Assertive vs. Submissive and Loving vs. Distrusting. Finally, the authors briefly review the results of six additional studies that involve ratings of the social behavior of persons ranging in age from four years through late adolescence.

When the results of these studies are adjusted to the framework of the two centroid factors noted above, the degree of concordance is accurately described by the authors as "remarkable."

The factorial studies mentioned above are not intended as an exhaustive summary of the available empirical knowledge bearing upon the question of the fundamental dimensions of social behavior. Other relevant studies could be cited to support the general trend indicated here; there may well be some that would not, although I am unaware of any frankly disconfirming evidence. On the whole, the conclusion seems justified that major portions of the domain of interpersonal behavior can profitably and reasonably accurately be conceived as involving variations on two independent, bipolar dimensions. One of these may be called a *dominance-submission* dimension; it includes dominant, assertive, ascendant, leading, controlling (etc.) behaviors on the one hand, and submissive, retiring, obsequious, unassertive, following (etc.) behaviors on the other. The poles of the second principal dimension are perhaps best approximated by the terms *hate* versus *love;* the former includes hateful, aggressive, rejecting, punishing, attacking, disaffiliative (etc.) behaviors, while the latter includes accepting, loving, affectionate, affiliative, friendly (etc.) social actions. Now, let us construct a hypothetical, two-dimensional space for the purpose of conceptualizing interpersonal behavior in these terms. We can do so by utilizing our dominance-submission and love-hate dimensions as Cartesian coordinates, with the point of intersection representing neutrality on each dimension—that is, their psychological midpoints. If we let the top and bottom of the vertical axis represent the dominant and submissive poles, and the extreme left and extreme right of the horizontal axis represent the hate and love poles, respectively, we will have developed four quadrants whose contents represent qualitatively distinct forms of social behavior. Starting at the upper left and proceeding clockwise, these may be described as (1) hostile dominance, (2) friendly dominance, (3) friendly submission, and (4) hostile submission.

Two other interesting properties of this model should not escape your attention. One is the possibility of representing intensity, as well as quality, of social behavior by means of a point in the hypothetical space which is jointly determined by degree and direction of movement from the neutral point of each dimension. Thus, if a particular sample of behavior involves, let us say, five units of *dominance* on the vertical dimension and three units of *love* on the horizontal dimension, the point of intersection of these measurements is representative of the quality of the behavior (Quadrant 2, friendly dominance) and also its "strength" or intensity, which would be proportional to the length of a vector running from the neutral or zero point of the two dimensions to the point of intersection of the measurements. It should be mentioned, however, that we are here dealing only with the conceptual aspects of the model. The precise meaning of a unit of measurement on these dimensions, in operational terms, is a rather complicated problem whose solution has only begun to be realized (Leary, 1957; Kogan and Fordyce, 1962). Another property of the model is that it suggests a circular space and a circular arrangement of interpersonal behavior. This raises the possibility of achieving an integration of factorial and circumplicial solutions in the interpersonal behavior domain, a possibility to which Leary (1957), Schaefer (1959), and Foa (1961), among others, have called attention. Foa has pointed out that a circumplex can always be described on two dimensions, but that not every two-factor domain will of necessity produce a true circumplex. Let us see what can be done with the available evidence.

EMPIRICAL STUDIES: CIRCUMPLICIAL

The initial suggestion that interpersonal behavior may be circumplicially ordered can be credited to the work of Leary (1957) and his colleagues at the Kaiser Foundation. These psychologists developed their ideas over a number of years with what appears in retrospect to have been an extraordinarily intuitive prescience. The framework they developed had no great empirical foundation at the time, but it has since proven to be very robust indeed in its capacity to predict and incorporate the subsequent empirical findings of other investigators. Because it seems to provide a very useful integration, I shall postpone its detailed presentation until we have completed a general survey of other relevant empirical findings.

One of the earlier empirical studies suggesting a circumplex ordering of interpersonal behavior is that of Borgatta, Cottrell and Mann (1958) which was referred to above. These authors examined the intercorrelations among their primary variables and noted that these intercorrelations might have made a circumplex ordering possible had their initial sample of variables contained more items having negative loadings on their two major factors. In other words, their trait sample from which subjects made their rankings of one another was biased in terms of a relative under-representation of items relating to submissive and unsociable (that is, hostile) behavior. Inspection of the trait samples utilized in the later (1960, 1964) Borgatta studies reveals that this bias persisted through all of them. This is actually an illustration of an important and more general point, upon which Leary (1957) has made some illuminating comments. It seems that the Kaiser Foundation group, in their own research, experienced considerable difficulty in discovering appropriate descriptive terms for behavior falling within particular ranges—a difficulty occasioned by the fact that our language appears to be significantly biased *against* adequate linguistic representation of certain forms of behavior. We shall have to remain alert to this potential source of distortion.

Schaefer (1959), on the basis of his review of the data mentioned earlier, describes the intervariable correlations of maternal behavior as approximating a circumplex ordering, although there is a small gap in the Unsociability area. Starting at the Control (dominance) pole, and reading clockwise in terms of the spatial model suggested earlier, Schaefer's circular ordering of maternal behavior variables is: [1] *Control* (Possessive), Overprotective, Protective-Indulgent, Overindulgent, *Love* (Accepting), Cooperative, Democratic, *Autonomy* (Freedom), Detached, Indifferent, Neglecting, *Hostility* (Rejecting), Demanding-Antagonistic, and Authoritarian-Dictatorial (thence back to *Control*). In a later review,

[1] In this and subsequent circular orderings of variables, I have taken the liberty of italicizing those variables which seem to approximate most closely the dominance, love, submission, and hate poles of the hypothetical two-factor space.

also mentioned above, Schaefer (1961) added, on the basis of the empirical intercorrelations at his disposal, a circumplex for child behavior. Utilizing the same format of presentation, the ordering of variables is as follows: *Extraversion* (dominance), Friendliness, *Love,* Conformity, *Introversion* (submission), Withdrawal, *Hostility,* and Aggressiveness. Schaefer and Bayley (1963) later elaborated this model and suggested separate behavior circles for boys and girls. For boys, the order is: *Bold,* Independent, Social in situation, *Friendly,* Tactful, Courteous, *Timid,* Reserved, Cold, *Hostile,* Rude, and Irritable. The order for girls is: *Bold,* Independent, Social, *Friendly,* Conscientious, Courteous, *Timid,* Calm, Popular, Reserved, Gloomy, Discontented, Sulky, *Hostile,* Defiant, and Irritable. The apparent expansion of the girl's circle in the hostile-submission quadrant may be at least partly an artifact of my having chosen, for the sake of consistency, to consider Timid as the *submissive* pole of this particular ordering. Calm, Popular, or Reserved might be a more realistic choice, but in any case the evident difference between the boys' and girls' circles is an interesting one and may reflect differences in sex-role expectancies.

Becker and Krug (1964), also utilizing data described above, present their own circumplex model of child behavior. The ordering of variables indicated by their research is as follows: *Assertive,* Sociable-Extraversion, *Loving,* Cooperative (Emotional Stability), Calm-Compliant, *Submissive,* Withdrawn-Introversion, *Distrusting,* Defiant-Hostile (Emotional Instability), and Emotional-Demanding. As was mentioned above, Becker and Krug also reviewed the data of six additional studies of child and adolescent behavior (none of them overlapping with those reported in this chapter). They were able quite readily to recast the results of these studies into the framework of their circumplex model, achieving a quite extraordinary degree of "fit." We shall not review these additional studies here.

Returning to nonparental, adult social behavior, Lorr and McNair (1963, 1965, 1966; Lorr, Bishop, and McNair, 1965) have carried out an extensive series of investigations in the development of their own version of an interpersonal behavior circle. Using as their basic rating instrument an Interpersonal Behavior Inventory which has undergone successive revision in the course of their work, they have gathered behavior ratings on diverse groups of subjects. Their various data pools consisted of ratings of 346 heterogeneous psychotherapy patients (provided by the patients' therapists) and 86 "normal" persons (1963); therapists' ratings of 525 patients undergoing extended psychotherapy with private practitioners and in various clinics (Lorr, Bishop, and McNair, 1965); therapists' ratings of a nationwide sample of 366 psychotherapy patients, psychology students' ratings of 290 nonpatients with whom they were familiar, and finally additional therapists' ratings on 60 "neurotic" persons (Lorr and McNair, 1965). The entire program of research has recently been reviewed and summarized by Lorr and McNair (1966). The latest form of the Interpersonal Behavior Inventory consists of 140 statements of manifest interpersonal behaviors which yield 15 category scores. The 15 variables array themselves in a circumplex order as follows: [2] *Dominance,* Exhibition, Sociability, *Affiliation,* Nurturance, Agreeableness, Deference, Succorance, *Submissiveness,* Abasement, Inhibition, Detachment, Mistrust, *Aggression,* and Recognition. Lorr and McNair's variables appear to be relatively heavily represented in the friendly submission and hostile submission quadrants of the two-factor space, and to have relatively light representation in the two dominance quadrants. The reason for this is unclear, but it is conceivable that their subject samples, containing large proportions of psychotherapy patients, were biased in the direction indicated.

Additional and essentially confirmatory evidence on the circular ordering of interpersonal behavior is provided by Slater (1962) and by Roe (1957). Despite minor variations and deviations, then, there is a quite impressive amount of agreement as to the structure and content of interpersonal behavior as represented in the relevant research literature. The categories of behavior with which we choose to work should reflect this generally concordant store of pertinent information. Let us now turn to the work of Leary and the Kaiser Foundation group in order to make

[2] The printed version of the circular ordering in the Lorr and McNair (1966) review apparently contains an error in respect to the placement of Abasement (see, for example, Lorr and McNair, 1965); I have used what I believe to be the correct ordering here.

some final decisions on this matter of categories, and to develop some further conceptual elaborations.

THE LEARY FRAMEWORK

The basic model of interpersonal behavior advanced by Leary (1957) and his associates is represented as a two-factor (Dominance vs. Submission and Hate vs. Love) circumplex having 16 distinctive, behaviorally defined segments. Qualitative variations in behavior are represented in terms of segment location within the circle, and behavioral strength or intensity is represented in terms of distance from the center. A graphic illustration of the model is presented in Figure 4.1, whose relationship to the preceding review of empirical research will, I trust, be clear. You will note that in the outer ring of Figure 4.1 the 16 categories are combined into distinctively labeled pairs, thus reducing the circle to eight categories. Leary and his associates have primarily concerned themselves with these "octant" categories. The dual labels for each octant share the characteristic that the first word indicates a mild or not intense form of the behavior in question, while the second refers to its extreme form. I propose to use these octant categories as our foremost means of coding interpersonal behavior in the remainder of this book. A brief description of each of these eight varieties of interpersonal behavior is therefore appropriate at this point.

Managerial-Autocratic Behavior. This behavior involves a dominant orientation shaded with elements of positive affect or friendliness. It includes all manner of activities indicating an implicit or explicit assumption of leadership, power, or expertise within an essentially collaborative context—that is, one in which there is presumed to be a correspondence in goals among parties to the interaction. Behavior in the managerial-autocratic range is strong, assertive, and confident in tone. It communicates the message, "I am a strong, competent, knowledgeable person on whom you may rely for effective guidance and leadership," and it tends to invite complementary behaviors involving obedience and respect (that is, behaviors in the Self-effacing and Docile range). The extreme forms of this behavior are suggestive of benevolent dictatorship and frequently take the form of an unyielding paternalism. Pedantry and dogmatic stances are included in this category.

Responsible-Hypernormal Behavior. Positive affect predominates in this behavior, but the friendliness is colored by a component of dominance. Its prototypic expression is therefore seen when

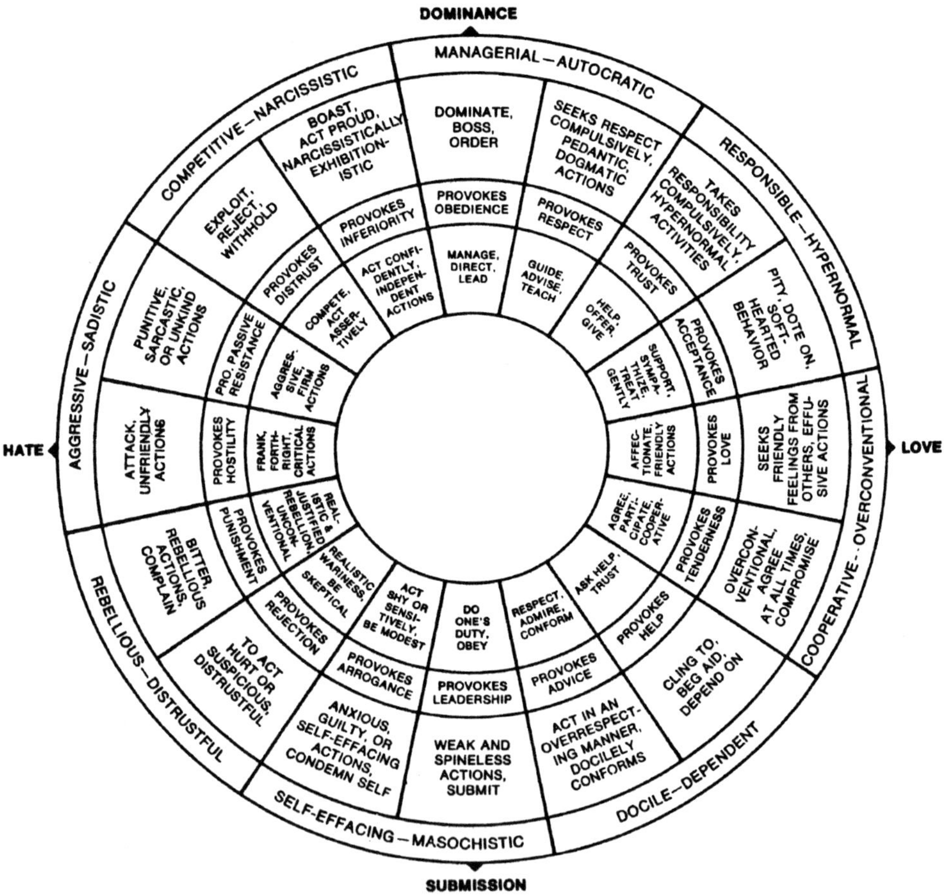

Figure 4.1. The Interpersonal Behavior Circle.

Adapted from Timothy Leary, *Interpersonal Diagnosis of Personality —A Functional Theory and Methodology for Personality Evaluation.* Copyright © 1957 The Ronald Press Company, New York.

help, support, and sympathy is offered to others. This behavior is also confident and strong in tone, but it takes a more "human-itarian" and personal form. It communicates the message, "I am a strong, competent, empathic person on whom you may count for understanding and emotional support," and it tends to invite others to respond with dependency and affection (that is, behaviors in the Docile and Cooperative range). The extreme of this behavior involves excessive displays of responsibility to others, self-sacrifice, and personal strength (thus *hyper*-normal), including inappropriate protectiveness and concern for the other's welfare.

Cooperative-Overconventional Behavior. The distinguishing feature of this behavior is the expression of positive, affiliative affect with an undertone of submissiveness. The keynote is affectionate cooperation and compromise, in which the maintenance of harmony appears to have assumed greater importance to the actor than any expression of personal or individual distinctiveness. The behavior is highly participative, agreeable, and affiliative, and it communicates the message, "I am an exceedingly friendly, agreeable, unchallenging person who would like you to like me." Such behavior tends to invite others to be supportive and friendly (that is, to engage in Responsible and Cooperative behavior). The extreme of this type of behavior involves inappropriate effusiveness, conventionality, and willingness to compromise in the face of potential disagreement.

Docile-Dependent Behavior. This behavior is primarily submissive in character, but includes an element of friendliness or affiliation. Its distinguishing feature is a display of help-inducing weakness in a context of implicitly or explicitly expressed trust, admiration, and respect for the other's strength. It conveys the message, "I am a weak and helpless person in need of your aid and support," often expressed in very poignant behavioral terms. It is, of course, an invitation for others to respond with advice, help, and support (that is, with behavior in the Managerial and Responsible ranges). The extreme of this form of behavior is a clinging, ingratiating dependency that may become very sticky indeed for the person toward whom it is directed.

Self-effacing–Masochistic Behavior. The predominantly submissive theme continues in this form of behavior, but it is here admixed with elements of aggression and hostility. It involves self-abnegation through obedience, submission, self-consciousness, and modesty. It tends to communicate to others the message, "I am a weak, deficient, unworthy person justly deserving of your domination, rejection, and contempt." The anxious, ashamed, self-deprecating behaviors tend to invite others to engage in arrogant, cruel, contemptuous, exploitative, self-enhancing reactions (that is, behavior in the Aggressive and Competitive ranges). In the extreme, this behavior takes the form of groveling weakness and self-condemnation and is called a depressive reaction in psychiatric terminology.

Rebellious-Distrustful Behavior. The keynote of this behavior is the expression of hostility and disaffiliation from a stance of relative passivity and powerlessness. It thus includes the congeries of actions whereby a person may indicate passive rejection and distrust of others. Cynical, wary, bitter, and provocatively unconventional behaviors are included within this category, as are all behaviors that suggest alienation from others and from societal norms, which, in this context, are commonly condemned as phony and hypocritical. This behavior communicates to others the message, "I reject and mistrust you, for you are, or are certain to become, unworthy of my affection and esteem." It tends to inspire rejection, indignation, and punitive measures in reaction (that is, behaviors in the Aggressive and Competitive ranges). The extreme of this form of behavior involves marked suspicion, bitterness, and uncompromising rejection of "authority." In the psychiatric area, the terms "paranoia" and "schizophrenia" (and their various derivatives) are often used in reference to extreme Rebellious-Distrustful behavior.

Aggressive-Sadistic Behavior. This behavior involves substantial, direct expression of hostility with an undertone of dominance. Included are all attacking behaviors, verbal and nonverbal. Bluntness, firmness, criticism, and sarcasm are frequent verbal manifestations; nonverbal manifestations are readily imagined and include the entire range of hostile actions. This category of behavior communicates the message, "I am a threatening and dangerous person, and you are a suitable target for my wrath." The "rationale" for this wrath, if it has any, may be almost any kind of failing in the other person, including moral failure. Behavior of this kind tends to inspire anxiety, fear, or guilt in others, and to invite others to be weak and submissively hostile (that is, to engage in behaviors in the Self-effacing and Rebellious ranges). The extremes of this behavior involve unmitigated cruelty and sadism.

Competitive-Narcissistic Behavior. This behavior returns to a preponderantly dominant theme, sharing this characteristic with the Managerial-Autocratic. The dominance in this case, however, has a distinctly aggressive component and involves an implicit devaluation of the other person. Proud, independent, self-assured, self-enhancing actions, in which the other is exploited or "put down," are included, as are all actions tending to display superiority in one or another attribute. The "one-upmanship" behaviors that Potter (1952) has amusingly described are also instances of this category. Competitive-Narcissistic behavior communicates the message, "I am superior to you, and you, being a lesser person, are hardly worthy of my serious consideration." Such behavior invites others to be submissively hostile and inferior in response (that is, to react in the Rebellious and Self-effacing ranges). In its extreme form, this behavior becomes inappropriately pompous, boastful, exhibitionistic, and blandly rejecting of the other's claim to respect and acknowledgement.

ADDITIONAL FEATURES OF LEARY'S SYSTEM

Leary and his colleagues, and others, have found that most interpersonal acts can be reliably coded within the framework of these eight categories. As might be expected the translation from act to category may not always be completely describable in digital terms, but the categories appear to have sufficient analogical clarity that difficulties in applying them to samples of behavior are rarely insurmountable. It would seem, then, that our goal of discovering a functional category system for interpersonal behavior has been achieved. Before moving on, however, we might profitably give some attention to certain additional pertinent aspects of the thinking of the Kaiser Foundation group, as presented by Leary (1957).

Individual Consistency. We would expect reasonably well-adjusted persons to be capable, in appropriate circumstances and with modulated intensity, of displaying behaviors across the entire range of the eight categories. It will usually be the case, however, that a particular person's social behavior will favor some segments of the circle more than others, thus giving his interpersonal behavior the distinctive coloration we ordinarily associate with the concept of *personality.* Within the framework of the interpersonal circle, psychological maladjustment usually manifests itself in the form of a rigid, inappropriate, inflexible reliance upon behaviors within a particular segment, which are often produced with great intensity. "In many cases the 'sicker' the patient, the more likely he is to have abandoned all interpersonal techniques except one—which he can handle with magnificent finesse" (Leary, 1957, p. 116).

Complementarity and "Purpose" in Interpersonal Behavior. You may have noted that, for each of the eight categories described above, a type of complementary behavior that tended to be elicited was mentioned. Thus, Competitive-Narcissistic behavior tends to "invite" a display of inferiority and submissive hostility. This idea is central to the Leary framework: interpersonal behaviors are viewed as being, in part, *security operations* (a Sullivanian term) employed by persons to maintain relative comfort, security, and freedom from anxiety in their interactions with others. The *purpose* of interpersonal behavior, in terms of its security-maintenance functions, is to induce from the other person behavior that is complementary to the behavior proffered. It is assumed that this induced, complementary behavior has current utility for the person inducing it, in the sense that it maximizes his momentary security. Leary suggests that we learn how to "train" others to respond to us in security-maintaining ways by acquiring the requisite behavioral "techniques," and that each of the eight categories of interpersonal behavior may be viewed as a distinctive set of learned operations for prompting desired behavior from others. Generally speaking, complementarity occurs on the basis of reciprocity in respect to the dominance-submission axis (dominance tends to induce submission, and vice versa), and on the basis of correspondence in respect to the hate-love axis (hate induces hate, and love induces love).

Foa (1961) has suggested an interesting elaboration of these notions. He writes, "an interpersonal act is an attempt to establish the emotional relationship of the actor toward himself and toward the other, as well as to establish the social relationship of the self and the other with respect to a larger reference group" (p. 350) and, "each behavior serves the purpose of giving or denying love *and* status to the self and to the other" (p. 351). Foa argues that, embedded within the dominance-submission and hate-love dimensions, there are three underlying "facets": (1) content (acceptance vs. rejection), (2) object (self vs. other), and (3) mode (emotional vs. social). He goes on to suggest (1965) that an interpersonal act may be represented as the Cartesian product of the three facets, each of which may take either of the two "values" indicated. Thus, eight (2 × 2 × 2) distinguishable interpersonal "profiles" emerge from this analysis. How do these eight profiles articulate with the Leary octants? Foa (1964, 1965) suggests that the fit is as follows:

Leary Octants	*Facet Profile*
Managerial-Autocratic	Social Acceptance of Other
Responsible-Hypernormal	Emotional Acceptance of Other
Cooperative-Overconventional	Emotional Acceptance of Self
Docile-Dependent	Social Acceptance of Self
Self-effacing–Masochistic	Social Rejection of Self
Rebellious-Distrustful	Emotional Rejection of Self
Aggressive-Sadistic	Emotional Rejection of Other
Competitive-Narcissistic	Social Rejection of Other

In Foa's terms, therefore, the eight types of interpersonal behavior we have identified convey implicit messages that give or deny love or status to the self or to the other person. Thus, Managerial behavior offers status to the other, Cooperative behavior offers love to the self, Self-effacing behavior denies status to the self, Aggressive behavior denies love to the other, and so forth. The notion of interpersonal behavioral complementarity is for the most part only implicit in Foa's analysis, but it is rather readily conceived in terms of confirmation of the conveyed message. For example, if Social Rejection of Self (Self-effacing) behavior is proffered, the specifically complementary behavior would be Social Rejection of Other (Competitive). If, on the other hand, Emotional Acceptance of Self (Cooperative) is proffered, specific complementarity would be achieved by an Emotional Acceptance of Other (Responsible) response. By and large, the complementarity hypotheses generated by this framework are consistent with those originally proposed by Leary, and with available empirical evidence (Leary, 1957). Any complete appraisal of Foa's reformulation of Leary's system, however, must await further research; as it stands, it is an intriguing idea that has an appealing simplicity and formal consistency.

"Levels" of Interpersonal Behavior. No summary of Leary's concepts would be complete if it did not include reference to the central notion of "levels" of behavior, of which there are said to be no less than five. In this book, we are predominantly concerned with only the first two levels: Level I, the level of Public Communication, and Level II, the level of Conscious Description. A person's Level I behavior is operationally defined in terms of descriptions of the behavior provided by *observers* other than himself; his Level II behavior is operationally defined in terms of his *own* descriptions of his and others' behavior. Both kinds of descriptions involve ratings on the same interpersonal circle variables, partly in order to facilitate interlevel comparisons. Functionally, therefore, Level I refers to a person's actual, objectively "real" interpersonal behavior (assuming observers independently agree in describing it), whereas Level II refers to his *perceptions* of interpersonal behavior—his own behavior and that of others. As is perhaps obvious, there is considerable possibility of perceptual distortions affecting Level II behavior. One consequence of this would be the occurrence of interlevel discrepancies in regard to a person's own behavior. Recalling our earlier discussion (in Chapter 1), it may also be noted that a person's response to another's behavior is not a response to that other's Level I acts, but is rather a response to his own Level II perception of those acts of the other. Level III in Leary's system is the level of Private Symbolization, which is operationally defined in terms of the content of a person's dreams, fantasies, and responses to projective tests. Level III behaviors are also coded in terms of the circle variables. Level IV is the level of

the Unexpressed, and consists of those segments of the circle that are unrepresented in the person's behavior at any other level; such behavior is presumably strongly inhibited, and is reminiscent of Sullivan's concept of the Not Me. Level V is the level of "Values," but this level is not given extended treatment in Leary's account of the system.

The Achievement and Maintenance of Interactional Balance

In the foregoing section there was introduced the important idea that an interpersonal act represents, in part, a prompt or "bid" to elicit response behaviors falling within a certain range of the interpersonal circle. Implicit in this idea is the notion that behavior complementary to the behavior proffered is in some way "rewarding," and that noncomplementary behavior is nonrewarding or perhaps even unpleasant—something to be actively avoided. Leary (1957), as we have seen, formulates this hedonic element in terms of the enhancement or disruption of "security," following Sullivan in this respect. This seems a reasonable formulation as far as it goes, but we are left with questions concerning the genesis and nature of the variations in hedonic outcome that appear to be dependent upon response complementarity. Two possibilities suggest themselves immediately, both of them derived from processes discussed in the preceding chapter.

In the first place, it is conceivable that certain kinds of behavior from others come to be "valued" on the basis of their having acquired secondary reinforcing properties through association learning. You may recall, for example, that the rewarding properties of "tender" behavior on the part of the other person were assumed to be learnable in this way. Learning of this kind is, of course, ultimately dependent upon the occurrence of primary reinforcement (such as, food, liquid, body contact), and we may incidentally note that, even at the adult level, certain behaviors of another may provide direct, primary reinforcement, as in sexual intercourse. On the negative side, it is also conceivable that certain kinds of behavior acquire negative value for the recipient by virtue of their learned capacity to cue unpleasant emotional responses, or anxiety. The person will therefore attempt to avoid the occurrence of such behavior in the other person. For example, Leary (1957) advances the hypothesis that a common antecedent of persistent Rebellious-Distrustful behavior is a learned *fear* of tenderness from others, the Rebelliousness serving to make the occurrence of tenderness unlikely; the relationship of this postulated process to Sullivan's concept of *malevolent transformation* is clear and direct.

The manner in which behavioral complementarity (or its absence) comes to have hedonic significance can also be conceptualized in terms of Plans and the interruption of their execution. In the preceding chapter it was noted that considerable evidence exists concerning the anxiety-inducing effect of an interruption of a planned sequence of behavior. The occurrence of a noncomplementary response to proffered behavior is, in effect, such an interruption, and we would suppose therefore that it might arouse anxiety. Presumably, the person is motivated to avoid such occurrences, and we would expect him, in general, to exercise care in the formulation and execution of his interpersonal Plans in order to maximize the likelihood of complementarity.

The two possibilities mentioned do not exhaust the available conceptions that might reasonably account for the apparently general tendency to desire certain kinds of interpersonal responses from others, and to find certain other kinds undersirable. Balance or congruency theory, as advocated by Secord and Backman (1961), is a case in point. Before we move to an examination of this interesting and useful framework, however, it should perhaps be emphasized that there is no fundamental incompatibility among these varying explanatory conceptions, and that it does not seem advisable, in the present state of our knowledge, to assume that any single mechanism is adequate to account for all instances in which a person appears to seek a particular form of social response from others.

BALANCE THEORY AND INTERPERSONAL RELATIONS

Secord and Backman's formulation, which is basically concerned with the problem of personality stability and change, is presented at length in their two major papers on this topic. The first of these (1961) outlines the theory in a more or less formal way and indicates the range of phenomena it is intended to encompass. The second (1965) and more ambitious work attempts to integrate theory with the findings of empirical research conducted by the authors and by others in a variety of areas in which the theory has relevance. In general, it may be said that the theory has substantial empirical support.

The general notion that persons have a need to maintain a "balance," or "consonance," or "congruency" among various currently salient aspects of themselves, such as their cognitions, their feelings, and their behaviors, has gained a wide and empirically justified acceptance among psychologists in recent years. The field of social psychology, especially, has seen a proliferation of theoretical developments organized around particular formulations of the general notion, and it has contributed to great advances in understanding in a number of areas. Secord and Backman take no stand with respect to the competing special theories as to how consistency needs operate, but are content with the now fairly unassailable observation that persons generally have them. They focus upon three elements or "components" which persons are said to strive for consistency among: (1) some aspect of the person's self concept (that is, a cognition that the person has concerning some aspect or attribute of himself); (2) the person's interpretation (perception, Level II) of those of his actions which relate to that aspect of his self concept; and (3) the person's perception (Level II) of the related aspects of the behavior of the other person with whom he is interacting. The term "self," as used here, refers to the phenomenal self, and is roughly coextensive with Sullivan's use of the same term.

Various types of inconsistency or incongruency among these three components are clearly possible, but the specifically *interpersonal* forms involve the functional relations existing between the third component and the other two. The person experiences congruency in the interpersonal sphere, then, only to the extent that his perception of the behavior of the other person is consistent with the relevant aspects of his self concept, and with his own interactional behavior, as he perceives it. If we assume that *incongruency* is experienced as an unpleasant state of affairs, the implication is that the person will strive to reduce it. There are several avenues open to him: He may change his self concept to bring it into line with his perception of the other's behavior toward him—an unlikely possibility under most circumstances. He may change his own behavior, or only his perception of it, in order to achieve interpersonal congruency—the limiting factor here being that any such change must concur with the self concept if *intrapersonal* incongruency is to be avoided. He may attempt to change the other's behavior toward him, or only his perception of it, to achieve the desired congruence. We should expect that any or all of these modes of interpersonal incongruency reduction might become operative under given circumstances. In general, however, some are more probable, or in the long run have greater adaptive merit, than others. Presumably there will be strong resistance to change in the self concept, for example, and solutions that require misperception of one's own or another's behavior contain an irrational element likely to become troublesome at some point in the interaction. Similarly, changing one's own "real" behavior might conflict with internal motivations, or with the self concept. It would seem, therefore, that attempting to induce changes in the other's "real" behavior has certain notable advantages as a method of interpersonal incongruency reduction; this being the case, we should expect to see it employed with considerable frequency. Secord and Backman (1961, 1965) refer to this method as "the evocation of congruent responses," and they note its similarity to Goffman's (1959) concepts relating to self-presentation and the staging of personal "performances," whose function is to create certain effects in the "audience."

THE ECONOMICS OF INTERACTION

Borrowing an analogy from the field of economics, Homans (1961) has pointed out that much of human interaction, reduced to its elementary forms, involves the exchange of goods and services between persons. In this chapter, we have identified a set of categories of social behavior and pointed out that, for each category, there would seem to be an identifiable and finite range of complementary behaviors. We have also suggested that, for various possible reasons, a person may be motivated to fashion his own interactive behavior in such a way as to prompt a particular kind of complementary behavior from others. If he succeeds in doing so, he is assumed to experience this as a rewarding state of affairs—that is to say, the other person has, in a sense, performed a service for him. On the other hand, a noncomplementary response is nonrewarding and may be experienced as unpleasant, giving rise to anxiety, or a sense of "incongruence." In this case, the person's behavior may be said to have incurred a "cost" for him, in the form of these unpleasant consequences. Moreover, the other person's noncomplementary response may be itself a prompt to engage in an altered form of behavior that would incur additional costs to the first person in terms of anxiety, insecurity, self-incongruence, and so on. Our first person is now at an impasse, confronted with two alternatives: (1) He can attempt to terminate the interaction. (2) He can try to salvage it by having another try at getting the other person's behavior into a more rewarding, or less costly, category. And so it goes.

This is an extremely oversimplified statement of a model of interaction that will occupy our attention for the remainder of the book. The next chapter is devoted to its more detailed explication and is based largely on the framework developed by Thibaut and Kelley in their influential book, *The Social Psychology of Groups* (1959).

REFERENCES

Allport, G. W., and Odbert, H. S. Trait names: A psycho-lexical study. *Psychological Monographs,* 1936, **47** (No. 211), 1–171.

Becker, W. C., and Krug, R. S. A circumplex model for social behavior in children. *Child Development,* 1964, **35**, 371–96.

Becker, W. C., Peterson, D. R., Luria, Z., Shoemaker, D. J., and Hellmer, L. A. Relations of factors derived from parent interview ratings to behavior problems of five-year-olds. *Child Development,* 1962, **33,** 509–53.

BORGATTA, E. F. Rankings and self-assessments: Some behavioral characteristics replication studies. *Journal of Social Psychology,* 1960, **52,** 297–307.

BORGATTA, E. F. The structure of personality characteristics. *Behavioral Science,* 1964, **9,** 8–17.

BORGATTA, E. F., COTTRELL, L. S., JR., and MANN, J. M. The spectrum of individual interaction characteristics: An interdimensional analysis. *Psychological Reports,* 1958, **4,** 279–319.

BROWN, R. *Social Psychology.* New York: Free Press, 1965.

CARTER, L. F. Evaluating the performance of individuals as members of small groups. *Personnel Psychology,* 1954, **7,** 477–84.

FOA, U. G. Convergences in the analysis of the structure of interpersonal behavior. *Psychological Review,* 1961, **68,** 341–53.

FOA, U. G. Cross-cultural similarity and difference in interpersonal behavior. *Journal of Abnormal and Social Psychology,* 1964, **68,** 517–22.

FOA, U. G. New developments in facet design and analysis. *Psychological Review,* 1965, **72,** 262–74.

GOFFMAN, E. *The presentation of self in everyday life.* Garden City, N.Y.: Doubleday Anchor, 1959.

HOMANS, G. C. *Social behavior: Its elementary forms.* New York: Harcourt, Brace & World, 1961.

KOGAN, W. S., and FORDYCE, W. E. The control for social desirability: A comparison of three different Q sorts and a check list, all composed of the same items. *Journal of Consulting Psychology,* 1962, **26,** 26–30.

LEARY, T. *Interpersonal diagnosis of personality.* New York: Ronald, 1957.

LORR, M., BISHOP, P. F., and MCNAIR, D. M. Interpersonal types among psychiatric patients. *Journal of Abnormal Psychology,* 1965, **70,** 468–72.

LORR, M., and MCNAIR, D. M. An interpersonal behavior circle. *Journal of Abnormal and Social Psychology,* 1963, **67,** 68–75.

LORR, M., and MCNAIR, D. M. Expansion of the interpersonal behavior circle. *Journal of Personality and Social Psychology,* 1965, **2,** 823–30.

LORR, M., and MCNAIR, D. M. Methods relating to evaluation of therapeutic outcome. In L. A. GOTTSCHALK and A. H. AUERBACH

(Eds.), *Methods of research in psychotherapy.* New York: Appleton-Century-Crofts, 1966. Pp. 573–94.

POTTER, S. *One-upmanship.* New York: Holt, Rinehart & Winston, 1952.

ROE, ANN. Early determinants of vocational choice. *Journal of Counseling Psychology*, 1957, **4,** 212–17.

SCHAEFER, E. S. A circumplex model for maternal behavior. *Journal of Abnormal and Social Psychology*, 1959, **59,** 226–35.

SCHAEFER, E. S. Converging conceptual models for maternal behavior and for child behavior. In J. C. GLIDEWELL (Ed.), *Parental attitudes and child behavior.* Springfield, Ill.: Charles C Thomas, 1961. Pp. 124–46.

SCHAEFER, E. S., and BAYLEY, N. Maternal behavior, child behavior, and their intercorrelations from infancy through adolescence. *Monographs of the Society for Research in Child Development*, 1963, **28** (No. 87), 1–127.

SECORD, P. F., and BACKMAN, C. W. Personality theory and the problem of stability and change in individual behavior: An interpersonal approach. *Psychological Review*, 1961, **68,** 21–32.

SECORD, P. F., and BACKMAN, C. W. An interpersonal approach to personality. In B. A. MAHER (Ed.), *Progress in experimental personality research,* Vol. 2. New York: Academic Press, 1965. Pp. 91–125.

SLATER, P. E. Parent behavior and the personality of the child. *Journal of Genetic Psychology*, 1962, **101,** 53–68.

THIBAUT, J. W., and KELLEY, H. H. *The social psychology of groups.* New York: Wiley, 1959.

CHAPTER 5

Negotiating Interpersonal Transactions

The theoretical analysis of interpersonal relations developed by Thibaut and Kelley (1959), like that of Homans (1961), rests basically upon an *exchange* view of human interaction. Their position in this regard is well illustrated in the following quotation:

> Perhaps it seems overly cynical, placing too much emphasis on the short-term bargaining or trading nature of . . . [interpersonal] relationships and overlooking some of the longer term satisfactions they often provide and the more subtle aspects of the interaction process necessary for the relationship to be satisfactory to both participants. The point should be made, however, that whatever the gratifications achieved in dyads, however lofty or fine the motives satisfied may be, the relationship may be viewed as a trading or bargaining one. The basic assumption running throughout our analysis is that every individual voluntarily enters and stays in any relationship only as long as it is

adequately satisfactory in terms of his rewards and costs. (p. 37)

The Thibaut and Kelley formulation of interpersonal relations is a quite ruthlessly hedonistic one that asserts the empirical law of effect as its fundamental operating principle. If the tender-hearted reader is offended by what may seem to be an attack upon his human sensibilities and values, I must ask that he suspend judgment and maintain his attentiveness until we have had the opportunity to expose the framework more fully and assess its usefulness in the analytical task confronting us. Our discussion throughout this chapter, although consistently oriented to available, relevant empirical knowledge, will of necessity be conducted almost exclusively at a conceptual level.

Rewards and Costs

The hedonic *outcome* attained by a person in any interaction with another person is calculated in terms of the *rewards* he receives and the *costs* he incurs in that interaction, and is perhaps best conceived in terms of a *net* magnitude, rewards minus costs. Thibaut and Kelley conceptualize the nature of rewards and costs in a quite general and straightforward way. A reward is any positively valued consequence accruing to the person from the interaction—such as the ability to engage in preferred behavior, need-satisfaction, consensual validation of one's attitudes, experiencing of personal acceptance by the other, and so forth. A cost is any negatively valued consequence incurred by the person in the interaction—such as the effort or energy expenditure required to make particular responses; the arousal of anxiety, embarrassment, or other unpleasant feelings; the simultaneous instigation of competing or conflicting responses; noncomplementary behavior in the other person, and so forth. Both rewards and costs may be either "exogenous" or "endogenous" in respect to interactional behavior. Exogenous outcomes are intrinsically related to the performance of any behavior and occur independently of the behavior of the other member of the dyad; they could be produced even if the person were behaving in isolation from others. Endogenous outcomes, on the other hand, depend upon the relationship, in the sense that the other person's behavior at least partially determines the rewards and/or costs experienced in consequence of behaving in any particular way.

I should like to expand very briefly upon and make explicit certain ideas about rewards and costs which are for the most part only implicit in Thibaut and Kelley's treatment. First, it requires very little imagination or presumption to note the interchangeability, across a broad range of applications, of reward-cost concepts and the Sullivanian conceptions of *satisfaction* and *security.* Enhancement of satisfaction (of biologically based or closely related needs) or of security (sense of well-being, self-esteem) is *rewarding,* whereas frustration and disruption of satisfaction or security is at best nonrewarding and may be *costly.* An appreciation of these parallels will help to tie in what has gone before with what is yet to come in our discussion. Even more important, I should like to warn against adopting a too-general and arbitrary set concerning what may constitute a reward or a cost in regard to any given instance of behavior. Most of us share very general notions about what is desirable behavior and what is undesirable behavior, both for ourselves and for others. The chances are that a majority of us would say that we prefer to engage in Responsible and Cooperative behavior and that we prefer to receive the same from others—that is, that this behavior is maximally rewarding to engage in and to receive. Conversely, most of us would regard Aggressive behavior as generally costly for both the actor and the recipient. But we also think that there are instances in which quite the reverse conditions would hold. For example, I suspect that most persons have at one time or another indulged in the prompting of a stern rebuke from another when they were feeling temporarily guilty or blameworthy; this particular ploy is common in the behavioral repertoire of adolescents in relation to their parents, and the complementary engagement produces an outcome increment for both participants, at least momentarily. The point is that the general social desirability of various kinds of behavior is correlated very imperfectly with the reward or cost value of the behavior as it is actually performed in given circumstances.

INTERACTION SEQUENCES

The unit of analysis adopted by Thibaut and Kelley in the study of interaction is called the *behavior sequence* or *set*. Each such unit represents an organized sequence of verbal and/or motor acts directed toward the attainment of some more or less immediate goal or state of affairs. The typical sequence involves acts with an instrumental function in moving the person toward his immediate objective, followed by other behaviors that are, broadly speaking, consummatory in nature—that is, they are involved with an appreciation or enjoyment of the attained goal. It is suggested that the individual maintains a given orientation or intention throughout any particular sequence, or in other words that he maintains a *set*. The repertoire of behaviors any person brings to an interaction consists of all the possible sets and combinations of sets he may perform. It should be obvious to the reader that the concept of *set*, as it is used by Thibaut and Kelley, is essentially similar to that of Miller, Galanter, and Pribram's (1960) *Plan* (see Chapter 3 of this book), and that behavior sequence or set units are readily conceived in terms of tactical-level TOTE units.

When two persons come together in interaction, then, each brings with him a repertoire of sets (or Plans) for the attainment of high reward–low cost outcomes, some of which he will execute in the immediate situation. If the two persons are strangers to each other, it may be assumed that, in the typical case, each will enact investigatory sets whose goals involve attempts to sample the potential outcomes available from the standpoint of currently salient motivations, and to gain information as to the sets that should be mobilized for subsequent enactment if maximum outcomes are to be realized. You may recall that in Chapter 3 we referred to this process in terms of the execution of search-and-solve Plans. Once begun, any particular interaction will presumably continue until the outcomes of either member drop below a satisfactory level, a situation that might be occasioned by a decrease in rewards (possibly owing to "satisfaction" of the instigations bringing the person to the interaction in the first place), an increase in costs, or both. A given interaction might therefore involve the execution of one or of many sequential sets by each party. By the same token, it may be suggested that a dyadic *relationship* may consist of a single or very many sequential interactions over time between the same two persons. The survival value of a relationship will be a function of the level of the outcomes experienced by each member in the course of their interactions. We shall have more to say about this matter presently.

THE INTERACTION-OUTCOME MATRIX

Dyadic interaction may be conceived as involving paired enactments of behavior, where each member of a pair represents a particular behavior sequence or set enacted by each party such that the two sets occur in a contiguous time relation to each other. The performances of the sets may overlap and occupy the same temporal period, or they may occur in immediately adjacent time periods, as when one of the persons executes a set in response to an immediately preceding set enacted by the other person. Because many, and typically the most significant, of the outcomes experienced in dyadic interactions are endogenous ones, the rewards and costs experienced by each member as he enacts his sets will be partly determined by the contiguous sets enacted by the other member.

In order to capture these interaction contingencies in a graphic manner, Thibaut and Kelley make extensive use of illustrative interaction-outcome matrixes, a prototypic example of which can be seen in Table 5.1. The possible sets that Person A may enact in interaction with Person B are arrayed along the horizontal axis at the top. The possible sets that Person B may enact are arrayed along the vertical axis at the left. Note that these possible sets are in each case coded in terms of the octant categories discussed in the preceding chapter. Thibaut and Kelley do not use these categories, and their analysis is variably conducted on both more abstract and more concrete levels than is intended here. The liberty has been taken of assuming that the possible sets that may be enacted by A or B, or *any* interacting persons, are encodable in these particular categorical terms. It would be useful also to include the behavior *intensity* variable (see page 107) in the matrix, perhaps as a third dimension, but this would seem to call for an unduly complicated display. The reader should, however, keep this additional variable in mind.

Each internal cell of the matrix depicted in Table 5.1 represents a potential contiguous intersection of one of A's sets with one of B's, and in the aggregate these cells may be conceived as constituting all of the possible contiguous pairings of A's and B's behavior sequences as they engage in interaction. Within each cell is noted the "outcome" consequence to A (above the diagonal) and to B (below the diagonal) of moving to that cell at a given point in their interaction. It is important to note that the outcomes depicted in the matrix are those which A and B will actually experience as a result of interacting in any given cell, and are not necessarily strongly correlated with what A or B may subjectively anticipate or predict as the outcome levels. In this sense, the outcomes depicted in the matrix are always "real" ones. On the other hand, however, the outcomes actually experienced by A or B—that is, those indicated in the matrix—are not necessarily "objective" in the sense that other persons would experience the same levels of rewards and costs under the same conditions. The outcome values entered into the matrix therefore refer to the subjective hedonic experience each person *will* have in the event that interaction takes place in a particular cell. Psychologists refer in a general way to such subjective values as *utilities*. Needless to say, the problem of devising suitable metric scales for the measurement of utilities is an extremely complicated one. We cannot hope to develop here any generally satisfactory solution to the problem in the present context. But it must be acknowledged as an important, although not crippling, limitation upon the power of our analysis.

One general property of the interaction-outcome matrix formulated here should be noted. The reward-cost factors in the various cells seem to be partly predetermined by the degree of inherent complementarity characterizing the intersecting behaviors of each

Table 5.1. Matrix of Possible Interactions and Outcomes

A's REPERTOIRE / B's REPERTOIRE	MANAGERIAL	RESPONSIBLE	COOPERATIVE	DOCILE	SELF-EFFACING	REBELLIOUS	AGGRESSIVE	COMPETITIVE
MANAGERIAL	r_A, c_A / r_B, c_B	ETC. / ETC.	. . . / . . .					
RESPONSIBLE	ETC. / ETC.							
COOPERATIVE	⋮ / ⋮							
DOCILE								
SELF-EFFACING								
REBELLIOUS								
AGGRESSIVE								
COMPETITIVE								

cell. Moreover, the distribution of these partially predetermined outcomes between the two interactants may often have a symmetrical character. For example, the intersection of Responsible behavior on A's part and Cooperative behavior on B's would represent a highly complementary interaction and would conceivably have some reward value to each partner on this basis alone, independent of the specific "content" of the behavior sequences enacted. If, on the other hand, A were to enact a Rebellious sequence contiguous with B's Cooperative one, the behaviors would be noncomplementary and would perhaps to that degree incur costs for each participant. For example, B's behavior might, at least analogically, convey a message of conventional, genial agreeability and affection, while A's conveyed one of bitter and cynical distrust. It is not a happy combination; you may recall from cocktail party behavior and the like the strain when two strangers happen to mesh in this way. The problem of complementarity and its relationship to outcomes is given more detailed consideration below.

THE EVALUATION OF OUTCOMES

It has been noted that the rewards and costs experienced by the members of a dyad have implications for the fate of their interactions and their relationship. Let us now be more specific about these matters. Thibaut and Kelley suggest two standards or reference points by means of which persons are guided in evaluating the outcomes they receive in interaction with others. One of these is the *Comparison Level* (CL). The CL is a kind of adaptation level that represents the neutral point for the person on a scale of goodness versus badness of outcome. It is his personal standard of evaluation for outcomes. The level of the CL may vary considerably between persons and even within the same person from time to time. Net outcomes (rewards minus costs) below the CL are experienced as unsatisfactory and as a poor return on one's investment in the relationship, while outcomes above the CL are experienced as a satisfactory and pleasant state of affairs. The level of the CL at any point in time may be influenced by a variety of factors, but in general it may be taken to be a modal or average value of the entire population of outcomes known to the person, including those he perceives as accruing to others, where each known outcome is "weighted" by its motivational salience for the person. It follows that if one's personal world is relatively bountiful, one's CL will be correspondingly high, and one will not be readily satisfied with low-outcome relationships. Conversely, the person whose outcome experience is relatively deprived will have a low CL and will be satisfied with outcomes that the person with a higher CL would find unattractive. The magnitude of the hedonic effect will in each case be proportional to the "distance" between outcomes and the CL. This concept of CL is an exceedingly important one in the domain of interpersonal relations, and it has a very broad range of explanatory power. One example with a certain contemporary pertinence is its usefulness in accounting for the seemingly increased subjective frustration of underprivileged groups, frustration that is, paradoxically, often observed subsequent to their making substantial progress in improving their outcomes.

While the ratio of outcomes to CL determines the attractiveness of relationships, it does not in itself determine their durability. Circumstances are sometimes such that they constrain a person to remain in a relationship he regards as manifestly unsatisfactory. Thibaut and Kelley conceive of this issue as relating essentially to the quality (in terms of outcomes) of alternative relationships available to the person, including the choice of remaining alone; the latter choice, of course, would not necessarily preclude imagined or fantasized relations with others. The concept of *Comparison Level for Alternatives* (CL_{alt}) is introduced to refer to this type of standard against which relationship outcomes are evaluated. The CL_{alt} represents the lowest outcome level a member of a dyad will accept in the light of the outcomes available to him in alternative relationships. If outcomes in a relationship drop below CL_{alt}, the person will leave the relationship in order to engage his current next-best alternative. The height of the CL_{alt} therefore depends mainly upon the reward-cost positions experienced or believed by the person to exist in the most satisfactory of the available alternatives to the present relationship, where, as in the case of the CL, these anticipated outcomes are weighted by their current salience for the person. While the height of the CL in relation to outcomes determines a person's *satisfaction* with a relationship, the height of his CL_{alt} may be said to determine his *dependence* upon the relationship. Thus, a person may be dependent upon a relationship even though finding it unattractive, simply because the outcomes he is experiencing, while unsatisfactory, are the best that he believes he can get at the time. The possibility that the person may, under certain circumstances, prefer isolation to any currently available real-world relationship suggests that he is able to provide outcomes for himself in excess of those he believes to be attainable in interaction with others. In general, the ability to produce high outcomes for oneself at costs that are competitive renders one independent of other persons, because the outcomes may be generated in isolation, or because they are "portable" from one relationship to another.

Three broad types of relationships can be distinguished on the basis of the differential levels obtaining among outcomes, CL, and CL_{alt}. In the first place, the CL may be below outcomes *and* CL_{alt} (with outcomes, of course, exceeding CL_{alt}). This is a happy circumstance for the person experiencing it, in that his attraction to, or satisfaction with, the relationship exceeds his dependence upon it. He could engage his next best alternative relationship and still remain above CL. Second, the CL may be below outcomes but above CL_{alt}. This is a situation in which the person's satisfaction with the relationship, while present in some degree, is exceeded by his dependence upon it. Such a circumstance renders the person vulnerable to a drop in outcomes below CL without being in a position to contemplate moving to a more satisfactory alternative relationship. The latter eventuality would be representative of the third relationship possibility, one in which the CL exceeds *both* outcomes and the CL_{alt}. It denotes the important class of *nonvoluntary* relationships, in which the person is constrained to remain in an unsatisfactory relationship because better outcome alternatives are unavailable to him, as is the case with prison inmates and other persons whose freedom of choice is restricted. A person may decide to remain in an unhappy marital relationship because the available alternatives are perceived as even less rewarding or more costly than the present situation, given the personal, social, and economic problems that may be occasioned by separation or divorce.

It is plain from these considerations that the formation and endurance of a dyadic relationship are dependent upon the existence of cells within the interaction-outcome matrix that yield outcomes exceeding each member's CL_{alt}, and upon elimination of interactions whose outcomes are below CL_{alt} for either member. This means, in effect, that certain positions highly desired by one member of the dyad might be denied to him because those same positions would fall below the other member's CL_{alt}. Dating relationships between young men and women frequently encounter strain because the form of interaction maximally desired by one of the parties is excessively costly for the other to enact. A person will achieve good outcomes in a relationship to the degree that the other person has a low CL_{alt}, and to the degree that his own and the other's outcomes are correlated across the various cells within which they may interact. In other words, a given relationship is likely to produce better outcomes than alternative relationships if each member can produce rewards for the other without incurring corresponding excessive costs. For a relationship to persist it must produce *jointly* experienced outcomes above each member's CL_{alt}, a condition that is tantamount to interdependence.

Interaction-Outcome Processes: Two Examples

Having considered the basic constructs of the Thibaut and Kelley framework, we are now in a position to fit it to some real-life examples of human interaction in order to examine in further detail the manner in which it "works." This discussion will also serve to summarize and make more explicit the character of the integration of "personality" and interactional concepts toward which we have gradually been moving throughout the earlier chapters of the book. We will rely upon interaction-outcome matrixes for illustrative purposes in much of what follows, and a standard format of presentation of these matrixes will be employed for the sake of convenience. The format has the following characteristics: (1) The octant categories will be collapsed into the four quadrants of *hostile dominance* (H-D, encompassing Aggressive and Competitive behaviors); *friendly dominance* (F-D, encompassing Managerial and Responsible behaviors); *friendly submission* (F-S, encompassing Cooperative and Docile behaviors); and *hostile submission* (H-S, encompassing Self-effacing and Rebellious behaviors). (2) We will forego separate representation of rewards and costs in the matrixes in favor of single-outcome magnitudes, which may be taken as the reward-minus-cost residual. (3) All outcomes will be scaled from the respective members' CL_{alts}, with a zero quantity indicating an outcome *at* the level of the CL_{alt}.

A HANDSOME LAD AND A PRETTY MAID

Let us take as our first example a somewhat expanded version of an interactional illustration suggested by Jones and Gerard (1967, Chapter 13). It concerns a "fleeting moment" during the initial meeting between a "handsome lad" and a "pretty maid." We will assume that each of the parties to the interaction has available a repertoire of four sets, each of which falls within one of the four interpersonal behavior quadrants, in respect to at least its analogical message value. (Real persons, of course, would have a large number of sets in each category.) The handsome lad's sets might be: an impassive stare (H-D), enthusiastic initiation of a conversational "line" (F-D), a warm grin (F-S), and a shy averting of his glance (H-S). And the pretty maid's available sets might be: a bored look (H-D), a smile and a wink (F-D), a smile without the wink (F-S), and a wary checking of the closure of the neckline of her blouse (H-S). These are the "opening" sets or Plans each of the parties brings to the interaction on the basis of his past experience and his perception of the current circumstances. Neither, of course, can predict with certainty what the other will do. What each will in fact do is dependent upon the nature and strength of the instigations that are salient at the time in respect to satisfaction and security needs, and upon each person's best guesses as to what the other may do. Both of these kinds of determining factors are in turn products of the immediate and remote past history of the participants in relation to situations that share some similar or common elements with the present one.

To simplify matters, let us assume further that both the handsome lad and the pretty maid are unencumbered by gross complications in their interpersonal functioning; that each would like to engage the other for mutual satisfaction in the realm of tenderness and sexuality, provided this can be accomplished without incurring undue costs; and that each has only "normal" requirements for the maintenance of his dignity and security in interpersonal relations, including average (although perhaps "Juvenile") needs to be "one-up" and to avoid being "one-down." The matrix depicted in Table 5.2 is intended to capture the essence of this particular fleeting moment. It has several interesting properties. Note first that the maximum outcome for both parties occurs in the cell representing the intersection of the lad's "line" and the maid's "smile" options. The occurrence of this interaction would get things off to a fine start, in that each person would receive maximum (current and anticipated) rewards at very minimal cost—even the "norm" of the boy's playing the "aggressive" role is happily fulfilled. But what are the chances of our two protagonists' managing to get themselves into his high payoff cell in their initial transaction? Several considerations indicate that its accomplishment is by no means certain.

The maid and the lad will each be aware that the other is capable of displaying a range of behaviors coordinately with their initial action, and that some of the possible combinations would be personally unpleasant, if not quite devastating. This is the meaning of the lad's − 3 outcome in that cell of the matrix in which his "line" is matched by a bored look. To the degree that either of them has been capable of making a realistic assessment of the interaction-outcome possibilities, they may not be willing to run the risk entailed in enacting the behavior that would produce the maximum joint outcome. Unless the instigation to interaction is quite strong, either one or both of them might choose a more cautious course of action. Moreover, since the maid is pretty and the lad is handsome, both will presumably have high CL_{alts} which is a limiting factor on the degree of risk they

Table 5.2. Interaction-Outcome Matrix for a Pretty Maid and a Handsome Lad in Their First Meeting

MAID'S OPTIONS / LAD'S OPTIONS	BORED LOOK (H-D)	SMILE AND WINK (F-D)	SMILE (F-S)	CHECK BLOUSE (H-S)
IMPASSIVE STARE (H-D)	0 / 0	−3 / +1	−2 / +1	−2 / +1
ENTHUSIASTIC "LINE" (F-D)	+1 / −3	+2 / +2	+3 / +3	+1 / −2
WARM GRIN (F-S)	+1 / −2	+2 / +3	+2 / +2	0 / −2
AVERTED GLANCE (H-S)	+1 / 0	−2 / +1	−1 / +1	−1 / 0

might be willing to undertake. If the possibility of embarrassment is very salient in the maid's mind, for example, her best alternative is the bored look, of which the worst consequence to her would be an outcome at her CL_{alt}. This choice might even afford a modest payoff in the form of being able to appear disdainful and sophisticated, assuming that this is a value she holds. The lad's situation is in many ways comparable, and, if we can assume that his perception of his potential outcomes is veridical (that is, as depicted in the matrix), he might enact the impassive stare as his best bet for salvaging a measure of specious self-enhancement while avoiding the possibility of a painful put-down. If both parties enact their "safe" H-D options, they will of course engage each other in the upper left-hand cell, which represents a kind of neutral standoff for both in respect to outcomes and which fails entirely of establishing a basis for the mutual satisfactions both desire.

Having found themselves in this awkward position in their initial transaction, they will still be able to alter the situation by an abrupt change of tactics. But notice that the enactment of a set that may encourage the other has now become more problematic for each of them. The H-D behaviors enacted by each tend to prompt further mutual behaviors in the hostile ranges, and even if the prompt is repudiated there is still the now-certain knowledge each has that the other is not averse to making an H-D response. Given this knowledge, it will take an act of considerable courage for either to move to their F-D or F-S options in enacting their succeeding sets. I shall leave it to the reader to puzzle out on his own a solution to the dilemma, but the somewhat sad tale of the momentary situation in which the lad and the maid find themselves illustrates a general point. That is, the dynamics of dyadic relationships are such that the two parties may be unable to effect maximum joint outcomes despite their having major interests that are highly correspondent.

MR. AND MRS. X: A MATRIX ANALYSIS

Our second example of the Thibaut and Kelley approach is a more complicated one, involving changes over time in a dyadic interaction. For it, we return to the distressed couple described in Chapter 1, Mr. and Mrs. X. You will recall that Mrs. X, a "helpful," Responsible (F-D) woman, developed a severe case of vaginismus (rejection, withholding—H-D), purportedly in response to her husband's exploitative indifference (H-D) to her, and that this precipitated a violent attack of "mental" symptoms (help-needing—F-S) in her husband, which in turn produced fear, anxiety, and probably guilt (H-S) in Mrs. X. Let us try to depict this series of interactions in terms of altering interaction-outcome matrixes. We may imagine that the adjustment initially worked out by Mr. and Mrs. X was somewhat along the lines indicated in Table 5.3. Mr. X mainly enacts his preferred H-D and F-D behaviors of an exploitative and dogmatic variety without great cost, and perhaps even with some reward, to Mrs. X. Mrs. X, on the other hand, can enact her Responsible F-D behaviors under conditions which are, in general, mutually rewarding. Neither has any reason to be enthusiastic about, or especially aversive toward, interactions in other cells of the matrix.

Table 5.3. Interaction-Outcome Matrix for Mr. and Mrs. X's Initial Accommodation to Each Other

MR. X's OPTIONS / MRS. X's OPTIONS	EXPLOITATIVE SELF INTEREST (H-D)	PEDANTIC AND DOGMATIC ACTIONS (F-D)	DEPENDENT, NEEDING HELP (F-S)	ACT HURT, COMPLAIN (H-S)
REJECT, WITHHOLD (H-D)	0 / 0	+1 / 0	0 / 0	0 / +1
RESPONSIBLE, HELPING ACTIONS (F-D)	+2 / 0	+1 / +2	+2 / +2	0 / +2
SUBMIT, COOPERATIVELY GIVE IN (F-S)	+3 / +1	+1 / +1	0 / +1	0 / 0
ANXIOUS, GUILTY, REPENTING ACTIONS (H-S)	+3 / +1	+1 / +1	0 / −1	0 / −1

We are led to believe that, in due course, Mrs. X comes to resent Mr. X's exploitative H-D behaviors toward her, perhaps especially in their sexual relations, in which he expects her to be Cooperative (F-S). In the meantime, we can imagine that his own enthusiasm for enacting H-D behaviors has continued unabated. The outcomes for Mrs. X under Mr. X's H-D option, however, have undergone quite drastic revision, with a large cost factor now involved in her enacting coordinate F-S behavior, and with a large potential reward available should she find some way of rejecting him (H-D) which will not simultaneously incur heavy costs. At the same time, the outcomes available to Mrs. X for enacting Responsible behavior have decreased because of her resentment. Table 5.4 approximates this set of circumstances in matrix form. The stage is now set for a significant alteration of Mrs. X's behavior in relation to her husband.

Our analysis does not necessarily require that Mrs. X achieve her vaginismus through a conscious, deliberate act of constricting the vaginal musculature, although that is far from incredible. It is enough for us to suppose that this musculature is subject to the influence of the "higher" neural processes, and it is possible that such influence could occur outside of awareness. In any case, Mrs. X is able eventually to fashion for herself a high-outcome response—vaginismus—to her husband's exploitative sexual demands. Consistent employment of this response by Mrs. X would be expected once again to alter the values of the interaction-outcome matrix characterizing the couple's relationship. Mr. X's penchant for H-D behavior now yields him chiefly frustration when it is exercised, because the only coordinate response providing an acceptable outcome for Mrs. X is her own covert form of H-D behavior. Even the less hostile varieties of Mr. X's domineering tendencies (F-D, pedantic and dogmatic actions) are less likely to be matched by submissiveness on the part of Mrs. X. In short, Mr. X is faced with a painful dilemma to the degree that his satisfaction and security rests upon his being able with impunity to enact behaviors in the dominant ranges. He must alter his tactics if he is to reassert a measure of control in the relationship. The conditions prevailing at this time are summarized in Table 5.5, which indicates the direction in

Table 5.4. Interaction-Outcome Matrix for Mr. and Mrs. X Immediately Prior to Mrs. X's Vaginismus

MR. X's OPTIONS / MRS. X's OPTIONS	EXPLOITATIVE SELF INTEREST (H-D)	PEDANTIC AND DOGMATIC ACTIONS (F-D)	DEPENDENT, NEEDING HELP (F-S)	ACT HURT, COMPLAIN (H-S)
REJECT, WITHHOLD (H-D)	0 / +3	+1 / +1	0 / +1	0 / +1
RESPONSIBLE, HELPING ACTIONS (F-D)	+2 / −1	+1 / +1	+2 / +1	0 / +1
SUBMIT, COOPERATIVELY GIVE IN (F-S)	+3 / −3	+1 / −1	0 / −1	0 / −1
ANXIOUS, GUILTY, REPENTING ACTIONS (H-S)	+3 / −1	+1 / −1	0 / −1	0 / −1

which Mr. X is likely to change. The matrix of Table 5.5 suggests that Mr. X's outcomes might be substantially increased by developing a "condition" requiring considerable help and support (F-S), and one that would also enable him to adopt the role of an injured party (H-S), whereby he might be able to alter the presently unfavorable matrix within which he and his wife are enmeshed.

And so, as we have seen, Mr. X becomes "sick." He manages to convey the impression that his mental health is in an exceed-

Table 5.5. Interaction-Outcome Matrix for Mr. and Mrs. X Immediately Prior to Mr. X's "Breakdown"

MR. X's OPTIONS / MRS. X's OPTIONS	EXPLOITATIVE SELF INTEREST (H-D)	PEDANTIC AND DOGMATIC ACTIONS (F-D)	DEPENDENT, NEEDING HELP (F-S)	ACT HURT, COMPLAIN (H-S)
REJECT, WITHHOLD (H-D)	−3 / +3	+1 / +1	0 / +1	0 / +1
RESPONSIBLE, HELPING ACTIONS (F-D)	+2 / −1	+1 / +1	+3 / +1	+2 / +1
SUBMIT, COOPERATIVELY GIVE IN (F-S)	+3 / −3	+1 / −1	+2 / −1	+2 / −1
ANXIOUS, GUILTY, REPENTING ACTIONS (H-S)	+3 / −1	+1 / −1	+3 / −1	+3 / −1

ingly tenuous state—a situation highly likely to inspire his wife to increase her nurturant, sympathetic efforts (F-D) in his behalf, and to behave in an anxious and repentant manner (H-S). The "resolution" of the impasse is depicted in Table 5.6. Mrs. X, being in a definitely "one-down" position, has reward and cost factors that largely limit her to her Responsible (F-D) and Self-effacing (H-S) options, with no resistance to their enactment even when Mr. X is enacting H-D. We may assume, however, that Mr. X will be cautious about enacting H-D in the sexual area out of

Table 5.6. Interaction-Outcome Matrix for Mr. and Mrs. X Following "Resolution" and Re-accommodation

MR. X's OPTIONS / MRS. X's OPTIONS	EXPLOITATIVE SELF INTEREST (H-D)	PEDANTIC AND DOGMATIC ACTIONS (F-D)	DEPENDENT, NEEDING HELP (F-S)	ACT HURT, COMPLAIN (H-S)
REJECT, WITHHOLD (H-D)	−3 / −1	−1 / −1	0 / −1	0 / −2
RESPONSIBLE, HELPING ACTIONS (F-D)	+2 / 0	−1 / +2	+3 / +3	+2 / +1
SUBMIT, COOPERATIVELY GIVE IN (F-S)	+3 / −3	−1 / −1	+2 / 0	+2 / 0
ANXIOUS, GUILTY, REPENTING ACTIONS (H-S)	+3 / +1	+1 / 0	+3 / 0	+3 / +1

fear of rejection; the latter response on the part of Mrs. X would be costly to her under the present circumstances, but not so costly as submission (F-S). It may be conjectured, then, that both will avoid a confrontation in this area. The cell yielding maximum mutual outcomes involves the coordination of Mrs. X's Responsible (F-D) option with Mr. X's Dependent (F-S) one, and we might expect a preponderance of interactions in this cell. Mr. X, however, will also presumably show some enthusiasm for his H-S option and the indirect accusation it conveys, partly to control and partly to punish Mrs. X. Mr. X's F-D option, on the other hand, will generally be somewhat costly for him to perform because it detracts from the convincingness of his "sick" performance. Again, it is not crucial for our analysis to assume that Mr. X consciously and deliberately fabricated his program of intimidation against Mrs. X, although, as Sullivan suggests (see page 52), and as Szasz (1961) asserts, it would be a mistake to conclude that such "hysterical" behavior is of necessity wholly unconsciously or automatically determined.

Generalized Interpersonal Styles and Their Interactional Aspects

The two illustrations of matrix conceptions considered thus far have been mainly concerned with relatively specific kinds of behavioral acts instigated by relatively specific conditions of interaction. It is undoubtedly true that persons generally vary their behavior in accord with the interactional conditions obtaining at a given time, but it is also true, as has been repeatedly suggested, that most persons develop favored interpersonal "styles" distinctive for them by virtue of the frequency and generality with which they display particular classes of behavior. "Style," as that term is used here, may be thought of as a discernible tendency to enact sets falling preponderantly, although often subtly, within a particular range of the interpersonal behavior circle. Thus, it was suggested that Mr. X was personally disposed toward the adoption of a Hostile-Dominant (Competitive) stance in relation to others, while Mrs. X was similarly disposed toward a Friendly-Dominant stance. As has also been suggested, it is this sort of generalized stylistic variation among persons to which the term "personality" chiefly refers.

INTERACTION OF PERSONAL STYLES: A MATRIX CONCEPTION

In a general way we have already considered the processes whereby personal styles may become more or less "habitual" as a consequence of experience. It seems reasonable to assume that the adoption by a person of a favored interpersonal style reflects the underlying circumstance that consistent enactment of the behaviors constituting this style produces, on the average, outcomes optimal for him in his relations with others. To put it another way, we may assume that characteristic styles of interpersonal behavior produce, over a broad range of interactions with others, higher rewards and/or lower costs for their purveyors than do other styles of behavior they might display. In Chapter 4 we developed the thesis that interpersonal behaviors could profitably be viewed as attempts to induce others to produce certain classes of behavior in response. The mechanisms involved in this type of attempt to influence the response of the other person to oneself are those of prompting and—very likely—"reinforcement." Both mechanisms appear to be based in large measure upon considerations of complementarity. If Person A enacts a given form of behavior, it may function both as a reinforcement (positive or negative, depending upon its degree of complementarity) for B's immediately preceding behavior, and as a prompt for B to respond in a complementary way. We may infer, then, that one of A's "purposes" in enacting a given form of behavior is that of producing in B a particular form of behavior in response. If A consistently enacts that same type of behavior over time, and with other persons as well, we are justified in assuming that the receipt of behavior which is complementary to it has generalized optimal outcome value for A, relative to other kinds of behavior he might receive. From this perspective, therefore, the suggestion that Mr. X experiences relatively high outcomes when others behave toward him in a Self-effacing–Masochistic way is a corollary of the suggestion that he has a Competitive-Narcissistic personality. The latter assertion is in no way intended to deny the possibility that engaging in Competitive behavior is intrinsically or "exogenously" rewarding to Mr. X. In fact, one might expect such behavior to become intrinsically rewarding through association learning if rewarding consequences have often occurred contiguously with its performance.

If we allow that the adoption of a particular interpersonal style in large part serves the function of producing a particular stance in the other person, there is still a question of why that stance in the other person should be more rewarding—or less cost-incurring—than alternative stances. Why is it, for example, that Mr. X experiences an optimal hedonic state when others are perhaps Self-effacing in relation to him. Or—to sharpen the issue somewhat—why does the Rebelliously disposed person appear to revel in punitive feedback and fear the possibility of affection and tenderness? The answer seems to lie in the area of security maintenance and enhancement. You will recall from Chapter 4 our analysis of interpersonal security in terms of the cue properties of the behavior the other person may display; the maintenance of uninterrupted sequences of Planned behavior; and the maintenance of congruent relations among one's self concept, one's own behavior (as perceived), and the behavior of the other person (again, as perceived).

We may conclude from these considerations that, in general, a person's prevailing interpersonal style (Competitive, Responsible, Docile, Rebellious, and so on), is, as Leary (1957) suggests, an aspect of his security-maintaining equipment. The successful prompting of complementary behavior in the other person may be assumed to have a security-enhancing reward value (for example, by confirming the self concept), while the failure of the other person to adopt a complementary stance might threaten or diminish security (for example, by disconfirming the self concept), and could thereby incur costs. We shall give considerably more attention to such processes in the following sections. For the moment, it may be noted that prompts of this general variety may be thought of as analogically coded metacommunications (see Chapter 1, pages 18-20) that seek to define the nature of the relationship currently obtaining between the interactants. Moreover, the fact that complementary responses have a statistically higher probability of occurrence than do other kinds of responses to the same evoking circumstances (Leary, 1957; Heller, Myers, and Kline, 1963) suggests that, other things being equal, it is more rewarding and/or less costly for persons to make complementary rather than noncomplementary responses to the prompts offered by their fellows. The qualifying phrase, "other things being equal," is of course crucial, for we know that other salient motivations of the responding person may frequently cause him to reject the first person's prompt and to enact noncomplementary behavior in response to it. These conceptions form the basis for the reference made earlier in this chapter to the existence of certain "inherent" reward-cost factors in the particular form of the interaction-outcome matrix we are using here as an analytical model. Let us now give some further attention to the issue of complementarity, on which our analysis ultimately depends.

Matrix complementarity. In the preceding chapter it was noted that, functionally speaking, complementarity tended to occur on the basis of reciprocity in respect to dominance-submission, and on the basis of correspondence in respect to hostility-affection. By and large, this conclusion is consistent with the Kaiser Foundation (Leary, 1957) research findings concerning the kind of behavior that tends to be provoked in the other person upon receiving behavior representative of one or another segment of the interpersonal circle, as is summarized in Figure 4.1 (page 108). Heller, Myers, and Kline (1963) provide additional empirical confirmation on this point. It is also essentially consistent with the implications for complementarity that may be drawn from Foa's (1964, 1965) "facet" reformulation of the circle variables, as has been noted (see pp. 113–114). The cells of our four-fold matrix that represent complementary interactions are therefore readily discernible. They are identified with dual plus signs in Table 5.7. The dual plus signs are intended to represent the likelihood that, in the typical case, the adoption of a particular interpersonal stance by A, and the adoption of a coordinate *complementary* stance by B, will produce some reward for both participants, independent of other reward-cost factors that may be involved in particular transactions between them. In essence, we are assuming that complementary interaction is in itself mutually rewarding to at least some degree, probably by way of enhancing the security of both participants.

Thus, four of the 16 cells of the matrix would appear to provide, in the typical case, a certain inherent reward mutually to any two persons who interact within them at any point in time. But what can be said of the remaining 12 cells? The simplest assumption to make, perhaps, is that they represent uniformly noncomplementary interactions with no inherent outcome implica-

Table 5.7. Mutual Rewards and Costs Based Upon "Inherent" Complementarity and Anticomplementarity

PERSON A'S OPTIONS / PERSON B'S OPTIONS	AGGRESSIVE/ COMPETITIVE BEHAVIORS (H-D)	MANAGERIAL/ RESPONSIBLE BEHAVIORS (F-D)	COOPERATIVE/DOCILE BEHAVIORS (F-S)	SELF-EFFACING/ REBELLIOUS BEHAVIORS (H-S)
AGGRESSIVE/ COMPETITIVE BEHAVIORS (H-D)		− / −		+ / +
MANAGERIAL/ RESPONSIBLE BEHAVIORS (F-D)	− / −		+ / +	
COOPERATIVE/DOCILE BEHAVIORS (F-S)		+ / +		− / −
SELF-EFFACING/ REBELLIOUS BEHAVIORS (H-S)	+ / +		− / −	

tions. Such an assumption, however, may be too hasty. Common experience suggests that some forms of noncomplementary interaction are, so to speak, more noncomplementary than others, in the sense that they produce for the participants (and sometimes even for uninvolved observers) a notable degree of strain, embarrassment, and other unpleasant emotional arousal. Unfortunately, with the exception of some almost casual observations made by the Kaiser Foundation research group (Leary, 1957), we are lacking any systematically derived knowledge about interactional collisions of this kind. In the absence of such knowledge, I should like to propose a working hypothesis concerning the general nature of these maximally noncomplementary interactions, one which—not accidentally—happens to accord with my own casual observations of social interaction. It is also largely in accord with the observations reported by Leary.

When a person "offers" behavior falling within any of the quadrants of the interpersonal circle, he is, in effect, "inviting" the other person to adopt a complementary stance in respect to *both* of the principal dimensions of the circle. Thus, if the person enacts H-D behavior, he is inviting the other to be *both* hostile and submissive. A corollary way of expressing this is that he is metacommunicatively proposing a definition of the relationship between himself and the other as one in which he is to have the higher "status" and in which the affective tone is to be relatively unfriendly. If the other person "accepts" both aspects of the invitation or proposal he adopts the complementary H-S position. However, the other person may accept only one of the component messages, as in an H-D or an F-S response. The latter circumstance, although lacking perfect complementarity, nevertheless leaves open a channel of potential transaction and negotiation. The H-D response is at least an acknowledgment that the interaction is an unfriendly one, and leaves open the possibility of an exhange of unfriendly messages in order to settle the matter of dominance as the interaction proceeds. Interactions of this kind are exceedingly common as "kidding" and "joshing" among persons who consider themselves to be basically friendly; it is a somewhat dangerous game, however, in that it not infrequently degenerates into a genuinely vicious struggle for the superior position. Similarly, the F-S response to an H-D overture acknowledges the responder's inferior position and leaves some room to both parties for negotiation on the issue of the affective quality that is to obtain in the relationship. A Docile, admiring response to a Competitive, exhibitionistic display represents an intersection of behaviors that is not wholly lacking as a basis of relationship. In contrast, consider the occurrence of F-D behavior as a response to an H-D overture. It is essentially a rejection of both components of the initiator's proposal, and as such it leaves very little ground upon which to effect a sustained engagement. When Managerial advice-giving or Responsible sympathy is offered in response to Aggressive bluntness or Competitive self-display, the mixture is apt to be a rather strained one, and it is difficult to imagine a relationship sustaining itself through very many transactions of this variety. Parallel considerations, of course, apply to combinations of H-S and F-S behaviors, in which there is also a dual mismatch of metacommunicative components. The person who enacts Self-effacing, weak behaviors is very likely to be made uncomfortable by one who enacts Docile, help-seeking behaviors, and vice versa.

We appear to have, then, two sets of quadrant combinations —H-D vs. F-D and H-S vs. F-S—which are especially noncomplementary. I propose to refer to interactions involving these combinations as *anticomplementary* ones. I further propose that the occurrence of interactions of this type is likely to incur endogenous costs for both parties. The initiator of an interaction in which an anticomplementary response occurs is confronted with a specific and relatively complete interruption of his Plans, a circumstance that is likely in itself to induce anxiety (see page 87). In addition he suffers a relatively complete repudiation of his definition of the interpersonal situation—a definition in which there is often a substantial security investment. The person who produces an anticomplementary response does so at the expense of risking an embarrassing impasse and subsequent retaliation from the other, and in many instances he violates strong normative pressures concerning the proper management of one's interpersonal affairs (Goffman, 1955). For these reasons, as has been suggested above, we would expect the occurrence of frankly anticomplementary responses only where their production is strongly motivated—that is, where contingent outcomes from other sources are anticipated to compensate for these cost factors. The costs to initiator and to responder believed to be associated with the occurrence of anticomplementary interactions constitute an additional set of outcomes that may be regarded as inherent in our matrix model; they are entered as dual minus signs in the relevant cells of Table 5.7.

Defining relationships. Table 5.7 represents an attempt to summarize the reward and cost factors that appear to be inherently and endogenously associated with dyadic intersections of the various categories of behavior we have chosen to deal with. These inherent outcome factors, it is suggested, operate in the main at a general, metacommunicative level, where basic definitions of the relationship of self to other are negotiated, and where basic security needs of persons are strongly engaged. They are therefore largely independent of more specific rewards and costs that may be experienced in consequence of the exchange of particular commodities. For example, a young lady who grants sexual intercourse to her suitor thereby provides one form of reward to him. His total outcomes from the situation, however, will be markedly affected by the style with which the young lady makes the specific reward available. If his security needs in this situation should require that he be Responsible (F-D) and that she be Docile (F-S), and if instead she "offers" herself in a style of Aggressive self- assertion (H-D)—thereby tending to invite him to be perhaps uncertain and self-conscious (H-S)—his net outcomes from the encounter might be minimal in spite of the sexual reward he obtains. Should these net outcomes be below his CL_{alt}, the young lady will presumably have lost a lover. I recall from my clinical practice several instances of young men who were rendered sexually impotent in situations similar to the one described, and it does not seem wholly unreasonable to entertain the possibility that this reaction was a manifestation of "involuntary" Hostile-Submissive compliance with the metacommunicative demand characteristics of the relationships in which these young men found themselves. If this were indeed the case, it would be an instance in which the metacommunicative demand proved more compelling than the available sexual rewards.

The existence of intrinsic outcome factors in interpersonal relations, as schematized in Table 5.7, provides an excellent mechanism whereby one person may "teach" another how to behave toward him, thus establishing the kind of relationship the first person prefers. For example, if a given person is so constituted that his security is markedly dependent upon his being able to appear weak and to avoid demands for personal strength being placed upon him, he may consistently enact Self-effacing (H-S) behavior. Note the options such a strategy would present to another person, based only on the outcomes depicted in Table 5.7. If Person A consistently enacts Self-effacing behaviors, perhaps in the form of clownishness or self-depreciatory statements, he imposes, in effect, certain constraints upon B's behavior toward him. For the purpose of illustration, let us assume that B is himself relatively uncommitted to any particular style of relating to others. Given the outcomes available to B in responding to A's persistent Self-effacement, he will find it difficult—that is, costly—to enact respectful, dependent, affiliative, (F-S) behaviors toward A, and he will be at least subtly propelled toward the adoption of a patronizing and arrogant stance (H-D) owing to the inherent complementarity reward available to him for doing so. In this manner, then, unless strong counterforces intervene, B will be trained by A over the course of perhaps several interactions to avoid making F-S responses to him and to emphasize the enactment of H-D responses. Of course, it would also be possible in an instance of this kind for A to introduce additional rewards and punishments in order to facilitate the "shaping up" of B's behavior toward him.

The acquisition of interpersonal style. These remarks may already have turned your thoughts to an interesting speculation regarding one possible antecedent in early childhood of the formation of enduring interpersonal styles. The young child, of course, has an exceedingly low, if not nonexistent, CL_{alt} in relation to his parents; he cannot normally turn away from them to engage alternative relationships, certainly not ones of comparable intensity and constancy. If the child's parents consistently and monolithically present a given interactional style in their relations with him, it is conceivable that they may, in the manner indicated, establish in him a tendency to enact behavior that is prevailingly complementary to their own, and to avoid the enactment of behavior that is anticomplementary to their own. Once established, moreover, a given interpersonal style tends for a variety of reasons (Secord and Backman, 1961, 1965) to become self-perpetuating. One of the more important processes involved is the encouragement of self-confirmatory (complementary) reactions in others, which are experienced by the person as reflected appraisal (see page 75).

If the plan of the present book had a more comprehensively developmental scope, if the behavior of children were less capricious than it is, if the literature on personality development in children were less intimidatingly voluminous and confused than it appears, and if the author were as conversant with this literature as he perhaps should be, it might be fun at this point to launch into a serious and scholarly evaluation of the extent to which this notion of personality (or interpersonal style) development would survive the stark light of empirical reality. Inasmuch as none of these conditions is fulfilled, however, it seems the better part of valor to content ourselves with two pertinent and well-established generalizations from the empirical literature on relations between parent behavior and personality development in the child. The first of these generalizations relates to the effect upon child behavior of variations in parent behavior on the hate-love dimension. Almost uniformly, studies in this area have come up with the same conclusion: hateful behavior in the parent begets hateful behavior in the child, and loving behavior in the parent begets loving behavior in the child. Although interpretable in other ways, this conclusion is clearly consistent with our hypothesis. The situation with parental dominance-submission, or what in this context is usually called strictness-permissiveness, is somewhat less clear cut. In general, however, the available evidence indicates that parental strictness has an inhibiting and suppressive effect upon the emerging personality of the child, and that parental permissiveness tends to be associated with ascendant, assertive, independent personality characteristics in the child. If we combine these two generalizations about the effects of parental behavior upon the developing youngster, we emerge with a picture that is highly concordant with our hypothesis.

The formation and survival of dyadic relationships. It is clear from the foregoing considerations that the "preferences" of persons for the adoption of given interpersonal styles will have a significant effect upon the choices they make in respect to interaction with other persons. The rewards and costs associated with complementarity and anticomplementarity in interaction, evaluated in terms of each participant's CL and CL_{alt}, would be expected to exert a substantial influence upon the formation and longevity of dyadic relationships. Thus, despite our fictional example of Mr. and Mrs. X, we would not often expect to see a relationship between a rigidly Competitive man and a rigidly Responsible women proceed to marriage. Such a man, other things being equal, would presumably be much more comfortable with a Self-effacing woman, and she with him. It is astonishing to see in real life the often remarkable survival value of marriages of this kind, which, in the extreme case, may appear to the external observer to be little more than institutionally sanctioned exhibitions of sado-masochism.

It may be conjectured that, within the first few minutes of newly formed dyadic relationships, considerable attention is given by the involved parties to determining the position each will take vis-à-vis the other in respect to dominance and affection. If the relationship promises to be a workable one from the standpoint of the level of complementarity of proffered stances, and from the standpoint of the apparent intensity or flexibility with which they are held, then the parties may go on to explore further the outcomes that may become mutually available to them through further interaction. On occasion, however, as is well known, an evident and costly collision of styles occurs practically immediately between two persons who seem otherwise to be socially adept; their outcomes with each other rapidly drop below CL_{alt}, and they terminate their incipient relationship with as much grace as can be managed. Now, if a person is not extraordinarily committed to some particular interpersonal stance, the possibility exists for him to adopt a nonpreferred stance, at least temporarily, in order to gain some other outcome objective in relation to the other person. For example, Hostile-Dominance is not a very adaptive posture for a young man undergoing an interview for a job, even though this may be his preferred style. Unless he happens to be "neurotic" about it, then, he will assume the Friendly-Submissive posture most Managers would expect of him. An amusing (to me) instance of the same sort of process sometimes occurs in dating relationships. On a certain university campus with which I am familiar it is alleged that the men prefer their women to be Docile and Cooperative in order that they may be comfortably Managerial and Responsible. It is also alleged, however, that very few of the women on this particular campus are in fact Docile and Cooperative in basic disposition, and on occasion a young man will even suggest that most are Competitive, especially in relation to young men. The girls, knowing about this and liking to have dates, are said to fabricate amazingly convincing performances of Docility during the earlier phases of their dating relations with the men, attempting thereby to keep the men above CL_{alt}.

COMPLEMENTARITY AS A PERSISTENT FORCE IN INTERACTION

The foregoing conceptions of complementarity and anticomplementarity are intended to suggest that these factors are more or less constantly in the background as reward and cost features of human interaction, and that they form something of a baseline condition in respect to the outcomes derived from interaction. More specific exchanges of goods, services, and disservices between persons have their own reward and cost factors associated with them, but the algebraic summation determining each party's total outcomes from any completed interactional set will in most instances contain a component from this complementarity source. For a given person, this more general source of outcomes assumes a fairly dominant role in his exchanges with the environment, if only because it comes into play repeatedly in virtually all of his interactions with others. Moreover, unless he is extraordinarily flexible or variable in style (and therefore in the kinds of experiences he finds rewarding or at least tolerable in relation to others), the level of these outcomes will be largely contingent upon his ability to control his interactions with other persons, limiting them to those cells in which his own outcomes are maximized. To some extent, this ability is undoubtedly a matter of diagnostic sensitivity and skill in the use of prompts and reinforcements, a skill that would seem to be a major component of what is called interpersonal competence. There seems to be little justification, at present, for considering such skill to be other than independent of stylistic preferences. Another, and not necessarily unrelated, aspect of the ability to control interaction is the amount of usable *power* the person is capable of generating in his relationships. The following section undertakes a brief analysis of interpersonal power, returning for this purpose to the specific formulations of Thibaut and

Kelley (1959). It may prevent confusion if we state at the outset that "power," as we shall be using the term, has almost nothing to do with dominance and submission, as we have been using those terms.

Power and Dependence in Dyadic Relationships

It was stated in an earlier section that a person's dependence upon a relationship was a function of the discrepancy between his CL_{alt} and his outcomes in the relationship. Power, in Thibaut and Kelley's (1959) terms, is simply the reverse side of the coin. Person A has power over Person B, and Person B is dependent upon Person A, to the extent that A can cause B to experience a wide range of outcomes above B's CL_{alt}. If B's outcomes, on the average, drop below his CL_{alt}, he will normally leave the relationship, and this factor constitutes one of several limitations upon the exercise of power in interpersonal relations. We shall consider some other such limitations presently. For the moment, however, note the implications of this formulation of power and dependence for our own analysis of personality in interpersonal terms. Power and its converse, dependence, will be a function of the degree to which one member of the dyad can, by his own actions, produce significant variations in the satisfaction and security experienced by the other member in the course of interaction between them. The resources utilized by the powerful person in maintaining the dependence of the other upon him may involve the manipulation of the other's satisfaction in respect to various of his needs, or the manipulation of his level of security, or both. The maintenance of power (or dependence) in a relationship will therefore be partly determined by the extent to which the personal characteristics (needs, security operations, and so on) of the two members of the dyad happen to mesh. The implications of this point will become clearer as our discussion develops.

FUNCTIONAL CHARACTERISTICS OF INTERPERSONAL POWER

We will begin our discussion of power and dependence at a fairly general level in order to illustrate the central concepts with maximum clarity. We will continue to employ the four-fold matrix, with outcomes scaled from CL_{alt}, for graphic representation of conditions of power and dependence, where the quadrant categories may be considered simply as a convenient means of coding various behaviors that may be enacted. Inasmuch as the behavioral consequences of conditions of power and dependence are maximally predictable only when the members of a dyad perceive the existence of these conditions, we will assume, unless otherwise indicated, that both members of the dyad have an accurate understanding of the content of their interaction matrix.

Three Varieties of Power. The definition of interpersonal power advanced by Thibaut and Kelley (1959), as well as other considerations, led these authors to describe two basic types of power relationships: *fate control* and *behavior control.* Working within the same framework, Jones and Gerard (1967) subsequently added a third type, called *contact control.* Let us consider each of these, roughly in order of apparent social complexity. They can be adequately represented by attending only to the outcomes of the dependent member of the dyad.

Contact control, illustrated in Table 5.8, occurs where the interaction-outcome conditions are such that one person's availability for interaction is sufficient in itself to make high outcomes possible for the other person. In Table 5.8, A has contact control over B because B is dependent for his high outcomes (+4) on the presence of A. For some reason, B is highly rewarded when he engages in H-D behavior in relation to A, relative to the rewards he can expect from engaging in H-D (or other) behavior in relation to his next most preferred partner (who can only provide outcomes which, by definition, do not exceed B's CL_{alt}). In this situation, A has power to keep B in the relationship, although his power does not extend to an ability to influence B's behavior in other ways; B's outcomes are independent of variations in A's behavior. A circumstance of this sort may at first blush seem rather unlikely and

Table 5.8. Matrix Illustration of Contact Control
(A has contact control over B)

PERSON A'S OPTIONS / PERSON B'S OPTIONS	AGGRESSIVE/ COMPETITIVE BEHAVIORS (H-D)	MANAGERIAL/ RESPONSIBLE BEHAVIORS (F-D)	COOPERATIVE/DOCILE BEHAVIORS (F-S)	SELF-EFFACING/ REBELLIOUS BEHAVIORS (H-S)
AGGRESSIVE/ COMPETITIVE BEHAVIORS (H-D)	+4	+4	+4	+4
MANAGERIAL/ RESPONSIBLE BEHAVIORS (F-D)	0	0	0	0
COOPERATIVE/DOCILE BEHAVIORS (F-S)	0	0	0	0
SELF-EFFACING/ REBELLIOUS BEHAVIORS (H-S)	0	0	0	0

bizarre, and in fact probably does not occur in pure form very frequently in real life. Nevertheless, there are certain real relationships in which this type of power is at least approximated—for example, where A is the only person in B's experience who will tolerate the role of recipient in respect to the particular form of H-D behavior in the enactment of which B finds so much pleasure.

Fate control is illustrated in Table 5.9. In this situation, B is unconditionally dependent upon A's behavior in the relationship. A is capable of moving B through a considerable range of out-

Table 5.9. Matrix Illustration of Fate Control (A has fate control over B)

PERSON B'S OPTIONS \ PERSON A'S OPTIONS	AGGRESSIVE/ COMPETITIVE BEHAVIORS (H-D)	MANAGERIAL/ RESPONSIBLE BEHAVIORS (F-D)	COOPERATIVE/DOCILE BEHAVIORS (F-S)	SELF-EFFACING/ REBELLIOUS BEHAVIORS (H-S)
AGGRESSIVE/ COMPETITIVE BEHAVIORS (H-D)	+4	0	0	0
MANAGERIAL/ RESPONSIBLE BEHAVIORS (F-D)	+4	0	0	0
COOPERATIVE/DOCILE BEHAVIORS (F-S)	+4	0	0	0
SELF-EFFACING/ REBELLIOUS BEHAVIORS (H-S)	+4	0	0	0

come magnitudes merely by virtue of his own behavioral choices, regardless of what B may do. The situation depicted is one in which, for some reason, B's outcomes are significantly greater under A's H-D option than under any other type of behavior in which A might engage. B's "fate" in the relationship is thus utterly dependent upon A's whim in choosing to enact, or not to enact, the H-D behavior B finds so rewarding.

Behavior control, illustrated in Table 5.10, is a condition in which B is contingently dependent upon A's behavior in relation to him.

Table 5.10. Matrix Illustration of Behavior Control (A has behavior control over B)

PERSON B'S OPTIONS \ PERSON A'S OPTIONS	AGGRESSIVE/ COMPETITIVE BEHAVIORS (H-D)	MANAGERIAL/ RESPONSIBLE BEHAVIORS (F-D)	COOPERATIVE/DOCILE BEHAVIORS (F-S)	SELF-EFFACING/ REBELLIOUS BEHAVIORS (H-S)
AGGRESSIVE/ COMPETITIVE BEHAVIORS (H-D)	0	0	0	+4
MANAGERIAL/ RESPONSIBLE BEHAVIORS (F-D)	0	0	+4	0
COOPERATIVE/DOCILE BEHAVIORS (F-S)	0	+4	0	0
SELF-EFFACING/ REBELLIOUS BEHAVIORS (H-S)	+4	0	0	0

B's outcomes are determined by neither his own behavior nor that of A, taken independently, but rather by particular conjunctions of the behaviors of each. The term "behavior control" refers to the contingency that, by varying his own behavior, A can motivate B to make corresponding changes in *his* behavior. In Table 5.10, the high-outcome conjunctions are depicted as complementary ones. While we would expect this to be, in fact, a frequent state of affairs, it is important to note that behavior control is not strictly limited to a complementarity (or anticomplementarity) basis. There are many other more specific sources of rewards and costs to which persons are contingently sensitive, any of which could come into play in the exercise of behavior control.

There is a fourth type of interpersonal power that represents a kind of mixture of fate and behavior control. Consider once again the fate control situation depicted in Table 5.9, where person B will presumably be highly motivated to obtain the desired H-D behavior from A. Person A is in a position here to use his fate control over B in order to control B's behavior. All that is required is that A withhold from B the desired behavior when B fails to do what A wishes, and that A perform the desired H-D response when B complies with A's wishes, whatever they might be. In this manner, A can "convert" his fate control over B to behavior control, and this type of process is therefore called *converted fate control.* The desired effect on B will occur, of course, only if A applies a systematic rule for matching his own behavior to that of B. Thibaut and Kelley point out that the extent of active monitoring required of A in order to apply effectively his matching rule will be a function of the relative emphasis given to augmentation of outcomes for B's compliance versus reduction of outcomes for his noncompliance. In the former case, B will be expected to monitor himself in order to be able to present evidence of his compliance to A, whereas in the latter case B will be interested in concealing evidence of noncompliance, which would require A to maintain active surveillance if he is to achieve his purpose.

Converted fate control may operate at any level of explicitness. In the extreme case, A may simply inform B in full detail of the matching rule he intends to apply in performing the behavior B desires from him. At the other extreme, A may apply the rule without informing B, and conceivably may even remain unaware of doing so. Where a highly implicit form of converted fate control is effective in producing behavior changes, as it demonstrably *can* be under certain circumstances (Sidowski, Wycoff, and Tabory, 1956; Kelley, Thibaut, Radloff, and Mundy, 1962), it becomes one of those apparently rare instances of truly "automatic" human instrumental learning (see Chapter 3). It might be noted in passing that the so-called "verbal conditioning" paradigm, in which the experimenter arbitrarily "rewards" the subject for performing a certain class of behavior, is essentially a type of converted fate control.

Usable Power. Our discussion to this point has assumed that the powerful person is disinterested in the effects upon his own outcomes of his exercise of power. While this assumption has been useful pedagogically, it is patently unrealistic. Power is usable in social interaction only to the extent that its use is consistent with the outcome interests of its possessor. The use of power may penalize the user directly, as when the behavior required for its exercise is for some reason not the behavior the powerful person would *prefer* to enact in that situation, or its use may be rendered undesirable in consequence of the counterpower held by the other member of the dyad. Consider once again the fate control situation depicted in Table 5.9 (page 157). If the matrix were filled in to include A's outcomes, and if these outcomes were consistently relatively low under his H-D option (for example, because the performing of such behavior would tend to cue anxiety in A), then A would be disinclined to use his fate control over B, or to convert it to behavior control. His *usable* power over B would be considerably less than what might be called his *potential* power.

Counterpower exists in a relationship to the extent that *both* members are dependent for their outcomes upon the behavior of the other, and power is equally distributed in a relationship to the extent that the range of outcome magnitudes through which each member can move the other (relative to their respective CL_{alts}) approximates equality. In general, this means that the member with the higher CL_{alt} will have relatively more power in a relationship, in that his higher baseline for the acceptability of outcomes will tend to restrict the range of outcomes through which the other person's behavior can move him. Seen from a slightly different perspective, the same considerations lead to the conclusion that the person who is most in need of the relationship (to obtain good outcomes) will have lesser power in it. We thus have the seeming paradox that the more powerful member of the dyad will often have outcomes below those of the less powerful member; it must be remembered, however, that this is partly conditional upon our scaling outcomes from the CL_{alt} of each member and indicates nothing about the "absolute" level of outcomes obtained, or about the degree of "satisfaction" (their magnitude in relation to the CL) they provide. Despite this qualification, it *is* nevertheless theoretically possible for the "absolute" outcomes of the low-power member to exceed those of the high-power member, although we would expect this circumstance to obtain relatively infrequently in real life. Given the possibility of power differentials in relationships, it may be suggested that the usability of power is partly determined by the excess of power one person has over the counterpower of the other.

For any variety of potential power one person holds over another, there are several possible varieties of counterpower the other may deploy if he has the resources to do so. The specific power relations obtaining between any two persons will depend upon the specific pattern of their interdependencies as these are reflected in their interaction-outcome matrix. The number of possible patterns of interdependency, even if reduced to the constraints of our four-fold matrix, are so legion that no attempt can be made here to catalogue them. The reader may find it interesting to work some of these out on his own by providing person A with various patterns of outcome in the illustrative tables on pages 156–158.

We should give some explicit attention to one additional point regarding interdependency. This is the matter of correspondence versus noncorrespondence of outcomes in interdependent dyads. These differing conditions are illustrated in Tables 5.11 and 5.12. Note that in each case A and B have equal power over each other's outcomes. In Table 5.11, these outcomes are perfectly correspondent, and, as depicted here, this perfect correspondence is in accord with complementarity expectations. In Table 5.12, on the other hand, the outcomes accruing to each equal-power partner are mainly noncorrespondent. B's outcomes, as in the former case, are tied to a complementarity base, whereas A's are not. For some reason, A obtains maximum rewards by always executing his H-S option, except when B enacts H-D, in which case A's preferred response becomes H-D also. Quite obviously, the degree of correspondence of outcomes obtaining in interdependent relationships is going to have a profound effect upon the character of those relationships. The A and B of our example in Table 5.11 should find it relatively easy to work out a harmonious relationship. Such

Table 5.11. Matrix Illustration of Interdependence with Correspondent Outcomes

PERSON A'S OPTIONS / PERSON B'S OPTIONS	AGGRESSIVE/ COMPETITIVE BEHAVIORS (H-D)	MANAGERIAL/ RESPONSIBLE BEHAVIORS (F-D)	COOPERATIVE/DOCILE BEHAVIORS (F-S)	SELF-EFFACING/ REBELLIOUS BEHAVIORS (H-S)
AGGRESSIVE/ COMPETITIVE BEHAVIORS (H-D)	+1 / +1	+1 / +1	+1 / +1	+4 / +4
MANAGERIAL/ RESPONSIBLE BEHAVIORS (F-D)	+1 / +1	+1 / +1	+4 / +4	+1 / +1
COOPERATIVE/DOCILE BEHAVIORS (F-S)	+1 / +1	+4 / +4	+1 / +1	+1 / +1
SELF-EFFACING/ REBELLIOUS BEHAVIORS (H-S)	+4 / +4	+1 / +1	+1 / +1	+1 / +1

is not the case with the A and B of Table 5.12, where each member, in order to maximize his own outcomes, must do so at the expense of the outcomes of his partner. The situation depicted in Table 5.11 is a cooperative one, whereas that in Table 5.12 is competive (note that we are here describing situations, not classes of behavior). The situations depicted are ones of relatively pure cooperation and competition, but the reader should be aware that various mixtures of cooperation and competition are possible in interaction matrixes, and in fact this kind of "mixed" situation is

Table 5.12. Matrix Illustration of Interdependence with Noncorrespondent Outcomes

PERSON B'S OPTIONS \ PERSON A'S OPTIONS	AGGRESSIVE/ COMPETITIVE BEHAVIORS (H-D)	MANAGERIAL/ RESPONSIBLE BEHAVIORS (F-D)	COOPERATIVE/DOCILE BEHAVIORS (F-S)	SELF-EFFACING/ REBELLIOUS BEHAVIORS (H-S)
AGGRESSIVE/ COMPETITIVE BEHAVIORS (H-D)	+4 / +1	+1 / +1	+1 / +1	+1 / +4
MANAGERIAL/ RESPONSIBLE BEHAVIORS (F-D)	+1 / +1	+1 / +1	+1 / +4	+4 / +1
COOPERATIVE/DOCILE BEHAVIORS (F-S)	+1 / +1	+1 / +4	+1 / +1	+4 / +1
SELF-EFFACING/ REBELLIOUS BEHAVIORS (H-S)	+1 / +4	+1 / +1	+1 / +1	+4 / +1

undoubtedly much more typical of interpersonal relations than is either pure case. The "handsome lad–pretty maid" matrix of Table 5.2 (page 135) provides a good example of "mixed" independence.

Excessive Use of Power. The possibility that power may be overused is a further limitation on the extent to which potential power can be exploited. A's power over B is a function of B's dependence upon the outcomes A supplies. If A, by exercising his power, rarely permits B actually to experience the favorable reward-cost positions otherwise available to him, B's dependence upon the relationship will decline, and, with it, A's power over him. For obvious reasons, this is most likely to occur under conditions in which outcomes for the two parties are relatively noncorrespondent, and especially where they are inversely correlated (as in the competitive situation of Table 5.12). Thibaut and Kelley state that, in general, the maintenance of power at a maximum level requires that it be used with discretion.

CONSEQUENCES OF POWER

As the mutual power which each member of the dyad holds over the other increases, so also does their interdependence. Highly interdependent dyads, in Thibaut and Kelley's (1959) terms, are highly *cohesive* ones. In a condition of high cohesiveness, each member wields high power over the other, but—just as importantly—each member has counterpower to blunt the other's demands upon him. This circumstance of mutual high power and mutual high capacity to resist the power of the other suggests, somewhat paradoxically, a high potentiality for conflict in the highly cohesive dyad. We would expect, however, that the promise of high mutual outcomes if accommodation can be reached would exert a constant pressure toward accommodation with continuing interdependence. Such accommodation might be in the form of developing an increased correspondence of outcomes for the pair, or it might be in the form of developing, implicitly or explicitly, contractual agreements regulating the distribution of outcomes to each of them. These two kinds of accommodation are, of course, not mutually exclusive. They are exceedingly important processes in interpersonal relations, and we shall deal with them in some detail in the next chapter. For now, we may simply note that the relevant empirical research, of which there is a substantial amount, strongly confirms this theoretical reasoning.

A condition of dyadic cohesiveness implies mutuality of power, where the power is approximately equally distributed between the two members. We may also consider the consequences of power when its distribution in the dyad is very unequal—that is, where one member is much more dependent upon the other than the other is upon him. Clearly, the high-power person in such a situation enjoys certain advantages. Inasmuch as he has more to give, or to take away, he is in a better position than is the low-power person to induce the other to behave in a manner he prefers. He should thereby be enabled more frequently to interact in those cells of the matrix that represent his best reward-cost positions. Related to this ability to reward or not reward on a grander scale is the high-power person's greater ability to predict the behavior of his partner; the likelihood that any behavior will be performed is proportional to the strength of the incentive for performing it. As Thibaut and Kelley suggest, this permits the high-power person to control the pace of the interaction and to initiate changes in its character. The high-power person will also find it less necessary than the low-power person to carefully monitor his own behavior, since he is relatively impervious to the effects of the other's attitudes and feelings toward him. The low-power person, conversely, has a greater need to avoid offending or annoying his partner, and the increased attentiveness required for this purpose probably adds measurably to the generalized costs he incurs in interaction.

THE REDUCTION OF POWER DIFFERENTIALS

It is clear from the foregoing that the position of the low-power person in a dyad is, for several reasons, a far from enviable one. We may expect, then, that the low-power person will frequently attempt to alter the unfavorable (to him) balance of power in the relationship. There are several avenues open to him whereby he might hope to do so. A brief consideration of some of the more important of these avenues follows. Our discussion generally follows the outline provided by Jones and Gerard (1967, pp. 577–89).

Compliance. The most obvious—if not the most impressive—strategy the low-power person might employ to ease his burden is that of complying with the desires of the high-power person. The fact that the high-power person prefers certain behaviors from the low-power person implies that the latter has some counterpower. While its influence is relatively weak, the exercise of this counterpower on the part of the low-power person does render his outcomes more predictable, and compliance does induce A to augment them. In itself, however, compliance does not change the relative distribution of power in the dyad; rather, it tends to perpetuate the status quo in this respect. It is likely, therefore, to be less than satisfactory as a long-run venture for the low-power person.

Raising the CL_{alt}. The low-power person can reduce the range of outcomes through which he can be moved by the high-power person (and thus reduce the power of the latter) by cultivating more attractive alternative relationships than he currently has available. If he is successful in doing so, and if he manages to communicate this success to the high-power person, he may justifiably expect the latter to eliminate from their interaction those matrix positions that are least favorable from the low-power person's standpoint, because it is these to which the alternative relationship offers strongest competition. In addition, the highest rewards the high-power person is in a position to offer will be reduced in relative potency by the emergence of an attractive alternative relationship for the low-power person.

Distorting the Value of Outcomes Received. The low-power person can neutralize the other's power over him to some extent by concealing the true hedonic effects of the other's behavior upon him, and by emitting false messages concerning these effects. Highly positive outcomes, for example, may be treated as routine, or they may even be publicly devalued by the low-power person. If the high-power person uses punishment in his control repertoire, the low-power person may minimize the hurt or pain inflicted, or he may exaggerate it in an attempt to induce the high-power person to employ more moderate tactics. Any of these maneuvers by the low-power person can have the effect of reducing the power of the high-power person by reducing the range of outcomes through which the latter believes he can move the person of lesser power.

Development of Resources. In a sustained relationship, the low-power person may devote a portion of his energies to the development of his own resources for affecting the outcomes of the other member. Any success in this venture would provide the low-power person with additional counterpower in the relationship. In many cases, such development of resources would probably take the form of acquiring increased expertise in the performance of behaviors valued by the high-power person, but other forms of resource development are clearly possible. The young lady who finds herself in a low-power position in respect to her boyfriend might be able to alter the power relation substantially by the simple expedient of placing herself on a weight-reduction program, thereby perhaps raising both her CL_{alt} and her capacity to deliver high rewards.

Propagandistic Enhancement of Behavior Products. Just as the low-power person can seek to devalue the products of the high-power person, so also can he attempt to build up the value of his own by skillful commentary, marketing, and "packaging." To the extent that the low-power person can convince the high-power person that the latter is getting from the former more than the objective facts warrant, the effective counterpower of the low-power person is increased.

Ingratiation. The low-power person may increase his attractiveness to the high-power person (and therefore his counterpower over him) at relatively low cost to himself by engaging in various kinds of ingratiation tactics. The surprisingly variegated area of ingratiation behavior has been thoroughly analyzed by Jones (1964), but we can do no more here than point out its rich possibilities as a means of neutralizing the power of another person.

POWER RELATIONS AND THE MAINTENANCE OF SECURITY

We can now attempt very briefly to point out the manner in which processes of power and dependence relate to the conception of personality developed within the framework employed in this book. We have taken the position that personality can in large measure be conceived in terms of the interpersonal behaviors a person enacts in order to maintain or enhance his security, and that his security is dependent upon the extent to which he is successful in inducing the other person with whom he interacts to produce certain classes of behavior in response. Power, as we have seen, is essentially the ability to produce variability in another person's outcomes. Theoretically, any need in the other person can be used as a basis of power over him, provided only that one has the resources to affect the extent to which the other's need is met.

Clearly, then, one important power source in interpersonal relationships is the capacity of one person to affect the security of another by producing behavior that enhances or diminishes that security. An important limitation on the use of this power source by any person, however, is imposed by his own security requirements. It will not be possible for A to exercise this kind of power over B, whose security requires, let us say, a Managerial stance from the other, if A's own security needs do not permit him to engage in Managerial behavior (or to risk the receipt of a complementary response to it). Less obviously, A's power over B will be limited if A's maintenance of security requires that he *always* be Managerial, for in this case he will be unable to *vary* B's outcomes in respect to receiving a Managerial response, except perhaps by leaving, or threatening to leave, the relationship. This would restrict A's power to a special, although commonly observed, type of contact control over B. If we consider only power as derived from ability to manipulate the other person's security in the manner suggested here, it would seem that, in general, a person is dependent in a relationship to the degree that his needs for a certain type of interpersonal response from the other are very great; and that a person is powerful in a relationship to the degree that he is able, at little cost to himself, to provide or refrain from providing (or perhaps even to provide a "punishing" anticomplementary response) the interpersonal stance desired of him by the other. Power in a relationship, therefore, is partly a function of the flexibility with which a person can adopt various stances—or, to put it another way, of the degree to which the person's security is not dependent upon the maintenance of a particular, narrowly limited interpersonal style.

Some interesting implications emerge if we consider the situation of the person whose security *is* dependent upon the consistent maintenance of a particular interpersonal style, and upon the adoption of a complementary style by others. You may recall that this was suggested earlier as one of the characteristics of many maladjusted or "mentally disordered" persons. By and large, for the reasons mentioned, such a person suffers a relative power decrement in his relations with others. Inasmuch as the forces driving him to get others into particular cells of interaction are very great, however, we might expect to see in these situations extensive deployment of compensatory counterpower strategies, including all of those suggested in the foregoing section. We will take up this matter in greater detail in Chapter 7, which extends our analysis into the area of disturbed behavior. I should like merely to note here that the extensive use of what Sullivan called "power operations" does indeed appear to characterize the behavior of many disturbed persons, and these operations are often carried out with great finesse and intensity in the relationships they form with others. Experienced psychotherapists are familiar with the discomfort occasioned by the patient who will go so far as to inflict injury upon himself (for example, by wrist-slashing, which can be an extremely "costly" outcome for the therapist) in order to force the therapist into a particular position, usually in this case a strongly Managerial-Responsible one.

One further implication of the line of thought developed here is worthy of note. Usable power is related to the level of the CL_{alt} of the person over whom it may be held, and also to the fact that certain types of interpersonal stances are evidently more popular than others and are therefore more readily available in the population if one should "need" them. In our culture, "loving" integrations with others are undoubtedly more readily obtained than are "hateful" ones, simply because there are many more persons whose security rests upon the maintenance of loving relationships than there are persons whose security rests upon the maintenance of hateful relationships. In general, then, persons whose security needs require interactions preponderantly on the Love side of the interpersonal circle will have higher CL_{alts} (and therefore will be less dependent in their relationships) than persons who require interactions within the Hate semicircle. This leads us to the interesting conclusion that interpersonal relationships based upon hostile interchange are likely to be characterized by a greater degree of interdependence than are those predominantly based upon affectionate interchange. Such a conclusion may seem quite startling at first, but I would urge you not to dismiss it too hastily on this ground alone. Unfortunately, there does not appear to be any systematic empirical evidence bearing on this issue. Casual observations, such as the one suggested earlier concerning the sometimes extraordinary longevity of seemingly sado-masochistic marriages, indicate that, under some conditions at least, the theoretical expectation seems to be confirmed. Other, similarly persistent relationships having a hateful quality include those sometimes obtaining between police officials and recidivist petty criminals, and between staff members and patients in certain old-style mental hospitals.

REFERENCES

FOA, U. G. Cross-cultural similarity and difference in interpersonal behavior. *Journal of Abnormal and Social Psychology*, 1964, **68**, 517–22.

FOA, U. G. New developments in facet design and analysis. *Psychological Review*, 1965, **72**, 262–74.

GOFFMAN, E. On face-work: An analysis of ritual elements in social interaction. *Psychiatry*, 1955, **18**, 213–31.

HELLER, K., MYERS, R. A., and KLINE, L. V. Interviewer behavior as a function of standardized client roles. *Journal of Consulting Psychology*, 1963, **27**, 117–22.

HOMANS, G. C. *Social behavior: Its elementary forms*. New York: Harcourt, Brace & World, 1961.

JONES, E. E. *Ingratiation: A social psychological analysis*. New York: Appleton-Century-Crofts, 1964.

JONES, E. E., and GERARD, H. B. *Foundations of social psychology*. New York: Wiley, 1967.

KELLEY, H. H., THIBAUT J. W., RADLOFF, R., and MUNDY, D. The development of cooperation in the "minimal social situation." *Psychological Monographs*, 1962, **76**, No. 19.

LEARY, T. *Interpersonal diagnosis of personality*. New York: Ronald, 1957.

MILLER, G. A., GALANTER, E., and PRIBRAM, K. H. *Plans and the structure of behavior*. New York: Holt, Rinehart & Winston, 1960.

SECORD, P. F., and BACKMAN, C. W. Personality theory and the problem of stability and change in individual behavior: An interpersonal approach. *Psychological Review*, 1961, **68**, 21–32.

SECORD, P. F., and BACKMAN, C. W. An interpersonal approach to personality. In B. A. MAHER (Ed.), *Progress in experimental personality research,* Vol. 2. New York: Academic Press, 1965. Pp. 91–125.

SIDOWSKI, J. B., WYCOFF, L. B., and TABORY, L. The influence of reinforcement and punishment in a minimal social situation. *Journal of Abnormal and Social Psychology,* 1956, **52,** 115–19.

SZASZ, T. S. *The myth of mental illness.* New York: Hoeber-Harper, 1961.

THIBAUT, J. W., and KELLEY, H. H. *The social psychology of groups.* New York: Wiley, 1959.

CHAPTER 6

Contractual Arrangements in Interpersonal Relations

The commodities persons exchange in their relations with each other are many and varied. Such exchanges are typically governed by "agreements," often tacit and implicit, which state more or less precisely the commodities to be traded and the "terms" of the trade. The terms are frequently concerned with the timing of the delivery of the respective commodities to each party. Generally speaking, mutual acceptance of such an agreement signifies that each party believes that the proposed exchange is at least equal in advantage to those he could effect with others capable of delivering the same desired commodity. (Note that this can be expressed in CL_{alt} terms.) The processes involved here are obvious elements in all "commercial" exchanges of money, goods, and services. It is perhaps less obvious that "noncommercial" exchanges between persons are also subject to the formation of such contractual agreements. It is these *noncommercial* interpersonal contractual arrangements with which the present chapter is largely concerned.

They are usually much less explicit than anything comparable to be found in the commercial realm, but, as we shall see, they exhibit many of the same properties.

For our purposes, and following Sullivan (see Chapter 2), we have divided up the "commodities" sought by persons into the two broad classes, *satisfaction* and *security*. One achieves satisfaction to the extent that one's internal, more or less "organic" irritations are reduced to a minimum, and one achieves security to the extent that one experiences a sense of well-being and freedom from anxiety. Our attention has chiefly been directed to the latter class of incentive, where the coin of the realm is the complementary (or self-confirming, or relationship-confirming) interpersonal response. It is clear that a person's achievement of either kind of goal will often require the cooperation of other persons. As has been suggested, these other persons will generally expect to be compensated in one way or another for their largesse—that is, they will require that the recipient of their "goods" or "services" perform various kinds of behavior which they, the providers, wish to have performed. One implication of these conceptions, as we have seen, is that interpersonal stances or positions constitute important commodities in the interpersonal marketplace, commodities that are subject to trade and exchange just as any others. Another implication is that we should expect, on occasion, to discover the existence of contractual arrangements regulating the noncommercial exchange of satisfaction- and security-producing behavior between persons.

Our approach in this chapter will be to consider first the development and function of normative rules *in general* in social behavior. We will then be in a position to discuss from that perspective the formation of *ad hoc* contractual arrangements between particular persons, where a specific norm is created within the dyad in order to maximize the outcomes to each member. From there we will go on to a class of interpersonal phenomena associated with the fraudulent proposing of interpersonal agreements. As will be shown, this is the essential characteristic of many of the interpersonal "games" described by Eric Berne in his well-known book, *Games People Play* (1964). Finally, we will undertake to examine certain types of persistent covert "arrangements" that characterize many stereotyped, maladaptive interpersonal relationships.

The Development of Norms

We turn again to Thibaut and Kelley (1959) for our fundamental conceptions of the regulation of interpersonal behavior by norm formation. A norm, according to Thibaut and Kelley, is a behavioral rule whose acceptance is shared in some degree by both members of the dyad. What are the conditions under which norms are likely to be generated? One such condition seems clear at the outset. If a norm is a mutually acceptable constraint on the behavior of at least one member of the dyad we should expect to find that it is mutually advantageous, in the sense that its operation promises to produce, on the whole, higher joint outcomes than could be obtained if it were not operative. A norm represents a special form of social control in which the person controlled typically agrees with and supports the legitimacy of the constraints imposed upon him. These constraints are, of course, often formulated in terms of very abstract, impersonal, "principles" of propriety, morality, justice, and so forth, although their explicit definition in such terms does not appear to be one of their essential features. Some norms are more crassly pragmatic, as in the case of those concerned with obeying traffic signals. It would seem that in order to understand the development of norms we need to understand the sources of the advantages they provide.

NORMS AND THE USE OF POWER

If the principal function of a norm is the regulation of social behavior, it is clearly not the exclusive means of accomplishing such regulation. The behavior of persons can also be controlled by the direct application of interpersonal power, as discussed at length in the preceding chapter. What are the advantages, if any, of normative control as opposed to control by means of interpersonal influence? Some of the reasons for the frequent substitution of the former for the latter type of control in social relations are perhaps already clear from our previous discussion concerning inherent limitations on the use of social power. Let us review these and add some additional considerations.

Advantages of Normative Control. We may look first at the situation in which the two members of the dyad have unequal power over one another—that is, where one member has greater ability to affect the outcomes received by the other. The low-power person in such a situation will quite obviously find it expedient to invoke normative regulations. At the very beginning of the relationship he may invoke norms of formality and etiquette in order to prevent, delay, or conceal his dependency upon the other. If the power differential becomes manifest despite these tactics, the low-power person will still be interested in using normative appeals to blunt the unbridled use of power by the high-power person. The capricious and whimsical use of power by the latter will reduce substantially the outcomes of the low-power person because he cannot under these circumstances carry out his behavior sequences to predictable conclusions. Moreover, should the low-power person call to the attention of the other his sad state of affairs, this may serve only to increase the salience of the power differential and thereby *increase* the functional power of the other over him. Under these conditions, we would expect the low-power person to attempt to impose a regularization of the relationship by appealing to extra-relationship, impersonal values—that is, to norms such as, "Do this because it is the right thing to do." No less obvious are the frequent advantages accruing to the high-power person by appealing to norms to control the other, rather than by directly and overtly exercising his power over him. As was pointed out in Chapter 5, power must be used sparingly in a relationship in order for it to be maintained; if the desired effects upon the other's behavior can be obtained by normative appeals, the power of the high-power person is not unnecessarily dissipated. At the same time the substitution of normative for personal influence enables the high-power person to reduce the cost of whatever surveillance he would need to maintain over the other in order to impose systematically the sanctions he controls. Thus, both the weaker and the stronger members of a dyad in which power is distributed unequally are likely to benefit from the formulation or importation of norms to regulate their relationship, obviating thereby the necessity of direct, uncoordinated, and obtrusive applications of power.

Norms may also help to smooth the way in dyads in which power is approximately equally distributed. As was mentioned in the preceding chapter, interdependent dyads having high cohesiveness (high mutual power) have a substantial potential for interpersonal conflict and for the development of unresolvable impasses. Each member may stand his ground, insist upon his own satisfaction, and block the satisfaction of the other. Insofar as each may perceive the other as the source of the difficulty by virtue of his "illegitimate" and "inconsiderate" use of power, costly argumentation may ensue which could easily have the effect of hardening positions rather than resolving the impasse. As Thibaut and Kelley note, this type of conflict can be avoided by the adoption of procedural agreements calling for each member to give up a portion of his own power in favor of the impersonal rule adopted as a norm. Very frequently the procedural rule adopted in situations of this kind states the correctness of an alternating sequence in the distribution of good outcomes to each member—that is, some form of "taking turns" is agreed upon. For example, if a married couple both enjoy occupying in their dealings with each other the same relatively extreme position on the dominance-submission continuum, neither stands much of a chance of gaining good outcomes in this respect, unless an alternating rule is adopted. In a case such as this we might imagine that an "arrangement" will be worked out whereby the wife is permitted to be submissive (or dominant) in certain of their activities together, while the husband gets *his* favored position in the course of other joint activities. The depersonalization of influence involved in norm formation permits both members of the dyad to avoid painful confrontations concerning the facts of their interdependence. In general, then, Thibaut and Kelley view norms as mechanisms for achieving functional behavioral constraints that would otherwise have to be provided through the informal and persistent use of interpersonal power. Note that there is no suggestion here that norms are deliberately developed in pursuit of this objective. On the contrary, it is likely that most norms are formed without a great deal of rational and explicit forethought or negotiation. It is suggested only that certain conditions existing in interpersonal relationships may form the basis for a type of collusion that renders these relationships more satisfactory for the participants; this collusion may be very open and formal, or it may be very covert and informal.

Conditions Favoring Norm Develpment. The circumstances leading to norm formation may now be briefly summarized. In general, the likelihood that norms will develop in a relationship increases with the degree of interdependence of its members. There is little necessity for regulation of behavior in relationships in which mutual dependence is at a minimum, inasmuch as the effect of one member's behavior upon the outcomes of the other is of a very low order. Norms are also unlikely to develop in relationships where the distribution of power is markedly uneven, as when one member has virtually no capacity to affect the outcomes of the other, but where that other is himself vested with very considerable power. We would expect the no-power person in such a relationship to attempt to invoke norms of "fair play" and so forth, but there may be little reason for the high-power person to accept the norm as applying in this case. Unilateral high power tends to make one immune to normative pressure unless the norm has been strongly "internalized."

Given a condition of interdependence, the likelihood of norm formation will also depend importantly upon the particular pattern of interdependence obtaining within the interaction-outcome matrix. If the outcomes to each member are highly correspondent (that is, highly correlated) over all of the cells of the matrix, then the behavior of one member can benefit or harm the other only to the degree that he is himself benefited or harmed by it. The exploitative use of power is largely precluded under these circumstances, a fact that renders the formation of norms unnecessary for other than minor purposes of behavioral coordination. Similarly, we would not expect to see extensive development of norms in relationships characterized by extreme, near-perfect *negative* correlation of the outcomes available to the two parties. If the inherent competitiveness of the relationship approaches this degree of severity, the members of the dyad may no longer be able to perceive *any* communality of interest in their dealings with each other, thereby providing little basis upon which to formulate agreements for regulating their interaction. Presumably, any such relationship would dissolve fairly rapidly in favor of each member's CL_{alt}. It would appear, then, that norms are most likely to be formed under conditions in which the outcomes in an interdependent dyad are imperfectly correlated over the various cells of the interaction-outcome matrix. Such a matrix will contain some cells in which the outcomes to the two parties are relatively correspondent, and some in which they are relatively discrepant. A relationship of this type contains structural elements of both "cooperation" and "competition," and is therefore sometimes called a *mixed-motive* relationship (Schelling, 1960). As was suggested in Chapter 5, most relationships between persons are of the mixed-motive variety.

Thibaut (1968) has recently reiterated and expanded upon a number of these points in the context of reporting a series of experiments on bargaining and the formation of contractual agreements in mixed-motive economic relationships. The experimental dyads created in these studies were potentially exploitative, interdependent ones in which each member was provided with a moderately attractive "alternative" relationship. The member having lesser "power" could therefore turn to this alternative in the face of threatened exploitation. Thus, each member of the dyad was equipped with an effective threat over the other, one based upon possible exploitation and the other upon possible withdrawal of loyalty. The likelihood of exploitation occurring in the relationship was experimentally manipulated, as was the likelihood of choosing the alternative relationship. It was predicted that the pressure to form contractual agreements regulating the distribution of outcomes and commitment to the relationship would be greatest under conditions of high likelihood of exploitation *and* high likelihood that the "disloyal" option would be exercised. The reasoning here was that the presence of strong mutual threats would motivate both parties to attempt to avoid victimization through appeals to formal regulatory rules, and that this shared motivation would produce optimal conditions for the development of contractual agreements concerning "fairness" and "loyalty," thus permitting maximum joint outcomes to be realized. In general, the results of the four experiments reviewed strongly support the theoretical prediction.

In addition to these studies emerging more or less directly out of the Thibaut and Kelley framework, there is a large and rapidly growing literature concerned in more general ways with the behavior of subjects in experimentally created mixed-motive relationships. The impetus for many of these studies has been provided by the importation into psychology of decision and (mathematical) "game" theory (Luce and Raiffa, 1957), and by a widening interest among psychologists in problems of international relations, which are commonly of mixed-motive nature. The subjects in these experiments typically "play" for imaginary or small monetary incentives. For the most part, these studies are only peripherally related to our major concerns in this chapter, and they are of sufficient quantity and diversity that no adequate review of them can be attempted here. A few of them, however, do provide highly relevant information on the consequences of an *absence* of adequate norm formation in relationships whose structure would make such norm formation an adaptive strategy. In general, the results of these studies, to the extent that they can be generalized beyond the experimental situation, are very sobering. Findings reported by Deutsch and Krauss (1960); Deutsch (1960); Scodel et al. (1959); Minas et al. (1960); Solomon (1960); Bixenstine and Wilson (1963); Komorita (1965); Lave (1965); and Shure, Meeker, and Hansford (1965) all indicate that persons often show pronounced tendencies to exploit a "cooperative" other, even where that is in the long run relatively costly to themselves. Permitting subjects to "communicate" with each other, either explicitly or tacitly (for example, through engaging in a discernible strategy that provides the other person with information as to intent), and thus opening the possibility of their forming "agreements," sometimes, but not always, reduces the apparently widespread tendency to be exploitative when the opportunity presents itself. The rather depressing conclusion to which these studies point should be tempered with the observation that these findings all derive from highly contrived laboratory settings, and that they may not be strongly representative of behavior under real life circumstances. Some recent evidence provided by Gallo (1966) suggests that, under certain conditions at least, such studies do produce misleading results. By increasing the real-world saliency of the payoff advantages of "cooperation," Gallo was able to reduce the self-defeating competitiveness of his subjects, as indicated by their pronounced willingness to form and adhere to a norm of cooperation.

THE HANDSOME LAD AND THE PRETTY MAID REVISITED

The initial encounter of the "handsome lad" and the "pretty maid," described in the preceding chapter and depicted in Table 5.2 (page 135), has the characteristics of a mixed-motive, interdependent relationship in which power is approximately equally distributed. Mutual threat exists in the capacity of each to exploit certain "opening gestures" either may make, and in the capacity of each to withdraw in favor of their respective CL_{alts}. It is, in short, a situation that should be highly conducive to norm formation. Insofar as the encounter of the lad and the maid is fairly typical of initial encounters of young men and women generally, we should expect to find that a system of normative control has evolved for the regulation of these budding relationships. Such is clearly the case. The norm that the boy should be the "aggressor," seen in this light, may be a lingering holdover from the age of chivalry—*he* takes the initial chances. Norms of formality, often invoked in such situations, have obvious adaptive aspects in permitting delayed commitment as the members of the dyad survey the probable consequences of offering more intimate exchanges. Even the "line" each employs may be highly stereotyped and ritualized, representing a type of formal normative regulation of the content of communication. In adhering to this norm (sometimes described as being "cool") each is spared the "dangers" of too early personal exposure and commitment, while retaining the option of capitalizing upon whatever opportunities may present themselves. Waller (1937) many years ago called attention to the elaborate norm structure that governs the progressive commitments involved as college couples move from casual dating through courtship to marriage. This is precisely what our analysis would lead us to expect; at every step along the way the possibilities of exploitation and "disloyalty" are clearly present and, if actualized, would be increasingly costly to the victim. The governing norms provide low-cost insurance to both parties.

ROLES

The concept of *role,* basic to many sociological analyses of behavior, has had an interesting and varied definitional history. The purposes of conceptual consistency and of convenience will be served, however, if we neglect these vicissitudes and subsume the concept within the general framework of our discussion of norms. Thibaut and Kelley provide a definition of role which accomplishes exactly that. A role, according to these authors, is "the class of one or more norms that applies to a person's behavior with regard to some specific external problem or in relation to a special class of other persons" (1959, p. 143). A role is therefore a special set of behavioral rules that apply to persons occupying a given formal *position* or *status* in a social system. Every person has several roles—at least one for every "system" (such as occupational, marital, familial, and peer group) in which he participates—a circumstance sometimes giving rise to role strain and conflict *within* the person. Smooth social interaction also requires that there be role reciprocity *between* persons as they interact. One cannot effectively enact the behaviors of the *teacher's* role, for example, unless the other person simultaneously enacts the behaviors normatively associated with the role of *student.* Quite obviously, we can apply here the same thinking as was developed in Chapter 5 in connection with the reward and cost features of high and low complementarity of interactional styles. More will be said about this matter in the following sections.

Relations Between Role and Personality. We can now begin to relate the foregoing conceptual orientation more directly to the phenomena of individual personality. Consider first the behaviors normatively associated with various social roles. Insofar as these behaviors are coherently organized—and role behaviors tend to be coherently organized—they are readily coded in terms of the octant categories of the interpersonal circle. Thus, the role of *teacher* involves normative sanctioning of predominantly Managerial behavior, while that of *student* involves normative sanctioning of predominantly Docile behavior. Similarly, the roles of *policeman* or *disciplinarian* relate to behaviors falling mainly in the Aggressive octant, while those of *"hippie"* and *purchasing agent* are mainly concerned with the Rebellious octant. Acknowledged attainment of a particular social status provides a person with a normatively sanctioned license, or obligation, to enact the behaviors considered appropriate to that status. When a person is acting *in role,* then, his role behavior is supported by normative rules, and corresponding normative rules usually specify also the appropriate reciprocal or counter-role behavior. This "appropriate" counter-role behavior, perhaps not surprisingly, is almost always very closely related to what we have been calling *complementary* behavior.

What we have here, then, is a situation in which relations between persons, as in the case of norms generally, are regulated by an impersonal power source, obviating recourse to the application of informal personal influence. The functional significance of roles in lubricating interpersonal processes essential to the maintenance of a culture has been well documented by sociological writers and is sufficiently obvious that we need not concern ourselves with it here. Of more direct pertinence to our task is the interesting fact that many roles specify interpersonal stances or positions *vis-à-vis* others which we would expect to be highly attractive to certain persons on the basis of their security-enhancing properties. If this is true, the achievement of a particular status in a social system, and the coordinate "right" to adopt the interpersonal stance appropriate to it, could be an extremely low-cost way of obtaining persistent security income in relationship to others who participate in that system. Impersonal normative power may be enlisted in this manner in the support of personal security requirements. It does not seem excessively conjectural, therefore, to suggest that persons often "drift." into roles that suit them from the standpoint of their preferred stance in relation to other persons. Sometimes, indeed, a role is carried out with such zest that it is impossible to believe that it is "just a job" for the person who enacts it. I have occasionally had encounters with policemen over minor traffic violations in which I have felt that way.

On the other hand, it seems necessary to caution that this idea could readily be overgeneralized. The antecedents of role acquisition are many and varied, and often have little or nothing to do with personal "needs." There are ample instances in everyday life in which a person is forced, by virtue of his formal status, to enact interpersonal behaviors and adopt interpersonal stances that are fairly obviously ill fitted to him. A role may be personally costly, as well as personally rewarding. We should expect that, over time, the role behavior of the occupant of a social position will tend to conform to the normative prescription, because the behavior of other persons toward him, when he is *in role*, will exert constant complementarity pressures in this direction. The new Ph.D. beginning his college teaching career observes, often to his amazement, that his students treat him like a professor; sooner or later, he begins to act like one. It may be too extreme to suggest that an acquired role may create the conditions for personality *change*, but something very much like this seems to happen occasionally.

Implicit Contracts in Dyadic Interaction

In the discussion to this point I have been concerned principally with normative processes *in general* in order to expose their functional characteristics and the conditions under which they tend to become operative. General, culture-wide norms arise as economical, ready-made solutions to widespread and recurrent problems of interpersonal articulation. Formal contracts of the type developed in mixed-motive commercial relationships represent an attempt to achieve—"artificially" as it were—a similar kind of solution to a more specialized variety of relationship problem. The form, content, and "enforcement" machinery of such contracts are, of course, subject to the regulation of more general cultural norms, which in this case have the status of metanorms (norms about norms). At a still more particularistic level, many informal norms develop within dyads as a means of coordinating actions and regulating the distribution of outcomes to the two parties. This is especially true where the relationship has a strongly mixed-motive character, as is often the case, and where there is therefore considerable advantage to both parties in coming to an "agreement" about how their relationship is to be conducted. Sometimes these agreements are explicitly negotiated, as when newlyweds work out by discussion the division of labor which is to apply in the accomplishment of various household tasks. Undoubtedly, however, many such agreements are arrived at in a very implicit, unverbalized way; the members of the dyad never quite state the "rules" under which they are operating, but the rules are there nevertheless, and they are often followed in an utterly reliable fashion by both participants. We would expect this type of implicit contract formation to be especially characteristic for transactions that are regarded as "sensitive," "delicate," or potentially embarrassing, as, for example, when a couple attempt to articulate their separate preferences for forms of sexual engagement. Implicit negotiation also seems to be the principal vehicle whereby members of a dyad arrive at informal complementary stances *vis-à-vis* each other in regard to the "positions" they will occupy within the space defined by the interpersonal circle. In relationships in which formal role assignments are absent or unclear, this becomes a negotiable issue of considerable importance in determining the outcome experience each member of the dyad will have in the course of their interaction. This section will focus particularly upon implicit contract formation in regard to the latter type of relationship issue.

THE PROBLEM OF STYLISTIC ARTICULATION

If persons were so constructed that they had no position preferences in their relations with others—that is, if there were no significant variations in hedonic outcomes associated with the adoption of one or another stance *vis-à-vis* others—then there would be no great problem in regulating interaction. Under these conditions, the only source of position-related rewards and costs would presumably be those associated with complementarity and anticomplementarity, as depicted in Table 5.7 (page 146). We assume that the outcomes from this source are distributed symmetrically to both members of the dyad—that is, that there is perfect outcome correspondence—and that the structure of the relationship is therefore completely "cooperative" in this respect. In line with our earlier reasoning, we would not expect norm formation to be of great importance under these conditions, except for the purpose of coordinating each person's actions with those of the other, as would be necessary in "switching" from one to another mutually desirable cell of interaction. As we have seen, however, persons in general do *not* exhibit this degree of flexibility. They do tend to have preferences of greater or lesser range in the positions they occupy in their interpersonal relations, and this factor, among others, introduces into any interaction reward and cost elements beyond those depicted in Table 5.7. These additional reward and cost features, moreover, will not (except by "accident") be correlated for the two members of the dyad over the various cells of their matrix, at least not in the initial phases of their relationship. They will therefore operate to distort the simple outcome symmetry of Table 5.7, producing varying degrees of noncorrespondence of outcomes and varying levels of structural "competition" as well as "cooperation."

Thus, while the proffering of Managerial behavior may be a powerful inducement for the other person to enact Docile behavior, it is not always a successful one. The target person may have other strong needs that exceed the strength of his need to comply with complementarity pressures. Unless the position preferences of the two members of a dyad happen to be exceptionally well matched, then, at least some of the cells of their interaction matrix will often involve noncorrespondent outcomes. If the matrix also contains cells in which outcomes *are* correspondent, as would usually be the case even if only by virtue of complementarity considerations, we have essentially the makings of a mixed-motive relationship in respect to the stances the members take *vis-à-vis* each other. Given the disadvantages of the direct and mutual use of interpersonal power to achieve desired positions, alluded to above, we would expect on occasion to see the emergence of implicit ad hoc norms within dyads in order to regulate the stances taken and the resulting distribution of outcomes to the two parties.

The emergence of such norms should have the general effect, over time, of increasing the correspondence of outcomes to the two members (Thibaut and Kelley, 1959, pp. 135–38).

THE AD HOC INTERPERSONAL CONTRACT

In undertaking to discuss the emergence of informal, ad hoc "arrangements" within dyads for the purpose of regulating interpersonal stances, we are necessarily treading on rather poorly charted ground. We have been brought to this point by the logical implications of our analysis of personality and interpersonal relations, and also, of course, by my conviction that the concept of an implicit ad hoc contract has a high degree of validity and potential power in accounting for various phenomena that can be observed in the interactions of persons. Consider, for example, three criteria listed by Thibaut and Kelley (p. 128) as warranting the inference that a norm exists within a dyad:

> (1) There would be regularity in behavior . . . [of the members of the dyad as they interacted].
> (2) In the event of disruption of this regularity, the "injured" person would attempt to restore it by appealing, at least initially, to the rule and he would exercise his personal power as an enforcer of the rule.
> (3) The person disrupting the regularity would be likely to feel some obligation to adhere to the agreement and might even exhibit some conflict or guilt about deviating from it, as if he were punishing himself for his nonconformity.

Needless to say, it seems to me that regularities *do* exist in the conjoint stances taken by members of a dyadic relationship toward each other, and that their disruption by one or the other member *does* frequently produce the effects described. However, the complexity and subtlety of this type of interactional "program (Plan) integration," to which Scheflen (1968), among others, has recently called attention, has evidently been sufficiently discouraging to researchers that we have available little directly pertinent and rigorously established empirical knowledge upon which to base a discussion of these matters. We will nevertheless proceed as best we can, recognizing the paucity of reliable observations we have.

We should expect the implicit ad hoc interpersonal contract to be basically similar to other forms of contractual agreement. That is, it should "state" the commodities to be exchanged, in this case the performance of certain behaviors within the relationship, and the terms and timing of their delivery. Various "contingency clauses" might be introduced into this basic pattern, but there will presumably be an upper limit on the complexity such contracts can have because of the deficiencies of the analogical language by means of which they are negotiated.

At the simplest level, we have the implied offer of a "contract" which is often contained in the initial, tentative behaviors enacted by the members of a newly formed dyad. Consider once again the meeting of the "handsome lad" and the "pretty maid" described in Chapter 5 (page 133). As has been noted, there is a reasonable chance in this situation that each of the parties will enact their "safe" options, probably thereby stopping the interaction practically at the point of its beginning. Let us suppose, however, that the lad takes the bull by the horns and initiates his "line." Seen from the perspective of the present discussion, this is a more complex interpersonal act than it might superficially appear to be. In enacting his line, the lad is, in effect, proposing a certain type of relationship with the maid. He is saying something like, "I am willing to be Responsible/Cooperative if you will be Cooperative/-Docile." The maid, of course, has the option of accepting or declining the lad's offer, and, as we have seen, the lad will have suffered a costly blow for his impetuosity should she choose the latter course. If, however, the maid meets his "offer" with a smile, she is, in effect, agreeing to his proposed definition of what is transpiring between them. She is saying something like, "I accept your offer. I agree to be Cooperative/Docile if you will continue to be Responsible/Cooperative." In short, the two will have formed a more or less binding agreement as to how their relationship is to proceed for at least some period of time into the immediate future. I am suggesting here that this "agreement" has a normative force not unlike that characterizing more formal contracts, and that the respective participants each feel at least some "moral" obligation to fulfill its terms. Violation of the terms of the contract by either party would be expected to have the predicted effects indicated above, unless there had been prior negotiation and agreement on a new contract stating a changed base of relationship. By taking advantage of the structure provided by such contracts, the problematical, mixed-motive aspects of the relationship can be circumvented, and the lad and the maid can maximize joint outcomes while minimizing the risk of exploitation and painful disconfirmations of perceived relative positions.

As the above example suggests, relationships may, and very probably often do, proceed from contract to contract, the terms being successively revised as additional facets or possibilities of the relationship become exposed in the course of interaction. It would seem, however, that many relationships are governed by a kind of overriding "master contract" which may persist in unaltered form for very long periods, despite minor revisions in the manner whereby the provisions of the master contract are fulfilled. Thus, in many long-term relationships such as marriage, there is usually some stability in the basic position that each member occupies *vis-à-vis* the other, even though there may be occasional readjustments of stances taken in various specific joint activities. These stable, basic positions are usually readily discernible even to the casual external observer. Of course, it sometimes happens that one or the other participant in such a stable arrangement discovers that the terms are not, after all, to his liking, in which case he may find it necessary to propose a new master contract, often by engaging in fairly flagrant violations of the present one. Divorce proceedings are made of such stuff, but sometimes such relationship crises result in altered master contracts that are more or less satisfactory to both parties as a basis for continuance, rather than negotiated liquidation, of joint ties.

An interesting example of a complex network of sustained, implicit, dyadic contracts which function in the life of a single person is provided in Elia Kazan's (1967) contemporary novel, *The Arrangement*. The hero of this work, Eddie Anderson, finds himself so deeply enmeshed in mutually contradictory, obligatory "agreements"—with his wife, his mistress, his parents, his employer, and so on—that he experiences a crisis of Selfhood. The author details in poignant terms the havoc created as Eddie attempts to break out of his complicated web of "arrangements" and to reassert some measure of personal control of his life. His co-contractors vigorously resist his attempts to change the rules, and his efforts to signal his own abandonment of them take on an increasingly urgent and bizarre character, so much so that he comes to be regarded as suffering from mental disorder. Kazan here pays metaphorical tribute to the element of moral compulsion often associated with these implicit agreements—no man in his right mind would dare flagrantly to violate them—and also to the apparent reluctance or inability of persons to communicate explicitly and digitally about the terms of many of their implicit, analogically negotiated contracts. We saw in the case of Mr. and Mrs. X (presented in Chapter 1 and analyzed further in Chapter 5) the breakdown of an initial "arrangement" followed by a complicated series of negotiations to establish a new contract, with all of these transactions being conducted in a highly analogical language mode. The binding force of many such interpersonal contracts is all the more astonishing in view of the inadequacies of the communication media utilized in negotiating them. But it may be this binding force, in part at least, that accounts for the reluctance of persons to utilize direct and straightforward means to renegotiate contracts they no longer find satisfactory.

Some implicit interpersonal contracts appear to be based on the "installment" or "lay-away" plan. Berne (1966) outlines the essential features of such arrangements in his characteristically amusing and intuitively compelling way in his discussion of "transactional trading stamps." He describes the response of a twelve-year-old-boy upon learning of this concept from his mother, a group therapy patient. The boy fashioned a roll of perforated stamps, a dispenser for them, and a small booklet whose pages were divided into squares. The legend at the top of the page read: "This page when full of stamps entitles you to one free suffer." The boy understood that it is sometimes possible to enjoy a favored position, even when the other person is reluctant, by "saving up" for it. The other person is thus compelled to acknowledge one's "right" to that position after having been induced to dispense a certain number of "stamps" redeemable in those terms.

Thus, "suffer" stamps are dispensed by A to B on each occasion in which A, usually with B's subtle encouragement, fails B in some way. When B has collected a sufficient number of these stamps he may cash them in for a free suffer—in our terms a "justifiable" indulgence in the self-sacrificial Hypernormal position. Free "mads" (Aggressive position), "guilts" (Self-effacing position), "loves" (Cooperative position), and so on may be negotiated in a similar manner. As Berne points out, saving stamps beyond the point where they may be cashed in for a small "prize" will usually entitle one to a big prize in the same category. Thus, the really determined stamp collector may be able to arrange for himself a veritable orgy of self- and relationship confirmation.

Fraudulent Interpersonal Contracts

We turn now to a species of human interaction in which the metanorms governing interpersonal contracts are more or less deliberately violated and exploited for the benefit of one member of the dyad. This can occur in a multitude of ways, but there appears to be an elementary basic structure in many of the variants. That structure can be described as follows: (1) A implicitly offers to B a relationship of a certain type, often one in which B may be expected to have a high degree of interest because of its seemingly favorable possibilities for satisfaction and security income. (2) B indicates acceptance of the implicit contract and initiates behaviors appropriate to its terms. (3) A then alters his own stance in the course of B's performance, destroying the complementarity that had existed and rendering B's performance obtrusively inappropriate under the circumstances. (4) A then assumes a position which is "justified" in the light of B's now exposed and vulnerable stance, forcing B into a new position of complementarity, and achieving the type of relationship that A had presumably *really* been seeking in the first place. The deviousness of the route utilized by A in achieving his objective apparently has the function of "setting up" B in such a way that A's coup produces a more dramatic and hedonically pleasing (to A) definition of relative positions than could be accomplished in a more straightforward manner.

SIMPLE TRANSACTIONAL REVERSALS

Eric Berne (1961) is the chief exponent of a theoretical framework of interpersonal relations called *transactional analysis*. This framework has much in common with the one developed here, although it is perhaps less systematically integrated and less directly tied to reliably established empirical knowledge. Its data base derives chiefly from anecdotal, clinical observations, albeit often very sensitive and penetrating ones, and its basic concepts (such as Child, Adult, and Parent "ego states") too frequently have a merely metaphorical relationship to observable behavioral events. It is not within the scope of our aims, however, to enter into a detailed discussion of transactional analysis here, much less to subject it to serious critical review. I wish rather to focus upon one aspect of transactional analysis, that of transactional "games," as treated at length in Berne's (1964) *Games People Play*. If we take a close look at many of the transactions described therein, the use of the term *game* to refer to them seems somewhat misleading. A "game," in the ordinary sense of the word, implies the active participation of at least two "sides," each of whose members follow a mutually agreeable and coordinated set of rules. Many of the "games" described by Berne, on the other hand, constitute in reality the victimization of one person by another through the use of fraudulent contract proposals. In other words, they operate according to the basic pattern indicated above, where the "victim" is in no sense an active and willing participant in his own victimization; he is merely playing according to another—and more normatively legitimate—set of rules, those originally proposed by his somewhat unscrupulous partner. We shall refer to these types of transactions as *simple reversals* to denote their one-handed aspect and to distinguish them from more complicated covert relationships of coordinated rule-following. Let us consider some examples of such simple reversals.

Why Don't You—Yes But (YDYB). YDYB is said to be the prototypic "game" in transactional analysis, and it is therefore fitting that we begin with this original model. Where appropriate, we will substitute our own terminology. The reversal is initiated when A (the perpetrator) adopts a Docile stance toward B (the victim) by presenting some life problem in such a manner that B is induced to offer advice—i.e., to adopt a Managerial counter-stance. A responds to this advice by saying, "Yes, but . . . ," and adding to that some information that renders B's advice irrelevant, erroneous, or gratuitous. If A's deflationary comment has been skillfully contrived and delivered, however, B will come back with an alternative solution, still believing that he has sincerely been offered the Managerial position. A shoots him down again. This may go on for several "rounds," until B finally realizes that he has been defeated, as manifested perhaps by an exasperated silence or a weak acknowledgment that A "sure has a tough problem there." A has demonstrated B's inadequacy, and B confirms it by assuming a Self-effacing position complementary to the Competitive position to which A has already switched. Note that A's Competitive position is anticomplementary to B's original Managerial one. In the face of his "demonstrated" lack of talent for the Managerial role, B is literally forced out of it. Needless to say, this reversal can be, and often is, deployed in a group setting, where there are several potential victims, and where an even sweeter Competitive victory can be fashioned by the skillful reverser.

Rapo. Rapo is another Competitive reversal, the "harder" forms of which, as Berne (1964) points out, sometimes have very serious and dire consequences in the lives of the participants. We will confine our attention to the milder forms. The initial matrix characterizing the start of a Rapo reversal is not unlike that used in our illustration of the "handsome lad" and the "pretty maid" (Table 5.2, page 135). The perpetrator of the Rapo reversal is traditionally, but not always, the female, and a rich but vulgar vocabulary has evolved to denote the type of woman who is a Rapo enthusiast. The traditional reversal begins when the woman emits strong Cooperative messages as to her possible availability for dalliance. We assume, however, that she typically will have scanned her proposed victim carefully beforehand, given the matrix possibilities of a costly rejection, or even of the victim's employing the male version of the same tactic. If all seems well, then, the woman deploys her siren song, and the man is soon producing delighted gestures to the effect that he gets the message and agrees to the contract. In colloquial terms, he "comes on strong," and becomes increasingly and eagerly committed to a Responsible position, perhaps suggesting a stroll in the garden or a "private" drink at his apartment. And then it happens. The woman displays alarm and shock that the man should have so badly misunderstood what kind of woman she was, perhaps hinting that only a fiend of some kind would mistake her friendship in that way. Her Competitive gratification is achieved through contemptuous rejection, while the man duly assumes the Self-effacing posture to which he has been led.

Now I've Got You, You Son of a Bitch (NIGYSOB). The picturesque title of this reversal reveals immediately that it is one involving an Aggressive payoff. The perpetrator of NIGYSOB initiates the reversal by placing himself in circumstances (often by adopting a strongly Self-effacing position) that invite Competitive exploitation from his victim. The victim, if he is unwise or unsophisticated in these matters, sooner or later accepts the proffered agreement and initiates a program of exploitation. At some point, however, he becomes careless, and/or the perpetrator suddenly increases his vigilance, and the exploitation is thereby publicly revealed in all of its nakedness. The perpetrator, with a suitable show of rage and indignation, assumes his justly deserved, Aggressive NIGYSOB position. The victim, if the reversal has been smoothly carried off, retires to the only positions left for him—withdrawn, bitter Rebelliousness, or guilty Self-effacement. It should be noted that sometimes the victim in this reversal is not quite as "innocent" or passive as this account suggests; in some instances he may be playing according to a coordinate set of rules, which would make the transaction a more complicated, two-handed one—in effect, a true sado-masochistic game. Any reversal can be converted to a game if the victim begins to "play."

These three examples should be sufficient to illustrate the manner in which fraudulently offered contracts are utilized for security enhancement in what we are here calling simple, one-handed reversals. A number of the other "games" described by Berne essentially fit the same pattern, including "Try and Collect,"

"Frigid Woman," "Schlemiel," and certain forms of "See What You Made Me Do." There are, however, at least two other classes of interpersonal phenomena Berne includes under the general rubric of "games." One of these is the more complex variety of coordinated two- (or more) handed arrangements persons sometimes work out for the purpose of secret or covert mutual gratification. We will deal with such true games presently. The remaining "miscellaneous" group of processes, as in the case of simple reversals, hardly seem to deserve to be called "games," except perhaps in the pejorative sense that they typically involve fraudulent or quasi-fraudulent elements. This is a rather mixed assortment of "illegitimate" but recognizable tactics sometimes employed by persons in the pursuit of satisfaction or of maintaining favored interpersonal positions. Two identifiable subclasses are briefly described below.

OTHER FRAUDULENT OPERATIONS

It is sometimes possible for persons to improve the level of their outcomes in interpersonal relations beyond what they could otherwise expect by essentially adopting a false *role*. In so doing they utilize the "power" of the normative sanctions associated with that role in order to induce others to permit them to engage in behavior or to occupy certain positions they find rewarding but otherwise unattainable. This is, then, a type of impersonation or imposturing. Szasz (1961), for example, argues strongly that "hysteria" (the type of "disorder," you will recall, that Mr. X had) represents the fraudulent adoption of a "sick" role for the purpose of coercing others to do one's bidding, most generally to be Responsible toward one. For Szasz, the hysteric is an imposter, although not necessarily a wholly conscious and deliberate one.

The "game" of *Wooden Leg* and its variants ("Indigent," "Veteran," "Stupid," and "Perversion"), as described by Berne (1964, 1966), seem to be based essentially on this type of fraudulent role-adoption process. The basic tactic involved is the strongly (though often analogically) communicated message, "What do you expect of a(n) . . . [man with a wooden leg] [stupid person] [person with such strong sex drives] [man who is insane] [man with a bad back] [ex-serviceman]?" Our society rightly relaxes its requirements for productivity and makes various other provisions for persons who become temporarily or permanently incapable of conventional performance or conduct by virtue of realistic misfortune. "Wooden Leg" tactics represent a subversion and exploitation of that important societal function by persons who claim special, normatively sanctioned considerations on the basis of counterfeit credentials. As is perhaps obvious, it is often difficult to distinguish counterfeit from real in this area, which is one of the reasons that the discrimination is usually considered to be the task of highly trained professionals. This is as it should be, but it is no guarantee that accurate discriminations will be made.

Finally, we should note a subclass of fraudulent operations that bears certain similarities to the "Wooden Leg" group. These are also operations in which deceitful self-presentations are offered for the purpose of gaining ulterior or covert outcomes, but they do not involve formally recognized social roles. The "games" of "Look How Hard I've Tried," "Sweetheart," "How Do You Get Out of Here," "I'm Only Trying to Help You," and certain forms of "Peasant" (Berne, 1964), for example, appear to be basically of this type. Various types of simple pretense are of course very common in life, and if their principal consequence is that of propping up a shaky security it is unlikely that they produce great harm. The more vicious forms of exploitative deceit, on the other hand, constitute a cynical and fraudulent manipulation of power relations, and they can be very harmful indeed.

Disordered Interpersonal Contracts

We have seen from the foregoing that certain types of complications and distortions of interpersonal relationships can be traced to the violation and exploitation of normative processes by particular persons acting in an independently self-interested way. By and large, adherence by persons to the terms of their interpersonal contracts is associated with the development of wholesome and mature interpersonal relations. It permits a maximization of joint outcomes within a context of cooperation and trust, it reduces the amount of energy expenditure required for the maintenance of surveillance and vigilance, and it encourages continuing mutual exploration of additional, as yet unrealized outcome possibilities in the relationship. There are, however, certain notable exceptions to this general rule. It sometimes happens that an implicit interpersonal contract whose provisions are scrupulously carried out by the members of a dyad nevertheless results in a more or less severely distorted—or even destructive—relationship. This section will focus upon such miscarriages of the contractual function.

As we have seen, contracts come into being as an efficient, low-cost means of insuring that the members of an interdependent dyad will interact in those cells of their matrix that provide, at a minimum, acceptable outcome levels to each of them. "Disordered" contracts serve the same purpose, but they have additional distinctive features that relate to the somewhat special needs of the persons who form them. Observations reported in the relevant literature indicate that there are at least two discriminable varieties of such contracts. These may be briefly described in general terms before we proceed to a consideration of specific examples.

The less complex of these two types of more sinister interpersonal contracts involves a process of *coordinated avoidance*. The coordinated avoidance contract tends to develop in relationships in which the interaction matrix contains cells having relatively high reward *and* cost factors for both members. In other words, these are cells characterized by a high degree of mutual *intrapersonal* conflict and ambivalence. The high joint rewards available in the cell(s) in question are a persistent source of "temptation," while the associated high cost factors are an equally persistent and salient source of frustration. The general effect of this tension-producing circumstance is to increase the cost to each member for remaining in the relationship. Sometimes, of course, the problem is resolved when this general cost factor reduces the outcomes of either member to a level below his CL_{alt}, whereupon the relationship terminates. Where this type of resolution is unavailable—for example, where the *average* outcomes to each member remain high in spite of their "problem," or where neither has a competitive CL_{alt}—it will be in their interests to find a means of neutralizing the effects of the conflictful portions of their matrix.

This can be done by "agreeing" to engage in interactions that reduce the reward values (or increase the cost values) of the troublesome cells to the point that they no longer constitute a serious source of temptation, thus forming a coordinated avoidance contract. The existence of such a contract produces certain unfortunate effects within a relationship. Most notably, it deprives the participants of any further opportunity to explore the troublesome area of their matrix, removing thereby the possibility of their finding a means to enjoy rewards in that area without incurring high costs. In addition, the avoidance behaviors the contract calls for, because of the extraneous function they serve, introduce a note of ritual into the interaction. As a consequence, these behaviors tend to become highly stereotyped and lacking in spontaneous zest, although they are often accompanied by strong emotional arousal. Finally, these contracted interactions are often of such a nature that their enactment in itself entails significant direct cost to the actors. These points may become clearer in the examples to be described below.

The second discernible class of disordered interpersonal contracts involves a more intricate and variegated interpersonal domain. Within this domain are included probably some of the most tragic and bizarre of the conceivable perversions of the human condition. The common element justifying their inclusion in a single class is the adoption of a trading agreement requiring of at least one member of the dyad the performance of behaviors that are self-injurious, deviant, or otherwise maladaptive. In return for behaving in this manner, the person is "rewarded" with behavior from the other that meets his needs—needs that are often extremely powerful and compelling. In effect, then, the other person in this situation is employing a potent variety of converted fate control within the framework of an ad hoc interpersonal contractual arrangement. Moreover, this condition sometimes exists bilaterally, in which case the contract may call for *both* parties to engage in self-defeating or eccentric behaviors. In describing the required behavior in this manner there is no intention to imply that the person engaging in it necessarily does so reluctantly or under protest; on the contrary, he is often a willing, if not an enthusiastic, participant. It seems reasonable to assume, however, that he is more oriented toward his payoff than toward his required performance. Bilaterally disordered contracts tend to be associated with conditions of high dyadic cohesiveness, because the payoff behaviors they call for are not widely available in the population generally. This circumstance, as has been noted earlier, would tend to maintain the CL_{alt} of both members of the dyad at a relatively low level, and to produce a condition of high mutual power and interdependence. These relationships are therefore sometimes extremely enduring and stable ones, despite their more or less bizarre character. The kinds of contracts described here may be termed contracts of *negotiated maladjustment*.

Both of these two types of disordered interpersonal contracts manifest themselves in actual relationships in various common forms. Some of these are considered below. Because of their greater importance, we shall give relatively more attention to contracts involving negotiated maladjustment. We begin, however, with a more concrete consideration of the coordinated avoidance type of contract.

ILLUSTRATIVE VARIETIES OF COORDINATED AVOIDANCE

It seems appropriate to turn initially to Berne (1964) once again for illustrative material. Berne includes processes of coordinated avoidance *and* negotiated maladjustment under his general rubric, "games." It is in this case an apt descriptive term, provided that it is stripped of any "fun" connotations. These processes, in contrast to the fraudulent tactics considered earlier, do involve coordinated interpersonal rule-following, the rules being the terms of the interpersonal contract according to which the members of the dyad conduct their interaction. It should perhaps be noted parenthetically that nearly all of the "games" which Berne discusses are everyday familiarities in the professional work of psychotherapists, although he of course deserves credit for systematically describing and cataloguing them.

At least two of Berne's (1964) games, "Uproar" and "Corner," represent a close category match with our coordinated avoidance paradigm. I suspect that it is not merely accidental that both these games have as their object the avoidance of intimate exchanges between the two "players,"—that is, the avoidance of joint occupation of positions toward the Love pole of the interpersonal circle. It seems to be the case that coordinated avoidance contracts are especially likely to develop as a means of aborting intimacy between persons who, for some reason, are both attracted to and repelled by the possibility of enjoying that state of affairs with each other. While I have occasionally seen evidence of the existence of coordinated avoidance contracts in relation to other kinds of potential interchanges, such as mutual hatred, these appear to be less common than the avoidance of intimacy variety. In any case, let us take a brief, closer look at "Corner" and "Uproar."

Corner. Corner is a game often played by married couples as a means of resolving tensions associated with the question of whether or not a romantic interlude is in store for them in the immediate future. Typically, both parties have current reservations about engaging in anything like that, or at least their willingness to do so is contingent upon the partner's approaching the matter from a particular stance. The member with the most serious reservations steers the conversation around to some issue in their lives that is known to be a "touchy" one, such as the state of imbalance of the family budget. The other party has two options: he can ignore this red herring, or he can become irritated. If he is "playing" too, he becomes irritated, whereupon the party of the first part says something like, "Well, if you're going to act like that you can just watch the late, late show tonight." If the party of the second part is still playing, he says, "Well, if that's the way you feel about it I will." Both parties adopt a stance of "justifiable" indignation, which renders any subsequent romance exceedingly unlikely. It is important to note that the sequence *could* have been interrupted by either party along the way. Instead, each "corners" the other by taking what he says at face value.

Uproar. Uproar is basically similar to Corner. The principal difference is that the intimacy-avoiding motivations are stronger and more persistent, and are indeed frequently reinforced by strong moral and legal sanctions. The disruptive behavior that functions to prevent intimacy is correspondingly more intense and dramatic. As Berne (1964) notes, the prototype Uproar game is played between fathers and their teenage daughters. The rules of the game are simple. One of the players, typically the daughter, "provokes" the other into a violent argument which is terminated when one or the other, or both, angrily departs from the scene. The provocation will usually be one that has been used before, and in fact is frequently one which has been so finely honed and tempered through practice that its effects are utterly predictable. Sometimes, on the other hand, a one-shot provocation may be so ingeniously fashioned that it cannot fail as a signal for the beginning of an Uproar game. A former teenage patient of mine, a determined Uproar player, came in from a date one evening and passed through the living room where her father was seated, carrying her underclothing in her hand. That is virtuosity!

On occasion, the provocation providing the lead-in to an Uproar game is a persisting "condition" rather than a specific act. Thus the daughter's hair length, or her wardrobe, or her preferences in young men become the visible battleground upon which the invisible war is fought. I have even seen it fought on the issue of diet and body weight. I have had the opportunity in recent years to study at close range the problem of obesity in a fairly large number of adolescent girls of a certain class. I do not wish to oversimplify this complex problem, but one of the most impressive common elements to be found without exception in this group of girls was the frequency with which they and their fathers played Uproar, usually using the girl's weight or eating habits as the inciting circumstances for the mutual adoption of "safe" Aggressive postures.

NEGOTIATED MALADJUSTMENT: "GAME" EXAMPLES

Certain of the games described by Berne (1964) are in themselves good examples of the operation of negotiated maladjustment contracts, while others (such as, "I'm Only Trying To Help You," "Indigent," "Try and Get Away With It," and "Psychiatry") are frequent component "parts" of such contracts. Probably the most illustrative of the full-scale variety are the games of "Alcoholic" and "Cops and Robbers." Let us begin our discussion of negotiated maladjustment with these.

Alcoholic. It should be noted at the outset that alcohol or alcohol addiction—if there is any such thing—is not an essential feature of the *game* of Alcoholic. This game can be played without alcohol; it can be played with other chemical substances, or indeed with such pharmacologically inert vehicles as women and race horses. The truly essential feature of Alcoholic, stated in our terms, is the devious achievement of a spectacularly Submissive position *vis-à-vis* particular other persons. These other persons receive their payoff in the assumption of a strongly Dominant position. Whether the Dominance-Submissive theme is played out predominantly in the Hate semicircle (Sadistic vs. Masochistic positions) or predominantly in the Love semicircle (Hypernormal vs. Dependent positions) is apparently largely a matter of the personal tastes of the players. Probably most players of the Submissive position in the Alcoholic game prefer a little of each, in which case they may be able to find a partner who can manage both complementary positions, punitive *and* caretaking. Failing that, they may be required to find or to cultivate two (or more) partners who will distribute the different counterpositions among them. Thus, the determined Submissive Alcoholic player might marry a woman who enjoys the stance of *moral persecutor,* while maintaining close relations with his mother, who is perhaps a confirmed *sympathizing rescuer*. It is a moot point as to who gets the most out of an Alcoholic game—the person who is degraded or the supporting players. It is a common experience of persons who try to break up games of Alcoholic that both sides resist it fiercely.

Alcohol (or women, or race horses) can of course provide hedonic outcomes independent of those involved in the Alcoholic game, and there is no intention to suggest that everyone who drinks (or wenches, or gambles) to excess is an Alcoholic player; some of my best friends do a bit of each without any notable tendency to convert these pastimes to the game of Alcoholic. The *game* represents a specific type of contractual interpersonal relationship in which one person "agrees" to be supremely degraded and helpless in return for various combinations of moral disgust, punitiveness, rescue, and forgiveness from others. It is a vicious arrangement, but its viciousness does not lie in overindulgence, which is seen from this perspective as being merely instrumental. The viciousness lies in the mutual exploitation of the unfortunately extreme position preferences of the players.

Cops and Robbers. Berne (1964) points out, I believe correctly, that there are at least two basic varieties of habitual criminals—those who engage in crime for profit, and those who do so in order to play Cops and Robbers. There is probably a middle group that does a little of each. Professional criminals, as opposed to Cops and Robbers players, are not found in great quantity in courtrooms and jails. Like professionals in most fields, they tend to be very purposeful and pragmatic in the exercise of their skills, and they do not often make amateurish mistakes. The confirmed Cops and Robbers player, on the other hand, does not get his payoff unless he is caught, and so he frequently manages to be incredibly "stupid" in the performance of his crimes. As a result, he is promptly apprehended and convicted, often many times throughout his life.

On the other side of the equation, there are probably at least two kinds of law-enforcement officers—professionals and players of Cops and Robbers. The professional derives his payoffs through the exercise of his skills; his work is coolly efficient and is directed to the single purpose of maintaining law and order. The Cops and Robbers criminal is a soft touch for him, and I imagine that he finds such "cases" dull and unchallenging. He does not engage in unnecessary violence, or in unnecessary surveillance procedures involving the more unpleasant varieties of entrapment. The officer who is a Cops and Robbers player, in contrast, derives his principal payoff from the interpersonal "position" he occupies *vis-à-vis* the criminal; his work is valued chiefly for the opportunity it provides him to be "legitimately" Aggressive. The Cops and Robbers officer is given to "checking" men's rooms and lover's lanes on his own initiative. Professional criminals, of course, rarely place themselves at the disposal of the Cops and Robbers officer, whereas Cops and Robbers criminals often do. It may not be too outrageous, therefore, to suggest that Cops and Robbers law-enforcement officers and Cops and Robbers criminals "need" each other.

The *game* of Cops and Robbers is not the exclusive province of criminals and policemen. An infidelity variant is a feature of some marriages, and adolescents and their parents sometimes play a form of the game revolving around the adolescent's activities while away from home. A college campus variety is not unfamiliar, with a predisposed dean and a certain type of incident-prone student playing the principal roles. A fair proportion of so-called sexual deviates, many of whom are "criminals" in only a special and arbitrary sense, seem more interested in playing Cops and Robbers than in the continued indulgence of eccentric sexual needs. The commodities exchanged in Cops and Robbers are the Aggressive-Sadistic position on the one hand, and the Rebellious-Distrustful or Self-effacing-Masochistic position on the other. In sustained, repetitive Cops and Robbers games, where both players remain constant, the implicit contract is of standard form and identifies each player. Many Cops and Robbers players, however, carry "blank" contracts with them, so to speak, in order to be prepared in the event that a suitable partner turns up in their environment. In such cases, the contract can be negotiated "on the spot," and the players can move immediately to their frequently grim proceedings. As has been intimated, Cops and Robbers players tend to place themselves in each other's paths in order to increase the likelihood of such happenings. Too much obviousness in this respect, though, may expose the game format and thereby cramp the style of the players. Berne (1964) suggests that there is a "hide and seek" element of basic importance in determining the quality of the outcomes the players experience.

NEGOTIATED MALADJUSTMENT AND DISTURBED FAMILY RELATIONS

Of all the research of recent years on the antecedents of personal maladjustment, one area of focus stands out as having major promise—research on the nature of interpersonal relationships within the families from which maladjusted persons emerge. The question of maladjustment per se will be considered in detail in the succeeding chapter. Our task in this section is to sketch out in broad terms certain *processes* that appear to be implicated in the acquisition of maladjustment within the family, and to relate these processes to our concept of the *negotiated maladjustment contract.* Most of the research findings as yet available in this area are derived from studies using relatively uncontrolled "participant observation" methods, and the findings of any particular study are therefore of somewhat uncertain reliability. Fortunately, there is a substantial degree of concordance in the findings reported by numerous, independent investigators, a fact that inspires greater confidence than would otherwise be warranted.

The central concept that, in my view, ties together all of this research is that of *family homeostasis,* as orginally propounded, I believe, by Don Jackson (1957). Stated very generally, Jackson's idea is that a family may be characterized, in part, as a "system" that maintains a relative constancy of internal environment despite continuous changes in the relations of its component parts to each other. In *disturbed* family systems, the maintenance of homeostasis sometimes requires that one or more family members act in peculiar or self-defeating ways. If this conception is a valid one, I would suggest that it describes conditions within the family that would be expected, on occasion, to lead to the development of implicit contracts of the type we have been calling *negotiated maladjustment.* In his original paper on family homeostasis, Jackson reported certain of the phenomena that led him to develop this concept. It may be helpful to consider some of these:

> (1) A young woman undergoing psychotherapy for recurrent depressions began to manifest increased self-assurance. Her husband, who initially was eager that she become less of a burden to him, called the psychiatrist rather frequently and generally alluded to her "worsening" condition. The therapist had not made an appraisal of the husband; and when the state of the husband's alarm became clear, he had become too antagonistic to enter therapy. He became more and more uneasy, finally calling the therapist one evening, fearful that his wife would commit suicide. The next morning he shot himself to death.
>
> (2) A husband urged his wife into psychotherapy because of her frigidity. After several months of therapy she felt less sexually inhibited, whereupon the husband became impotent.
>
> (3) A young woman with anorexia nervosa ("unexplained" loss of appetite, accompanied by other distinctive features) was persuaded to enter psychotherapy by her

husband. Following a period of intense, rather dangerous, acting out, she began to relate more intimately to her husband. The husband's initial pleasure at her response was marred by his developing a duodenal ulcer.

(4) A young woman requested psychotherapy for a variety of reasons, *none* of which included dissatisfaction with her marriage. Her mother had died when she was two years old, as had the mother of her husband. The couple married in their late teens and, after a stormy beginning, apparently had made a pleasant, if markedly symbiotic (interdependent), adjustment. The wife was fearful of having a child, but both she and her husband wanted one, and hoped therapy would make it possible to have one. With a good deal more information than there is time to present, the psychiatrist felt that therapy for her alone would endanger the marriage, and that if she became pregnant, the husband, unsupported, might become seriously disturbed. The husband agreed to start psychotherapy with another psychiatrist; and a somewhat stormy, but eventually fruitful, time was had by all. (Jackson, 1957, pp. 88–89)

The reader may be assured, once again, that phenomena such as those described here are by no means rare and exotic. They occur with distressing frequency in the professional work of psychotherapists, the wisest of whom, as in the fourth case, anticipate the potential unfortunate outcomes. In each of the above cases, change or the threat of change in the behavior of one member of a marital dyad, *in the direction of functional enhancement,* was followed by actual or anticipated deterioration in the "adjustment" of the other member. Does it not appear that the "problem" in these instances was at least as important to the adaptation of the member who did not have it as it was to that of the member who did? Let us consider some additional observations by other investigators.

Evidence of interdependence, even where it involves the production of maladjusted behavior for the benefit of another person, does not in itself necessarily imply the existence of a *contractually regulated* relationship between the producer and the "consumer" of the behavior. If there is a contract, we should, as has been noted, expect to see some "guilt" or similar reaction on the part of the person who violates its terms, and some efforts or appeals on the part of the injured party to re-institute them. Since we are dealing here with very implicit contracts, however, these reactions to violation should be less than completely obvious. Consider the following excerpt from an interview with the mother of a schizophrenic young man. The interview occurred shortly after the family visited the young man in the hospital.

> He had put the bolster up in front of him so he didn't see Jean (his girl friend) at all, and all she saw of him was his feet, and I leaned over to him and said very quietly, "Eddie, have you thought what you would like to have us get for you to give to Jean for Christmas?" Quietly, so she couldn't hear us. And he said, "I don't want to get her anything." And I said, "She'd feel very badly if you didn't." And he said loudly enough so you could hear him across the hall—I mean he wasn't hollering or anything, but he spoke right out and he said, "Unless I can buy my own Christmas presents and do my own Christmas shopping it's not Christmas as far as I'm concerned." He said, "This business of having everything done for you. You can't do anything for yourself." And then he was vulgar—it's the first time I've ever heard him talk like that—he said "You can't even—" he said, "as far as I'm concerned I can't even shit for myself." It was shocking for me—I mean I wasn't—I mean I was shocked at the fact that he felt the need to express himself that way, and I said, "Well, it's perfectly all right if you don't want me to. We won't do it. It's entirely up to you." . . . And a little while later I said to him, "Eddie," I said, "I believe the doctors out here—I just want to say that I can appreciate—we can all appreciate what you are going through and that it's a pretty tough time, and the doctors say that sometimes these things become pretty painful—not physically, but pretty painful to you mentally, and we do understand and appreciate that, and everybody around here does too." And he said, "Well, what do they want me to

> do?" And I said, "Well, I don't know what anybody wants you to do, Eddie, but everybody, regardless of what you think, they want you to do what you want to do." But I said that "there are so many times that *you don't express yourself,* and if you don't tell us and if you don't tell the doctors here what you want, unless you say definitely that you do or you don't. There isn't any way of anybody knowing what you want unless you let us know." And he said, "Well, what do they want me to do? What do I have to do to get well?" I said, "Well, the only thing that I could suggest that might help is to *talk to them* just like you are talking to me now. *Tell them* how you feel about things." And he said, "Why do I have to talk to them?" He said, "Are they God? Did they make me? Am I required to tell them my innermost feelings?" I started to say something and forgot what it was. Anyway, before I could say anything he said in a very controlled, and restrained, and courteous voice, as you would speak to an utter stranger on the streetcar, he said, "Would you please leave now." I said to him, "What did you say?" I couldn't believe my ears. He said, "I said, would you please leave now." And I said, "Eddie, you don't want me to go now. We've been looking forward to this visit all week, and I *know that you have too.*" And he stood up and said, "Well, if you won't leave I will have to." He left the room and walked all the way down the corridor as far as he could possibly go . . . the very last door down there. So then we went outside. (Wynne, Ryckoff, Day, and Hirsch, 1958, p. 218. Emphasis added.)

Following this episode, the patient became completely mute and catatonic, a condition that endured for 13 months.

Wynne et al. (1958), to whom we are indebted for this remarkable example, interpret the episode as a disruption and restoration, on a changed basis, of a certain type of stereotyped emotional relationship among the members of the family. Their term for this type of stereotyped emotional relationship is *pseudo-mutuality.* Pseudo-mutuality exists in family relationships to the degree that family members find it more important to maintain a sense of having relationships of a certain type with each other than to recognize or acknowledge the personal identity and individuality of each of the members. Thus, in the present example, the mother is apparently unable to acknowledge that the son is asserting an identity other than that of an inhibited, dependent child. When he expresses himself in no uncertain terms, she accuses him of *not* expressing himself, and then she suggests that if he has feelings to express he should express them to the doctors (and not to those toward whom they are felt). When Eddie makes his violation of the "rules" undeniable, the mother is initially wholly stymied. Wynne et al. inform us, however, that this is merely temporary. Eddie's parents subsequently re-interpret his 13-month withdrawal as anger at the nursing staff, and as having nothing whatever to do with them. But Wynne et al. also suggest that Eddie's withdrawal represents his own contribution to the re-establishment of a ruptured pseudo-mutuality, albeit on a different basis. He is no longer aggressive, but rather a passive, helpless, silent, vegetable-like person—a suitable object of "loving" and devoted parental concern. Does this sound like the re-establishment of a broken contract?

The context within which the above observations were made was a large-scale, clinical investigation project on the family relations of schizophrenic persons, conducted under the auspices of the National Institute of Mental Health. Wynne and his colleagues have since continued to refine and expand their conceptions of what is going on within these disturbed families (Ryckoff, Day, and Wynne, 1959; Schaffer, Wynne, Day, Ryckoff, and Halperin, 1962; Wynne and Singer, 1963; Singer and Wynne, 1965; Wynne, 1965). We cannot take time to review their interesting findings here. It may suffice to say that they have been moderately successful in relating certain of the more bizarre phenomena of schizophrenia to identifiable forces operating within the relationships among family members. More apropos of our present concerns, Wynne continues to be impressed with the rigidity of organization of disturbed families, a rigidity I am inclined to attribute to the operation of negotiated maladjustment contracts. In one of his more recent papers, Wynne (1965) writes, "The homeostatic, self-regulatory capacities of families as social subsystems . . . are very considerable. Indeed, [disturbed] *families have a staggering capacity to remain the same*" (p. 321; Wynne's italics).

Let us look briefly at one more clinical example, this one supplied by Haley (1959a), who was a prominent member of a different research team working in the same area. The material consists of a recorded conversation among a schizophrenic young man, his parents, and the patient's psychotherapist. The patient had previously sent his mother a Mother's Day card which contained the inscription, "For Someone Who Has Been Like a Mother to Me." The mother was disturbed by this card and confronted the son concerning the inappropriate inscription. The son initially feigns perplexity as to why mother should be upset. Father attempts to interpret the whole matter as a mistake, but mother persists. We pick up the conversation at this point:

> *Patient*: Well, I meant to sting you just a tiny bit by that outside phrase.
>
> *Mother*: You see I'm a little bit of a psychiatrist too, Simon, I happen to be—(laughing). So I felt so—when you talked to (the therapist) I brought along that card—I wanted to know what's behind your head. And I wanted to know—or you made it on purposely to hurt me—Well, if you did, I—I . . .
>
> *Patient*: (interrupting) Not entirely, not entire . . .
>
> *Mother*: (interrupting and overlapping) I'll take all—Simon, believe me. I'll take all the hurt in the world if it will help you—you see what I mean?
>
> *Therapist*: How can you . . .
>
> *Mother*: (continuing) Because I never meant to hurt you—Huh?
>
> *Therapist*: How can you hurt anybody who is perfectly willing to be hurt? (short pause)
>
> *Father*: What's that?

Mother: I uh—a mother sacrifices—if you would be—maybe a mother you would know too. Because a mother is just a martyr, she's sacrificing—like even with Jesus with his mother—she sacrificed too. So that's the way it goes on, a mother takes over anything what she can help . . .

Therapist: (interrupting) What mother?

Mother: (continuing) her children.

Patient: (interrupting and overlapping) Well, uh, I'll tell you Ma—listen, Ma, I didn't mean to—to sting you exactly that outside part there.

Therapist: Well, you said so.

Patient: Oh, all right, but it—it wasn't that exactly. No, I'm not giving ground—uh—it's hard to explain this thing. Uh—uh—what was I going to say? Now I forgot what I was going to say. (short pause) I mean I felt that this—this is what I mean, uh—that I felt that you could have been a better mother to me than you were. See there were things.

Mother: Uh . . .

Father: Well you said . . .

Patient: (interrupting) You could have been better than you were. So that's why—that's that—I felt—it was, uh—uh, was all right to send it that way.

Mother: Well, if you meant it that way that's perf—that's what I wanted to know—and that's all I care you see. But I still say, Simon, that if you would take your father and mother just like they're plain people—you just came here and you went through life like anybody else went through—and—and don't keep picking on them and picking them to pieces—but just leave them alone—and go along with them the way they are—and don't change them—you'll be able to get along with everybody, I assure you.

Patient: (interrupting) I mean after all a card is a card—why I'd—it seems to me kind of silly (anguish in his voice and near weeping) to bring that thing in here—they have sold them at the canteen, Ma . . .

Therapist: Are you anxious now . . .

Patient: Why . . .

Therapist: Are you anxious now because she said . . .

Patient: I shouldn't be blamed for a thing like that, it's so small . . .

Mother: (overlapping) I'm not blaming you.

Patient: (continuing) I don't even remember exactly what the thing was.

Mother: (overlapping) Well, that's all I wanted to know (laughs)

Patient: (continuing) I didn't want to—to—to—to blame you or nothing. (Haley, 1959a, p. 360)

This conversation continues in similar vein until the patient, utterly defeated by the joint efforts of both of his parents, finally concedes that all he meant was that his mother had been a *real* mother to him, a suggestion made by his father. The distinctive feature of the entire conversation, as Haley points out, is that no member of the family affirms what any other member has said except when the son is behaving in a "symptomatic" way—either by claiming amnesia or by falsifying reality. The pressure put upon the son to (in our terms) repair the breach of contract is enormous, the mother not hesitating even to draw a comparison between her own suffering and that of Christ's mother. In acquiescing to these demands the son exhibits "pathological" behavior—behavior that is evidently more tolerable to his parents than is calling a spade a spade.

The research group with which Haley has been associated has concerned itself chiefly with communication processes in disturbed families (Bateson, Jackson, Haley, and Weakland, 1956; Bateson, 1960; Weakland, 1960; Haley, 1959b, 1963). The principal concepts of this group revolve around the notion of interpersonal "control" through the use of metacommunicative signals. Without going into detail it may be said that the conceptual framework developed by this group is highly compatible with the one advanced here. Their focus, however, has been on the means whereby normative, contractual sanctions are subtly invoked and manipulated in families containing a schizophrenic member.

The findings of one more large-scale project on family relations in schizophrenia should be included in this somewhat cursory review. This project, which involved very intensive study of a small number of families, was conducted at Yale University by Theodore Lidz and his colleagues (Lidz, Cornelison, Fleck, and Terry, 1957a, 1957b; Lidz, 1958; Lidz, Cornelison, Terry, and Fleck, 1958; Lidz, Fleck, Cornelison, and Terry, 1958; Fleck, Lidz, Cornelison, Schafer, and Terry, 1959; Lidz and Fleck, 1960; Lidz, Schafer, Fleck, Cornelison, and Terry, 1962; Lidz, Fleck, Alanen, and Cornelison, 1963). Fleck (1960) has provided a brief summary of the major findings of the project. Among the findings was the discovery of two types of family pattern that tended to be associated with the development of schizophrenia in the offspring. One of these was the *schismatic* family, marked by chronic strife and argumentation, primarily between the parents. A careful review of the descriptions supplied by the investigators convinces me that many of these schismatic families were operating according to what we have termed *coordinated avoidance* contracts. The other pattern was that of family *skew*. Skewed families show more or less severe distortions of thought and behavior, apparently resulting from compromises necessitated by the peculiarities of one or more members. Unlike schismatic families, skewed families frequently have a peaceful and harmonious—if rather odd—external appearance. They are described by Lidz et al. (1957b) as follows:

> In all of these [skewed] families, one partner who was extremely dependent or masochistic had married a spouse who had appeared to be a strong and protecting parental figure. The dependent partner would go along with or even support the weaknesses or psychopathologic distortions of the parental partner because dependency or masochistic needs were met. In contrast to the marriages with overt schism,

> one partner could gratify rather than combat a spouse's narcissistic needs. It may be significant that no member of these six marriages had intense emotional bonds to the parental family, and it is possible that the absence of such alternative sources of gratification tended to hold these spouses together. A striking feature in all cases was the psychopathology of the partner who appeared to be dominant, creating an abnormal environment which, being accepted by the "healthier" spouse, may have seemed to be a normal environment to the children. (p. 246)

Does this sound like *negotiated maladjustment* to you? It sounds very much like it to me. Lidz et al. (1957b) note that, on occasion, the entire family, including the children, actively participate in and support the aberrant behavior and thinking of the "dominant" member, for which, presumably, they receive in their turn due rewards. A strikingly similar picture emerges from the findings of yet another large-scale investigation of family relations and schizophrenia, as reported in part by Bowen, Dysinger, and Basamania (1959) and by Brodey (1959). We will not, however, take additional time to review these findings.

It should be plain that the argument presented in this section is a relatively weak one. We have had to rely, in the main, upon uncontrolled observations and anecdotal accounts of clinical investigators, albeit highly credible and responsible ones. Moreover, these observations were never made for the purposes to which we have put them, and they are therefore fitted into our framework only with some degree of strain. To reiterate a point made in the very first chapter, no claim of proof is made on the basis of clinical examples. On the other hand, the case is not wholly without empirical support. I look forward eagerly to the research of future years, which should settle the question for us.

A Final Word

I know that I am not the first author to experience some misgivings in writing about such matters as strategies, games, and implicit contracts in human relationships. The sources of these misgivings are not difficult to locate. They arise out of an awareness that the existence of such processes in relations between persons justifies for some the adoption of a markedly cynical and wary attitude in regard to people in general. This is especially true where, as in this chapter, the *misuses* of these processes tend to be emphasized, if only for pedagogical reasons. The fact is, however, that there are many good strategies, games, and contracts that do not rob people of their spontaneity and self-determination, and that encourage the development of a level of genuineness and intimacy between persons that would otherwise be difficult of attainment. I hope that I have not caused the reader to lose sight of this important fact.

REFERENCES

BATESON, G. Minimal requirements for a theory of schizophrenia. *A.M.A. Archives of General Psychiatry*, 1960, **2,** 477–91.

BATESON, G., JACKSON, D. D., HALEY, J., and WEAKLAND, J. Toward a theory of schizophrenia. *Behavioral Science*, 1956, **1,** 251–64.

BERNE, E. *Transactional analysis in psychotherapy*. New York: Grove Press, 1961.

BERNE, E. *Games people play*. New York: Grove Press, 1964.

BERNE, E. *Principles of group treatment*. New York: Oxford University Press, 1966.

BIXENSTINE, V. E., and WILSON, K. V. Effects of level of cooperative choice by the other player on choices in a prisoner's dilemma game. *Journal of Abnormal and Social Psychology*, 1963, **67,** 139–48.

BOWEN, M., DYSINGER, R. H., and BASAMANIA, B. The role of the father in families with a schizophrenic patient. *American Journal of Psychiatry*, 1959, **115,** 1017–20.

BRODEY, W. M. Some family operations and schizophrenia. *A.M.A. Archives of General Psychiatry*, 1959, **1,** 379–402.

DEUTSCH, M. The effect of motivational orientation upon trust and suspicion. *Human Relations*, 1960, **13,** 123–39.

DEUTSCH, M., and KRAUSS, R. M. The effect of threat on interpersonal bargaining. *Journal of Abnormal and Social Psychology*, 1960, **61,** 181–89.

FLECK, S. Family dynamics and origin of schizophrenia. *Psychosomatic Medicine*, 1960, **22,** 333–44.

FLECK, S., LIDZ, T., CORNELISON, A., SCHAFER, S., and TERRY, D. The intrafamilial environment of the schizophrenic patient. In J. H. MASSERMAN (Ed.), *Individual and family dynamics.* New York: Grune & Stratton, 1959. Pp. 142–59.

GALLO, P. S. Effects of increased incentives upon the use of threat in bargaining. *Journal of Personality and Social Psychology*, 1966, **4,** 14–20.

HALEY, J. The family of the schizophrenic: A model system. *Journal of Nervous and Mental Disease,* 1959(a), **129,** 357–74.

HALEY, J. An interactional description of schizophrenia. *Psychiatry,* 1959(b), **22,** 321–32.

HALEY, J. *Strategies of psychotherapy.* New York: Grune & Stratton, 1963.

JACKSON, D. D. The question of family homeostasis. *Psychiatric Quarterly Supplement*, 1957, **31,** 79–90.

KAZAN, E. *The arrangement.* New York: Stein and Day, 1967.

KOMORITA, S. S. Cooperative choice in a prisoner's dilemma game. *Journal of Personality and Social Psychology*, 1965, **2,** 741–45.

LAVE, L. B. Factors affecting cooperation in the prisoner's dilemma. *Behavioral Science*, 1965, **10,** 26–38.

LIDZ, T. Schizophrenia and the family. *Psychiatry,* 1958, **21,** 21–27.

LIDZ, T., CORNELISON, A., FLECK, S., and TERRY, D. The intrafamilial environment of the schizophrenic patient: I. The father. *Psychiatry*, 1957(a), **20,** 329–42.

LIDZ, T., CORNELISON, A., FLECK, S., and TERRY, D. The intrafamilial environment of schizophrenic patients: II. Marital schism and marital skew. *American Journal of Psychiatry*, 1957(b), **114,** 241–48.

LIDZ, T., CORNELISON, A., TERRY, D., and FLECK, S. Intrafamilial environment of the schizophrenic patient: VI. The transmission of irrationality. *A.M.A. Archives of Neurology and Psychiatry,* 1958, **79,** 305–16.

LIDZ, T., and FLECK, S. Schizophrenia, human integration, and the role of the family. In D. D. JACKSON (Ed.), *The etiology of schizophrenia.* New York: Basic Books, 1960. Pp. 323–45.

LIDZ, T., FLECK, S., ALANEN, Y. O., and CORNELISON, A. Schizophrenic patients and their siblings. *Psychiatry,* 1963, **26,** 1–18.

LIDZ, T., FLECK, S., CORNELISON, A., and TERRY, D. The intrafamilial environment of the schizophrenic patient: IV. Parental personalities and family interaction. *American Journal of Orthopsychiatry*, 1958, **28,** 764–76.

LIDZ, T., SCHAFER, S., FLECK, S., CORNELISON, A., and TERRY, D. Ego differentiation and schizophrenic symptom formation in identical twins. *Journal of the American Psychoanalytic Association*, 1962, **10,** 74–90.

LUCE, R. D., and RAIFFA, H. *Games and decisions.* New York: Wiley, 1957.

MINAS, J. S., SCODEL, A., MARLOWE, D., and RAWSON, H. Some descriptive aspects of two-person non-zero-sum games. II. *Journal of Conflict Resolution*, 1960, **4,** 193–97.

RYCKOFF, I., DAY, J., and WYNNE, L. C. Maintenance of stereotyped roles in the families of schizophrenics. *A.M.A. Archives of General Psychiatry*, 1959, **1,** 93–98.

SCHAFFER, L., WYNNE, L. C., DAY, J., RYCKOFF, I., and HALPERIN, A. On the nature of the psychiatrists' experience with the family of the schizophrenic. *Psychiatry*, 1962, **25,** 32–45.

SCHEFLEN, A. E. Human communication: Behavioral programs and their integration in interaction. *Behavioral Science*, 1968, **13,** 44–55.

SCHELLING, T. C. *The strategy of conflict.* Cambridge: Harvard University Press, 1960.

SCODEL, A., MINAS, J. S., RATOOSH, P., and LIPETZ, M. Some descriptive aspects of two-person non-zero-sum games. I. *Journal of Conflict Resolution*, 1959, **3,** 114–19.

SHURE, G. H., MEEKER, R. J., and HANSFORD, E. A. The effectiveness of pacifist strategies in bargaining games. *Journal of Conflict Resolution*, 1965, **9,** 106–17.

SINGER, M. T., and WYNNE, L. C. Thought disorder and family relations of schizophrenics. III. Methodology using projective techniques. *A.M.A. Archives of General Psychiatry*, 1965, **12,** 187–200.

SOLOMON, L. The influence of some types of power relationships and game strategies upon the development of interpersonal trust. *Journal of Abnormal and Social Psychology*, 1960, **61,** 223–30.

SZASZ, T. S. *The myth of mental illness.* New York: Hoeber-Harper, 1961.

THIBAUT, J. The development of contractual norms in bargaining: Replication and variation. *Journal of Conflict Resolution*, 1968, **12,** 102–12.

THIBAUT, J. W., and KELLEY, H. H. *The social psychology of groups.* New York: Wiley, 1959.

WALLER, W. The rating and dating complex. *American Sociological Review*, 1937, **2,** 727–34.

WEAKLAND, J. "The double bind" hypothesis of schizophrenia and three-party interaction. In D. D. JACKSON (Ed.), *The etiology of schizophrenia.* New York: Basic Books, 1960. Pp. 373–88.

WYNNE, L. C. Some indications and contraindications for exploratory family therapy. In I. BOSZORMENYI-NAGY and J. L. FRAMO (Eds.), *Intensive family therapy.* New York: Harper & Row, 1965. Pp. 289–322.

WYNNE, L. C., RYCKOFF, I. M., DAY, J., and HIRSCH, S. I. Pseudo-mutuality in the family relations of schizophrenics. *Psychiatry,* 1958, **21,** 205–20.

WYNNE, L. C., and SINGER, M. T. Thought disorder and family relations of schizophrenics. II. A classification of forms of thinking. *A.M.A. Archives of General Psychiatry*, 1963, **9,** 199–206.

CHAPTER 7

"Personality Disorder": Extranormative Efforts at Relationship

The field of mental health, including the various scientific and professional disciplines associated with it, is in the midst of a revolution of enormous scope and significance. The dimensions of this revolution cannot readily be described in brief and simple terms, but it involves nothing less than a radical redefinition of the nature of the phenomena that constitute the proper concern of workers in the mental health area. If there is a common theme in all of this, it is one of disillusionment with the so-called "medical model" of personality disorder, as evidenced by such terms as "mental disease," "mental illness," and "psychopathology." According to this model, disordered behavior is the result of "pathogenic" factors existing inside of persons (in their minds or psyches) in a manner similar to a locus of infection or an organic structural defect; "treatment" within this framework therefore becomes a matter of excising, altering, or suppressing the malfunctioning mental element so that it will no longer cause trouble. The task of the professional helper is to "fix" the passive victim of the disease. This may be done by "deep" psychological probing, powerful pharmacological agents, electricity passed through the brain, or even surgical destruction of brain tissue. Treatment efforts geared to this model, while not without their occasional positive (or at least "calming") effects, have been considerably less than impressive in their rate of production of "cures"; they frequently create as many problems as they solve.[1]

The conception of behavior disturbance as an illness has also, of course, had its favorable features. It is a distinct improvement over the concept of demonic possession, for which the recommended "treatment" was exorcism by torture and even burning at the stake. As Sarbin (1967) has pointed out, however, the entirely metaphorical concept of mental illness makes no more sense logically than does that of "possession." There are, in fact, some striking similarities between these two types of (pseudo-) explanations of odd behavior—not the least being that they are both highly pejorative and more or less permanently stigmatizing as "diagnoses." Adams (1964) has recently reviewed a period of American and British psychiatric history in which an alternative to the possession and disease conceptions was widely held. This was the era of "moral therapy," roughly from 1800 to 1860. The guiding principle of moral therapy was that behavior disturbances resulted from problems in human relationships and could therefore best be ameliorated through the highly personalized provision of new and wholesome relationships. Making allowances for the shortcomings of old hospital records, it would appear that moral therapy was incomparably more successful than subsequent therapies based on the now-widespread view of mental disorder as a kind of foreign agent intruding itself into the mind of the diseased host. In very

[1] See, for example, Maher (1966, Chapter 17) for an unbiased discussion of the results produced by the "biological" therapies. *Reliable* evidence on the effectiveness of "depth" (that is, classical psychoanalytic) psychotherapy is nowhere to be found, but the admittedly inadequate knowledge that we do have relating to this question provides no great reason for confidence; see Strupp's (1963) review and Eysenck's (1964) rejoinder for an up-to-date discussion of the evidence.

recent years moral therapy has returned to the mental hospital in the guise of what is called "milieu therapy," and there is as a result the encouraging prospect that we may again approach the apparently impressive rate of success in dealing with severe behavior disturbance that may well have been fairly common in 1840!

Unfortunately, the issues we are addressing in these comments are readily obfuscated by controversies arising out of interprofessional rivalries and jurisdictional disputes. Obviously, there are *real* diseases of the brain or other organs that can produce or contribute to the development of behavioral "symptoms"; and problems of human relationships very often do have *real* pathological effects at the organic level in the form of psychosomatic illnesses. Physical malfunction is properly the domain of the physician, who, by virtue of his particular training and experience, is equipped to perform those biological manipulations needed to effect an interruption or reversal of the (physical) pathological process. These matters are not our concern. Disorders of behavior, in the overwhelming majority of instances, are unrelated to physical pathology unless one retreats to the somewhat tedious and unhelpful position that behavior of any kind must bear an isomorphic relationship to events in the central nervous system. Our concern is with disorders of behavior conceived as learned patterns of action, or more specifically as learned patterns of relating to the social environment. Such patterns are typically "stored" in brains that are entirely "healthy" by any reasonable criterion. Nonpathological variations in the characteristics of the biological equipment of persons are seen from this perspective as merely one of the factors determining the interpersonal experiences an individual will have and also, to some degree, his ability to make use of those experiences in the construction of a functional Image of his universe. Their causal significance in most behavior disorder is at best merely contributory and indirect.

Lest the message be misunderstood, I should point out that an attack on the medical model of behavior disorders does not constitute an attack on the legitimacy of physicians interested in these problems. Indeed, the changed perspective is due in no small measure to the leadership of a fairly large group of thoughtful, innovative physicians. To take just two examples, Harry Stack Sullivan, whose views have provided our own point of departure in this book, may also be justly credited with inaugurating the modern era of milieu therapy; and the brilliant analyses of Thomas Szasz (1961, 1963), another psychiatrist, have contributed much of the intellectual force toward inducing these changes. The issue, therefore, is not really one of professional or disciplinary hegemony. Large numbers of psychiatrist-physicians have never been persuaded that the search for "the pathogenic factor" in most behavior disorders was anything but a search for a chimera. The target of the mental health revolution is not medicine or psychologically oriented physicians, but rather the grossly oversimplified way of thinking about behavior disorder implied in the "medical model." Psychiatrists, perhaps understandably, have been reluctant to relinquish their "medical prerogatives" in the field of behavior disorder, but this should not blind us to the fact that a very substantial proportion of them do not subscribe to the medical model in their professional activities.

Abandonment of the concept of "mental illness" as an explanation for the deviant behavior of biologically healthy, physically intact persons has many profound implications, some of them possibly disturbing. The destruction of a cherished cultural myth, especially one that is in many ways highly functional,[2] is never accomplished with great ease. One of the most basic—and least comfortable—of the implications concerns the question of voluntary action. It is somehow easier for us to believe people act "that way" because they can't help it, because they are "sick," than to believe they do so "on purpose." It is sometimes suggested, indeed,

[2] One of the more important functions of the mental illness myth is its provision of an escape route for avoiding the fundamental philosophical, ethical, and legal questions raised by the existence of persistent behavioral deviance, and by society's need to fabricate some means of coping pragmatically with it. It seems likely that in the long run we will do better to confront these issues directly in attempting to find solutions; reliance upon conceptual sleight-of-hand may be sufficiently mystifying to obscure these painful issues temporarily, but in the meantime it impedes progress toward a more wholesome and genuine understanding. See Szasz (1963) and Sarbin (1967) for cogent discussions of some of these problems.

that to hold the latter belief is to take a step backward in time to the period when persons were held responsible, and were therefore punished, for their behavioral noncomformity.

The issue we are dealing with here is a very subtle and complex one. Let us be careful to make the appropriate discriminations. It is one thing to say a person enacts odd and (objectively) self-defeating behavior because, under the circumstances, that is the best outcome exchange he can manage with the environment. It is quite another to say he does so because he is malevolent, or stubborn, or "manipulative." He may, in a certain sense, be all of those; but these are descriptive terms, not causal ones. The person who behaves strangely because that is the only way he can maintain a tolerable relationship to the world is entitled to at least as much compassion and sympathy as the person who does so involuntarily because he is "sick." The altered perspective implies the necessity of many changes in the manner in which we deal with "mental disorder," but it does *not* justify a cynical and punitive attitude toward disordered persons.

The essential error of viewing the disordered person as a helpless victim of mysterious psychic forces is well illustrated in a recent study by Braginsky and Braginsky (1967). The subjects of this study were 30 long-term inmates of a mental hospital, all of them considered to be "chronic schizophrenics." Chronic schizophrenia is generally regarded as the most severe form of personality disturbance. One would anticipate therefore that, if any class of mental patients is truly irrational and helpless in respect to their "crazy" behavior, the Braginskys' subjects would show these characteristics in abundance. The authors hypothesized, however, that these randomly selected patients would have the goals of remaining in the hospital and retaining their "open ward" privileges, and that furthermore they would be capable of engaging in self-presentational strategies designed to realize those goals. The 30 patients were randomly divided into three experimental groups and were individually subjected to brief evaluative interviews conducted by a staff psychologist who was unaware of the group to which any patient belonged. The independent variable in the study was the "reason" for the interview, as casually mentioned to each patient immediately prior to its occurrence. One group was informed that the interviewer was interested in determining whether patients "might be ready for discharge" from the hospital. Another group was informed that the interviewer was interested to see whether patients "should be on open or closed wards" (all of the patients were at the time residing on open wards). The third group was told that the purpose of the interview was to determine "how you are feeling and getting along in the hospital," a reason that would be interpreted in this context as comparable to the evaluation-for-discharge reason. The investigators predicted that patients in the *open ward status* interview condition would give the impression of being mentally healthy (in order to retain their open ward privileges), while those in the other two interview conditions would give the impression of being mentally ill (in order to be able to remain in the hospital). The interviews were tape recorded, and each interview was subsequently monitored by three psychiatrists. The psychiatrists, who had no knowledge of the experiment, were asked to make ratings of each patient in regard to his degree of illness, his degree of need for hospital control, and various symptomatic behaviors. The ratings of the psychiatrists, who incidentally agreed quite well among themselves, were entirely in accord with the investigators' predictions. Patients in the *ward status* condition turned out quite "healthy," while those in the other conditions turned out quite "ill." Interestingly, none of the *ward status* patients mentioned delusions or hallucinations in their interviews, but nine of the 20 patients in the other two conditions spontaneously indicated that they were troubled with these relatively "serious" symptoms. Artiss (1959), in another connection, has made the point that the alleged hallucinations of schizophrenic persons might sometimes be merely lies, not *qualitatively* different from, "I couldn't come to school yesterday because I was sick" (p. 202). In any case, additional research findings reported by Braginsky and his colleagues (Braginsky, Grosse, and Ring, 1966; Braginsky, Holzberg, Finison, and Ring, 1967; Braginsky, Holzberg, Ridley, and Braginsky, 1968) strengthen further the suggestion that traditional viewpoints have severely underestimated the adaptive skill of the typical hospitalized mental patient. Confirmatory evidence on this point is supplied by Fontana and Klein (1968), who have demonstrated the strategical aspects of a type of "deficit" in reaction time traditionally alleged to be characteristic of schizophrenics.

As these introductory remarks have probably already made clear, the approach we shall take in discussing disorders of personality will be somewhat unorthodox. One of the more important departures from convention will be a relative lack of concern with the traditional diagnostic "entities" or "syndromes" of disorder. I regard these classifications of behavior (such as schizophrenia and obsessional neurosis) as being very nearly meaningless when used in anything but a purely descriptive way, and in general they are descriptively inadequate. I doubt that anyone is capable of specifying their category limits with sufficient precision to permit reasonably reliable (consensually valid) "diagnoses" to be made. But even if that proved to be within the realm of possibility the presumption of a specific, common "underlying pathology" implicit in these traditional categorizations flies in the face of much empirical knowledge to the contrary, and—worse—it diverts attention from the interpersonal processes that are, in my view, the sum and substance of the disorder. To the degree that behavioral categorizations are needed, we shall stick with our interpersonal circle variables. We have already seen something of the manner in which these can be used to code "abnormal" behavior. Let us now try to be more specific about what constitutes abnormality and personality disorder.

The Definition of Personality Disorder

It may be helpful to begin with what personality disorder is *not*. It is not co-extensive with personal feelings of anxiety, unhappiness, or despair. Life is hard, and we will all experience our share of suffering and quiet desperation in trying to cope with it. A certain amount of fear and unhappiness (insecurity) has always been part of the human condition and it always will be. This is a point made very forcefully by Schofield (1964). He roundly criticizes mental health propaganda suggesting that it is abnormal to be unhappy, or that the latter is in itself a suitable reason for seeking "treatment." He argues that Americans have been taught to feel anxious about anxiety, resulting in an artificial inflation of the incidence of self-diagnosed maladjustment and thereby creating further strain on an already badly strained mental health services delivery system. Among some groups, he notes, it is even considered fashionable to be "in" therapy or analysis, to say nothing of the advantages this affords as a means of excusing childish or inconsiderate behavior toward others. Schofield acknowledges that unhappy persons can and should be helped by seeking sympathetic interpersonal relationships, but he denies there are any mental health implications in this. He specifically rejects the idea that such problems require the services of highly trained mental health professionals. Schofield perhaps overstates the case somewhat, but it seems to me that he is basically correct in his insistence that most anxiety is an entirely normal phenomenon.

As a general rule, private feelings and experiences, and even behaviors performed in private, will not suffice as a basis for defining personality disorder. If they did, my guess would be that personality disorder would have to be considered a near-universal —and therefore "normal"—phenomenon. Personality disorder, if the term is to have any meaning, is a matter of how one *behaves* (including what one *says*) in the presence of others; its definition is public and social in nature. Subjective anxiety and unhappiness do not in themselves constitute personality disorder, although they are, needless to say, frequent accompaniments of it. Not even very intense levels of anxiety or despair, which can certainly be so severe as to exceed any person's tolerance, can be taken as indications of disorder unless the individual behaves in some irregular or unusual way. Often, of course, irregular or unusual behavior is determined in part by such internal emotional states.

PERSONALITY DISORDER AS "NAIVELY" DESCRIBED

If we wish to limit the definition of personality disorder to publicly observable behavior, we still have the problem of deciding what kinds of behavior we shall take as indications that a condition of disorder exists. This is a somewhat problematic issue. As many observers have pointed out, the descriptive language ordinarily employed in discussions of "abnormal" behavior is so thoroughly suffused with medical terms and metaphors that it invites prejudgment on important questions of interpretation. Psychologists, who should be sensitive to this problem, typically have not been. Fortunately, a number of sociologists, among them most notably Goffman (1962), have in recent years interested themselves in the "status" of mental patienthood. Their descriptions of what it is to be "mentally ill" more nearly approximate the ideal of conceptual neutrality, and we shall for that reason adopt their perspective in our search for a workable definition of personality disorder.

The identification of a person as disordered is made on the basis of his social behavior. Moreover, the *criteria* defining disordered or abnormal behavior are essentially the products of social custom and convention. What is irregular or unusual in one culture may be routine and standard in another. In certain times and places the public assertion of having had "spontaneous" hallucinatory experiences has been sufficient to elevate a person to a position of great fame and prestige; and anthropologists have described entire societies whose members displayed a level of aggressiveness or competitiveness (or other behavioral style) that would be regarded in our culture as abnormal. The incidence of personal disorder does not appear to vary a great deal from culture to culture, but criterial specifications defining behavioral abnormality do show very substantial intercultural variation. With the possible exception of "wild" behavior or frenzy, which is quite generally recognized as disordered (or the cultural equivalent thereof), it is doubtful that one could find *any* instance of behavior *universally* considered to be the product of "abnormal" processes. By and large, then, the "reality" of abnormality or personality disturbance is a purely social reality; it is a question of the kinds of explanatory constructs or *causal attributions* (Kelley, 1967) a society evolves in respect to particular kinds of behavior—or more specifically particular kinds of public, deviant (norm-violating) behavior.

There are many kinds of public norm violations that do not earn the attribution of "personality disorder," criminal acts and lapses in etiquette being familiar examples. As Scheff (1966) has pointed out, the violation of cultural norms that are more or less explicitly recognized and codified *as such*, as in the case of laws and rules of etiquette, does not normally lead to an attribution of mental disorder. Some norms of a culture, however, are so basic that they are not considered to be norms—they become reified. These norms have to do with the culture's basic assumptions about the nature of reality and decency. Deliberate violation of such norms is unthinkable for most of the society's members. The occurrence of these violations is therefore to a large extent *inexplicable*, giving rise to causal attributions of an extraordinary or even supernatural nature (such as witchcraft and mental illness).[3] Scheff refers to these special, unnamable norms as "residual" ones, and to their violation as "residual rule-breaking."

Residual rule-breaking in a public (interpersonal) context appears to be a *necessary* condition for the attribution of mental or personality disorder. Is it also a *sufficient* one? A considerable amount of evidence indicates that it is not. Scheff (1966) reviews a variety of epidemiological research findings that show, virtually without exception, an absolute prevalence of such behavior in ostensibly "normal" populations higher than the number of "cases" found in their subpopulations of diagnosed deviants. Most residual rule-breaking, it seems, is selectively inattended, ignored, denied, or regarded as having merely transitory significance. What distinguishes the "normal" rule-breaker from the "abnormal" one? Scheff's answer is based on an earlier idea suggested by Becker (1963): it is the *response* of the witnesses to the deviation. In the final analysis the causal attributions made by the witnesses (including perhaps the perpetrator of the act himself) in "explaining" the behavior establishes its degree of abnormality. This is essentially a matter of labeling. Beyond that, however, the response of others toward rule-breaking behavior also has hedonic significance for the rule-breaker. In most instances the "public" response to residual rule-breaking is, at best, indifference; often, we may surmise, it is (objectively) punitive. The usual response to rule-breaking would tend to discourage its recurrence. But what if the response were in some way "satisfying" (that is, provided an outcome well above CL) to the rule-breaker? Suppose, for ex-

[3] I am indebted to Thomas D. Cook for discussion which led to clarification of some of these ideas.

ample, it enabled him to enjoy a favored interpersonal position without incurring the possible costs involved in acknowledging that he was seeking that position. Or suppose the "value" of the position were directly enhanced by the stigmatizing and pejorative label of "abnormality." Or suppose, finally, that the desired position had characteristics so extreme that its attainment presupposed residual rule violation. Scheff's analysis does not emphasize the element of possible hedonic payoff accruing to the rule-breaker from the social response to his deviant behavior. It does, however, make a strong case for the *deviation-amplifying* character of much of the social feedback attending various kinds of residual rule-breaking—a type of feedback that may under certain conditions encourage the rule-breaker to launch a "career" as a mental patient.

The disordered person can thus be described as someone who breaks residual rules in such a spectacular and/or persistent way that it is impossible for others to ignore the rule-breaking, or to discover "normal" reasons for its occurrence. But how can we account for the persistence of a type of behavior that is normally (although not always) frowned upon and punished by the sundry other persons who are exposed to it? This question is absolutely basic, and is, in fact, tantamount to asking why personality disorder is not a self-limiting condition. Our answer must be obvious: the reactive punishment is somehow not experienced as being sufficiently costly to outweigh the overall outcomes accruing to the rule-breaker as a consequence of his rule-breaking behavior. The persistently disordered person's modal payoff matrix with the environment is one delivering *relatively* high outcomes to him for enacting particular kinds of rule-breaking behavior. In many cases the process can be conceived as a renunciation of modest tactical benefits in favor of superior strategical advantages.

It may be noted in this connection that acquisition of the label "mentally ill" is not invariably greeted as a major disaster by the person so labeled. For example, it is an excellent "cover story" for various types of rule-breaking ("it's not me who is doing this —it's my illness"), including that special variety associated with the violation of the terms of interpersonal contracts. "Copping out on the nut" is a legal tactic used by some delinquents and criminals. Some allegedly mentally ill persons, in other words, find this label useful in the employment of "Wooden Leg" (p. 194) tactics. The label is even functional in a certain sense for those unfortunate, confused persons who are residual rule-breakers because they never learned what the rules *are,* having grown up in weird family environments (see, for example, Lidz et al., 1958; Laing, 1965). Under these circumstances, *any* explanation for repeated failures in interpersonal relations might be eagerly grasped —even such an extreme one. Given society's need for a seemingly rational "explanation" of rule-breaking, there is sometimes an implicit collusion between the rule-breaker and society concerning the definition of what is going on between them. Unfortunately, the "sick" definition is one that in many instances encourages a continuation—or even an augmentation—of the difficulty.

To sum up, personality disorder may be described as a condition of residual rule-breaking in interpersonal behavior, where the rule-breaking is so extreme or persistent that it cannot be ignored or explained by reference to normal processes. It must be assumed that the experienced or anticipated outcomes accruing to the disordered person from his rule-breaking behavior are the best currently available to him, *despite* cost components that may be involved in a punitive environmental response; the *actual* punitiveness of such reactions (such as the labeling of the person as mentally ill), as experienced by the rule-breaker, is often not as great as it may appear to the external obserer.

THE SPECIFIC "CONTENT" OF DISORDERED BEHAVIOR

Granting that extreme and/or persistent residual rule-breaking in public is the common element or principle involved in the "diagnosis" of personality disorder, there remains a question of the distinctive forms such rule-breaking may take. We shall attempt a detailed cataloguing of disordered rule-breaking processes in a later section. At a general level, it may be noted here that most—if not all—disordered rule-breaking is associated with the achievement and maintenance of relatively extreme interpersonal positions in respect to real or imagined other persons. There is method in madness. Persons who are considered disordered do not typically rush about breaking rules in a random and haphazard fashion. On the contrary, the behavior of disordered persons exhibits regularity and individual distinctiveness in a manner similar to that of normal persons. In fact, the behavior of most disordered persons is extraordinarily regular, not to say rigid. In many instances, the rule-breaking is in concrete terms nothing more than a persistent rigidity or stereotypy of behavior, such that the person repeatedly enacts the same type of interpersonal behavior independent of its "appropriateness" to the circumstances. The behavior itself may be considered normal and unremarkable when it is displayed in contexts permitting "normal" causal attributions to be made concerning it—as when a person under attack by another produces aggressive behavior in response. It becomes an indication of personal disorder only when it is repeatedly enacted in situations where it does not "fit."

Many persons are thus identified as disordered because they seem "stuck" or "hung up" in the maintenance of a particular interpersonal stance, even though the behavior they display is not in itself considered especially notable. In other cases, a person is judged to be disordered because, in achieving a particular position, he displays behavior that is more or less intrinsically rule-breaking. The qualification "more or less" is inserted out of respect for the fact that *context* can be a factor in attributions made concerning even the most bizarre behavior. At any rate, some types of behavior are so devoid of "normal" explanations that the person enacting them is judged as disordered on the basis of a single occurrence. The popular, "unofficial" attributions of mental illness made immediately following the recent acts of assassination against public figures in the United States provide a noteworthy example. In most such instances, the attribution of abnormality is made principally on the basis of the norm-exceeding *intensity* or *amplitude* of the behavior. Qualitatively similar behavior (in terms of the interpersonal circle) of more modulated intensity is considered normal, unless of course it is repeatedly enacted under inappropriate circumstances. Rule-breaking in respect to behavioral intensity, on the one hand, and behavioral rigidity, on the other, appear to be moderately strongly correlated in the population at large, and so we should expect to find many disordered persons exhibiting both kinds of deviation.

We have seen throughout this book that a person's interpersonal behavior may profitably be conceived as being, in large measure, an attempt to assume a certain stance or occupy a certain position *vis-à-vis* other persons. His outcomes in that effort are conjointly determined by his own and the other's behavior. Is there any reason to believe that the situation is in any way different for disordered persons? I do not think so. The disordered person is distinguished only by the fact that he obtrusively breaks rules in gaining or maintaining interactions in optimum-outcome cells. Unless his "partners" are entirely imaginary and subject to his own whim, moreover, his outcomes are dependent upon his ability to induce them to limit *their* behavior to his best-outcome cells. He does so, in part, by breaking rules, attempting thereby to force the issue. If he is sufficiently desperate, he is usually able to find compliant partners, reluctant or otherwise. The willingness of the truly desperate person to break the rules gives him an enormous power advantage in obtaining the kinds of relationships he needs. If all else fails, he can, and sometimes does, commit suicide or retire to relationships with purely fantastic others who "interact" with him in ways that fulfill his needs. In connection with the latter, however, it must be remembered that *claiming* to have hallucinations is an excellent strategy for maintaining the degraded, masochistic interpersonal position associated with the "psychotic" or "insane" role. As was indicated earlier, the "volunteering" of such information may not be a completely reliable indication of reality.

Considered in terms of the interpersonal circle, it appears that any octant segment may come to represent a position preference of such overriding "attractiveness" to a person that he will break residual rules in order to obtain or maintain it. The position is usually one toward the outer (extreme behavior) rim of the circle, reflecting the great strength of the interpersonal needs commonly involved. A correspondingly intense form of complementary behavior from the other person would presumably have optimum outcome value, as a general rule. While any qualitative variety of interpersonal behavior can thus provide the "content" of a disordered condition, the actual, observed distribution of disorder is quite markedly out of balance in this respect. There is a pronounced tendency for disordered behavior to be involved chiefly with the Hateful and Submissive ranges of the circle. I would speculate that this is due in large part to the fact that, in our culture at least, residual rules relating to Hateful and Submissive behavior are more stringent (and therefore more readily broken) than those relating to other forms of behavior. The imbalance, in other words, may be an artifact of our conventions concerning proper social behavior.

Our analysis points to the following tentative definition of "personality disorder": *Personality disorder consists of the pursuit of a particular, stable interpersonal position in relation to real or imagined others in ways that publicly violate the residual rules of a culture.* The definition is regarded as tentative because its limits have by no means been adequately tested. Having been fashioned within the framework presented here, it is obviously bound by it. Ultimately, its value as a definition rests on the value of the conceptions from which it derives.

Causal Factors in Personality Disorder

Having delimited the field of inquiry, we may now move to a consideration of *why* certain individuals behave in a personally disordered way. Why do they break rules in establishing their positions in relationship to other persons? Clearly, a considerable degree of circumspection is called for in any attempt to answer this question. Proven facts are hard to come by in this field, which already abounds in fanciful, speculative, and doctrinaire pronouncements. I should not like to add measurably to the existing folklore, but on the other hand I do feel compelled to marshal some of the implications of our analysis in an attempt to gain perspective on the problem. Our discussion will focus upon more immediate causal factors in personality disorder. We shall largely ignore possible "remote" causes, such as childhood traumas, although I do not wish to imply thereby that I think they are irrelevant; I do suspect they have been overrated as determiners of current, adult disorder.

THE PROBLEM OF ANXIETY

It was suggested above that there is no reason to assume a special set of motivations for the disordered person's interpersonal behavior. He, like the rest of us, is trying to make the most out of the interaction matrixes available to him. While basically sound, this view of the situation requires some further elaboration in order to account for the special characteristics of disordered behavior. If preferred interactional styles (or interpersonal positions) are primarily instrumentalities of security maintenance, as has been argued at length, how much more urgent must the problem of security maintenance be for the disordered person, relative to the person who stays within the rules. This appears to be the core of the issue—the disordered person's security is so extremely vulnerable that he overplays (in repetitiveness and/or intensity) his principal devices for keeping it propped up. Insecurity, of course, is experienced phenomenologically as *anxiety*.

We have noted that anxiety is *not* personality disorder. There is no denying, however, that it is deeply implicated in most—if not all—instances of disorder. Freud (1936) considered anxiety to be the "central problem" of neurosis, and virtually all personality theorists since that time—including Sullivan—have given it a prominent place in their conceptions of disorder. Clinical experience with disordered persons amply justifies this conceptual prominence. They either *are* very anxious a good part of the time, or they can rapidly be made so by denying to them their favored positions. (The latter, by the way, usually requires considerably more skill and stamina than untrained persons are likely to possess; the disordered person, in his own special way, is frequently a "pro.") To put the matter very simply, it appears that the disordered person breaks rules in order to avoid or minimize the severe anxiety to which he is, for some reason, especially prone.

We should digress briefly at this point to clarify some possible sources of confusion concerning anxiety. Contemporary behavioral scientists use the term "anxiety" in at least two quite distinct ways, and it is important that you appreciate the difference. Spielberger and his students (Spielberger, 1966; Hodges, 1968; Johnson, 1968) have contributed notably to making the distinction clear. According to their analysis, one type of anxiety, *trait anxiety,* is a generalized disposition to respond to situations in an anxious way —especially situations in which self-esteem is threatened. Trait anxiety is measured by questionnaire items asking the subject how anxious he feels *generally.* I have argued elsewhere (Carson, 1969) that questionnaires of this type can most accurately and parsimoniously be interpreted as providing the subject with a structured opportunity for self-presentation: if he *says* he is an anxious person, what we know about him thereby is only that he is a person who says he is anxious. The correlates of a tendency to present oneself as an anxious person can be established through appropriate empirical investigation, but by no means should it be assumed on an *a priori* basis that *being* anxious a good part of the time is necessarily one of them. Support for the view that trait anxiety questionnaires measure something other than anxiety is provided by Kimble and Posnick (1967). These investigators found it rather easy to construct a questionnaire *devoid of items relating to anxiety* which nevertheless did an excellent job of predicting subjects' responses to the most widely used trait anxiety questionnaire. The items of their instrument have no anxiety content, but they do have grammatical structure, emotional intensity, and social (un-)acceptability comparable to those included in trait anxiety questionnaires. The common *functional* feature, it seems to me, is that the items provide the subject with an opportunity to portray himself in Self-effacing terms. In other words, I am suggesting that so-called trait anxiety is basically the same thing as the Self-effacing interpersonal stance. The trait anxiety questionnaire is merely a rough but structured way of quantifying it. It may indeed be true, as Spielberger and his associates contend, that the high trait anxiety person is "prone" to attacks of (real) anxiety; but that is merely a correlate, not the essence, of trait anxiety as it is typically measured.

Real anxiety, or what Spielberger calls the *anxiety state,* is operationally defined in terms of autonomic nervous system arousal *and* simultaneous reports of subjective tension and distress.[4] We are all more or less familiar with the phenomenological aspects of this state, and so there seems little need for me to attempt to convince you of how unpleasant it can be. It is practically indistinguishable from fright, and its most severe manifestations are therefore experienced as being akin to panic. It is this extreme level of anxiety state, presumably, that the disordered person attempts to avoid through his unusual interpersonal behavior. Use of the term "anxiety" in what follows should always be taken to mean the anxiety *state,* unless otherwise indicated.

ANXIETY (INSECURITY) AS THREAT TO SELF

What is the source of the anxiety or insecurity driving the disordered person to break rules in establishing his relationship to the social environment? Once again, there seems to be no reason to assume the processes involved are in any way unique or qualitatively different for the disordered person relative to his more fortunate fellows. We should expect that the disordered person is made anxious by the same sorts of things that make all of us anxious—but him more so. As we have seen, there are several possible ways of approaching this question of the sources of anxiety. It can be thought of as a type of conditioned response cued by certain stimulus configurations (including internally generated ones) impinging on the person's receptor apparatus. It can be conceived as a product of conflicting, frustrated, or interrupted Plans. Or finally it can be conceived as a special type of incongruency experience, especially one relating to the phenomenal Self. These varying conceptualizations, as has been noted, are not necessarily

[4] Subjective reports of tension and distress are, like responses to trait anxiety questionnaires, subject to the influence of self-presentational biases. This may complicate the interpretation of experimental findings. For example, it is conceivable that high trait anxiety subjects would *increase* their Self-effacement by reporting "state" anxiety under certain types of "ego threatening" conditions (for example, where enhanced performance is demanded of them). Inconsistent findings reported by Hodges (1968) can be interpreted in this manner.

mutually exclusive, and they appear to a large extent to be interchangeable as explanations of most instances of anxiety arousal in persons. Choosing among them becomes largely a matter of theoretical emphasis and the "level" of construct with which one may prefer to work. My own choice of the incongruency model in what follows results from a conviction of its superior integrating properties within the general framework that I have been trying to set forth.

Anxiety and Self-Congruence. You will recall that Sullivan postulated an intimate relationship between the experience of anxiety and the structural aspect of personality he called the *self dynamism* (see Chaper 2). Specifically, he held that the self dynamism—the repository of the individual's conceptions of himself as a person—develops as a means of controlling anxiety, largely through the control of awareness. Its governing principle is that of *consistency:* experiences consistent with the Self are security-enhancing and are admitted to awareness; experiences inconsistent with the Self are anxiety-producing and require defensive measures to diminish or obliterate their potentially noxious effects. For Sullivan, anxiety is the response of the person to becoming more or less aware of an incongruence between some current experience and the current contents of the self dynamism. Starting from a very different conceptual base, Rogers (1959) developed out of his own clinical experience a practically identical formulation.

> Anxiety is phenomenologically a state of uneasiness or tension whose cause is unknown. From an external frame of reference, anxiety is a state in which the incongruence between the concept of self and the total experience of the individual is approaching symbolization (representation) in awareness. When experience is *obviously* discrepant from the self-concept, a defensive response to threat becomes increasingly difficult. Anxiety is the response of the organism to the "subception" (discrimination without representation in awareness) that such discrepancy may enter awareness, thus forcing a change in the self-concept. (p. 204)

Generalizing from the conceptions of these two gifted clinicians, we may assume that the severe anxiety against which the disordered person appears to be defending himself is somehow related to the high level of threat posed to his Self-system by the experience he may encounter. Combining this with our earlier observations, we conclude that—*in general*—the disordered person is driven to break rules in the pursuit of particular interpersonal positions *vis-à-vis* others because any recognition by himself of his occupation of *other* positions would at the time constitute a serious violation of his Self-system, exposing him to anxiety. Why does the Self-system of the disordered person become so narrowly and rigidly constraining? I have pondered and combed the research literature for an answer to this question for several years, without coming to any very satisfactory or confidence-inspiring solution. Perhaps it is simply as Sullivan and Rogers, among others, have suggested—that the early life of the disordered person has been one in which the approval and disapproval of significant others (chiefly parents) was to an extraordinary degree conditional upon the child's exhibiting particular kinds of Self-defining interpersonal behavior.

THE SELF, ANXIETY, AND THE SECORD-BACKMAN THEORY

Consider once again the Secord and Backman (1961, 1965) theory of personality and interpersonal relations presented in Chapter 4 (pages 116–118). The central idea of this theory is that a state of tension is generated whenever there is a condition of imbalance or incongruence among some aspect of the person's phenomenal Self, relevant perceived aspects of his own behavior, and relevant perceived aspects of the behavior of another toward him. The "tension" Secord and Backman speak of is considered to be unpleasant, but they do not specifically identify it as anxiety. There seems little doubt that "cognitive" tensions of the sort they appear to have in mind do indeed exist, and that in many contexts such cognitive tensions are at best only remotely related to the *anxiety state* as conceived here. In the light of the above discussion, however, we shall make the assumption that the specific tension of anxiety is aroused whenever a condition of incongruity would constitute a significant threat to the Self, as in fact it usually would. The Self may be considered to be the "anchor" of the Self –own behavior–other's behavior triad, presumably being the element least subject to alteration.

Having made this integration of clinical Self theory with the Secord and Backman formulation, we are now in a position to use the latter as a system for cataloguing the various forms of rule-breaking in which disordered persons may engage in their efforts to maintain—at least phenomenologically—their Self-protective interpersonal positions.

Varieties of Residual Rule-Breaking

Secord and Backman (1965) identify and review the pertinent research relating to five processes utilized by persons in their efforts to achieve and maintain congruency in interpersonal relations. They are: (1) cognitive restructuring, (2) selective evaluation, (3) selective interaction, (4) evocation of congruent responses—as mentioned earlier—and (5) congruency by comparison. Secord and Backman are chiefly concerned with the "normal" use of these methods of congruency maintenance by persons who are not manifestly disordered. It would appear, however, that each of these methods can be employed "normally" only within a certain range of application. If that range is exceeded, residual rules are necessarily violated, and if the violation is severe and/or persistent, the violator will be considered disordered. I would suggest that the Secord and Backman listing of methods of congruency maintenance, while not necessarily exhaustive, includes all of the principal means whereby disordered persons, through excessive utilization, break the residual rules of their culture. Apparently inadvertently, these authors have provided us with a fresh perspective on "types" of processes underlying the more obvious and overt manifestations of personality disorder. An illustrative overview of rule-breaking in each of the five modes follows.

DISORDERED COGNITIVE RESTRUCTURING

As was noted in earlier chapters, the cognitive processes, including perception, are subject to influence from certain sources of bias. Motives arising from threats to the Self are one of the more important of such sources, calling into play processes of selective inattention and selective enhancement (distortions of category accessibility) that may seriously affect the formation of any cognitions having relevance for the Self. The person whose self-system is endangered by past, current, or anticipated interpersonal transactions may misinterpret various internal or external events so as to achieve a reassuring congruency and relieve the impending threat. He may "restructure" his cognitive representation of his own actions, the actions of the other, or the actions of *both* participants to bring them into line with his current Self. Should the misinterpretation be of a very gross order (lacking in consensual validity), and should it be revealed in an obtrusive manner to others, the person will be considered disordered. Relatively mild cognitive deviations may cause the person to be regarded as exhibiting "neurotic" manifestations, such as displacement, repression, parataxic distortion, transference, or the like. If he becomes markedly insistent about his peculiar version of reality, it will be considered "delusional," and he may thereby earn himself the label "psychotic" for his too-liberal trifling with rules concerning the rendering of consensually valid accounts of reality.

Cognitive restructuring on a scale that exceeds normal limits is an extremely common form of disordered behavior. It may be employed by the disordered person as his principal method of Self-protection or as an adjunct to other methods. Occasionally, social support for restructured cognitions is traded as an item in implicit interpersonal contracts of the negotiated maladjustment variety, as when one member of a dyad affirms the eccentric interpretations of the other in return for outcomes the other is capable of delivering to him. The latter is a frequent occurrence among the members of disturbed families, as suggested in the preceding chapter. Many forms of disordered cognitive restructuring essentially involve the formulation of invalid causal attributions to "explain" one's own behavior or that of the other.

DISORDERED SELECTIVE EVALUATION

The Self-threatening aspects of a state of incongruency may be mitigated to some degree by selectively enhancing the personal "value" of components of experience that are Self-congruent, and by selectively devaluing or derogating incongruent components. It may be surmised that in most instances the critical component to be enhanced or devalued is the other person and his behavior, depending upon whether or not they confirm or disconfirm the Self. There is a considerable amount of evidence, most of it reviewed by Secord and Backman (1965), that normal persons routinely practice selective evaluation of this kind in making value judgments about others. Significantly, the effect does not appear to be confined to the case in which the maintenance of a "favorable" self-concept is at issue; normal persons having a depreciated self-concept are apt to find substantial merit in persons who behave toward them in a depreciatory way, and to be relatively disparaging of those who display the opposite attitude. Even among normal persons, then, the need to maintain Self-congruency can override any needs for "positive" feedback from others.

Selective evaluation to the extent that residual rules are broken in the process is not an especially salient form of disordered behavior, partly because rules in this area tend to be lax ("to each his own" in the matter of tastes), and partly because it is rarely observed in isolation from other, more dramatic types of deviance. Its most common manifestation is probably the use of inappropriate or extreme forms of disparagement of the content or source of Self-threatening interpersonal communications. Many clinicians, for example, have noted that in working with schizophrenics they sometimes have the feeling that they are being "toyed with" and subtly ridiculed. Haley (1965) has been very explicit on this point, suggesting that the schizophrenic has acquired many devices for blunting by subtle derogation any suggestion that he can be treated as a rational and respect-worthy person. Consider the following brief conversation between a schizophrenic patient and two clinicians (Laffal, Lenkoski, and Ameen, 1956, p. 411):

Dr. X: Peter, I want to ask you something. I'm holding a pipe here in my hand. Do you see this pipe?

Patient: No.

Dr. X: Dr. Y, do you see this pipe?

Dr. Y: Yes, I see the pipe.

Dr. X: Peter, how is it when I show you the pipe, you say, no you don't see it, and Dr. Y says yes, he does see it. How is it he says yes and you say no?

Patient: Well . . . the doctor says he don't see it?

Dr. Y: I do see it.

Patient: You do see it?

Dr. X: What do you say, Peter?

Patient: I do see the pipe.

Dr. X: You do see the pipe?

Patient: Unnnhhh.

Dr. X: Now, wait, you tell me. I've got the pipe in my hand. Do you see the pipe?

Patient: Nope, I don't see it.

One is tempted to ask who is kidding whom in this exchange.[5]

[5] It should be noted that the excerpt quoted is from an interview in which the patient was supposedly under the influence of sodium amytal (sometimes inaccurately called "truth serum"); his behavior, as indicated here, was not substantially different from his behavior when not drugged. Laffal, Lenkoski, and Ameen use this and other observations to support their contention that the patient's "opposite speech" was inadvertent and unintentional, although they do note that it had the effect of producing "confusion and dismay in the listener" and of "reducing communication and effectively rejecting others" (p. 412). I do not find persuasive their case for the "automatic" nature of the disruptive behavior.

My opinion is that Peter wins hands down. By making patently preposterous responses to the doctors' doubtless well-intentioned (if somewhat patronizing) efforts to communicate with him *as though* he were sane, he devalues the apparently threatening implicit message that he is other than a degraded and wholly unreliable person. I suspect that much of the seemingly "crazy" behavior demonstrated by schizophrenics generally is at least in part Self-protective in the same fashion as is suggested here.

Psychotherapists are familiar with another type of disparagement of their efforts. Most "schools" of psychotherapy emphasize that the therapist should be warm, empathic, permissive, and nondirective toward his patient—that is, that he should occupy a position somewhat toward the Submissive pole in the Love semicircle. Most patients who are unsophisticated about psychotherapy initially find this confusing and distressing; their experience has been that you go to the doctor for direct advice and "management" of your condition, and that he provides these amenities in a straightforward, matter-of-fact way (assuming the Managerial position). Typically, the psychotherapy patient must be "taught" to assume sufficient initiative to place himself on a democratic footing with the therapist, and to tolerate a warm and personal relationship. Fortunately, many patients prove capable of doing so. A large proportion do not, because their security and self-systems are severely threatened by the position preferences of the therapist. Many persons from the lower social classes, for example, find this type of relationship with a middle-class therapist quite intolerable. It is probably fair to say that this remains one of the great unsolved problems of psychotherapy. Many persons who could doubtless benefit from psychotherapy find it so threatening that they disparage therapy and the therapist, and they terminate the relationship before it effectively begins. To the extent that disregard of competent professional advice is rule-breaking, such relationship-disrupting behavior might itself be considered disordered. Of course, it is the responsibility of professional psychotherapists to seek some means of coping with this serious problem.

DISORDERED SELECTIVE INTERACTION

Self-congruity may be maintained or enhanced by attempting to limit one's interactions with others to persons whose behavior is Self-confirmatory. Such selective interaction is again a common feature of the everyday life of normal persons, as seen in the free choices made by persons in deciding with whom to interact. It is frequently augmented, as we have seen, through the adoption of formal social roles that encourage complementary behavior in one's role-partners. Incongruent interactions produce outcome decrements that tend rapidly to fall below CL_{alt}, terminating the relationship. Quite obviously, it is possible for interaction selectivity to become so extreme or stringent that it constitutes a violation of residual rules. Severe, rule-breaking constriction of the range of the person's interactions is a common means of defending against marked self-system vulnerability.

The most dramatic form of disordered selective interaction is undoubtedly that in which the person terminates his relationships with real others and engages virtually exclusively in interaction with the products of his own fantasy. Apparently, these interactions can become so vivid and compelling that they lose their *as if* quality and are experienced as real, as in hallucinations. In these fantastic relationships the person presumably "enjoys" positions that are either unavailable or available only at an unbearable cost to the Self in his interaction matrixes with real persons. Thus, the person may fancy himself as being pursued by homosexual seducers, where any seeking of the same or a similar "position" in real life might violate the self-system and induce panic. White (1964) provides an instructive example of the process in an excerpt from the writings of an intelligent, chronically schizophrenic patient:

> There is . . . a large unconscious male person who is suspended upright by straps, framework, etc., and who is also "tied up" to the writer by . . . strange "soul connections." Whatever sensation this male person is caused to feel, the writer himself feels just as strongly. By causing the closed

> fingers of the said male person's hand to spread apart, the writer's fingers are thereby also made to spread apart against the writer's will. By manipulating his magnetic hands near the genitals of the said male person, a pursuer is able to give both the male person and the writer involuntary erections of the penis. This has been of frequent occurrence. Such business must be stopped. (p. 78)

One may reasonably doubt the sincerity of this patient's protestations concerning the activities of his tormentors, but there is essentially no doubt at all that he has exercised a rather drastic and rule-breaking "selection" in respect to his interaction partners. It may be noted in passing that his decision to "publish" an account of these strange interactions affects in certain predictable ways the character of his relationships with *real* persons. I think it is profitable to assume that he was aware of this, and that it constitutes selective interaction of a slightly different sort—with mental hospital personnel; the Masochistic *position,* however, is retained.

Many instances of disordered selective interaction are not so extreme as to involve a preponderance of social intercourse with purely imaginary others. The others may be real enough, but so severely circumscribed as to acceptable characteristics that the person's social life is for the most part limited to a very few relationships, perhaps just within his immediate family, or within some type of *total institution* (Goffman, 1962), such as a mental hospital or prison. The person cannot risk the uncertainty of other relationships, where there may be pressure for him to adopt a Self-incongruent position. In effect, such a person is rendered extremely dependent upon the Self-confirming relationships he does have. Clinical experience suggests that this sort of pattern is a frequent causal element in many so-called *phobias,* including the not uncommon school variety found in children. The phobic person may so restrict the range of his interactions with others that he becomes essentially incapacitated, exhibiting—or at any rate claiming—various irrational fears. An unbiased functional analysis of these fears often reveals that they prevent the person from abandoning, even temporarily, the secure confines of a strongly Self-confirming relationship. The presence of some source of urgent temptation to do so seems to be an underlying factor in many of these cases; for example, a housewife attracted to (but repelled by) the prospect of being "picked up" by strange men might develop fears of inconsequential characteristics of the outside environment—fears that keep her confined to the home.

Disordered selective interaction, needless to say, often occurs under the auspices of unilateral or bilateral negotiated maladjustment contracts. The frequently intense interdependencies involved in these relationships encourage the development of implicit norms that serve to regulate loyalty and outcome distribution.

DISORDERED EVOCATION OF CONGRUENT RESPONSES

We have already given considerable attention to the evocation of congruent responses by both normal and rule-breaking means, and so we shall deal with it here in a more cursory manner than its importance would otherwise merit. Based in large part upon the *power* (outcome control) deriving from complementarity pressures, congruent response evocation may be regarded as the basic method of congruency maintenance for disordered as well as for normal persons. It is extensively and consistently employed by both groups in their efforts at Self-confirmation.

In its normal form it is a marvelously suave mechanism whereby the other person is led to offer, more or less voluntarily, a class of social responses that supports and confirms the interpersonal position claimed by the initiator. Unless the interests of the two parties are markedly discrepant—as they perhaps would be only in the event of a direct clash of anticomplementary position preferences—a smooth and relatively unforced articulation can usually be achieved; neither person is absolutely and unswervingly committed to his most preferred stance. The *disordered* form of congruent response evocation occurs where at least one of the parties *does* have such a commitment. Here, the methods employed to evoke a confirming response are likely to have a more grim and compelling nature, and the options of the other person are correspondingly reduced. The disordered person, by breaking the rules, literally forces the other into a narrowly complementary, relationship-confirming stance. The intensity and/or rigidity of his behavioral insistence tends to preclude a "negotiated" settlement concerning the differential positions to be occupied by himself and the other. The other person's only available alternative, should his own Self be threatened by the demand made upon him, may be to escape from the relationship—which is one of the reasons why disordered persons are not noted for the large number of voluntary friendships they are able to sustain.

The disordered person's efforts to enforce congruent responses may be manifested in specific "symptomatic" behaviors as well as in an unduly vigorous enactment of a particular, generalized interpersonal style. We have already seen how phobic symptoms can function in strategies of selective interaction; they also, of course, embody a message of incapacity and helplessness and may therefore have the tactical function of evoking care-taking behavior in the other. Certain forms of so-called obsessional neurosis, in which the person may do little else but express indecision and worry about trivial matters, seem to have a similar functional significance. A more sinister variant of symptomatic obsessionalism occurs where the expressed worries and doubts essentially represent a lead-in to a "Why Don't You—Yes But" reversal, the victim being conned into an involuntary confirmation of the reverser's Narcissistic stance. "Hysterical" symptoms, as has been noted at length, are frequently directly interpretable as interpersonal position ploys. In short, many of the specific types of symptoms traditionally associated with the class of disorders known as neurosis function as devices for evoking congruent responses, a function notably enhanced by the commonly held belief that these "symptom"-like rule violations must be a manifestation of illness and are therefore utterly involuntary. The traditional view of such symptomatic behaviors emphasizes their supposed "primary gain" in reducing internal motivational conflicts and tends to give small recognition to the "secondary gain" emphasized in the more thoroughgoing interpersonal approach taken here. The limits of the interpersonal approach to neurotic symptoms are not precisely known at this time, and it must be acknowledged that certain types of classical (although actually quite rare) symptomatic behaviors—such as compulsive hand-washing—are not readily accounted for in any obvious way within a strictly interpersonal framework. In general, however, it can be said that the analysis of specific neurotic symptoms in terms of their interpersonal functions will often yield data essential to their full understanding.

As has been noted, *any* interpersonal position can come to assume sufficient importance for a person that he will break residual rules in order to occupy it. While the rules are more likely to be violated in respect to attainment of positions in the Hate and Submissive sectors of the interpersonal circle, even position preferences within the Friendly-Dominant quadrant (Managerial and Responsible positions) are occasionally so extreme as to lead to recognizably deviant behavior—usually in the form of disordered attempts at congruent response evocation. The person becomes so intensely Autocratic or Hypernormal that he violates uncodified rules relating to acceptable and proper Friendly-Dominant behavior. Now, note that the violation of rules *in itself* constitutes a powerful interpersonal message of a certain type—namely, a Rebellious-Distrustful one. Such manifestations of Rebellion-Distrust tend to evoke the relevant complementary response of punishment and rejection from others. Thus, the person enacting an inappropriately intense level of Hypernormality in the hope of forcing a Self-confirming response of appreciation and trust runs a risk of receiving instead a specifically disconfirming response of punitive rejection. The general point is that disordered behavior of any form tends to produce a uniform, "higher order" response of punitive rejection specific to the disordered person's incidental occupation of a Rebellious-Distrustful position. In many instances of disorder, of course, occupation of the Rebellious-Distrustful position is not entirely incidental, but is rather the person's basic position preference; in such cases the response to his rule-breaking per se is merely an additional source of confirmatory feedback. Where the person is basically seeking another type of feedback, however, his inadvertent and simultaneous assumption of a Rebellious-Distrustful stance may produce a response quite rudely shocking to him, so much so that he may alter his rule-breaking behavior. This analysis would lead to the prediction that disorders in which the social feedback from rule-breaking is compatible with the apparent position preference of the person will be more intractable and persistent than those in which it is not. The prediction appears to be amply confirmed in the "prognoses" attaching to various forms of disordered behavior. With rare exception, the most chronic of the personality disorders have been found to be those in which the person characteristically occupies a position in the lower left quadrant of the interpersonal circle.

DISORDERED SOCIAL COMPARISON

Incongruent information concerning the Self may be subjected to a transformation of meaning through social comparison processes. In its most common form, this is accomplished via a cognitively engineered displacement of the subjective scale used to make judgments about one's own characteristics relative to those of others, shifting the scale as needed in order to move its "normal" or "average" point to the location yielding a maximally congruent interpretation of Self-relevant information. Thus, Bramel (1962) has shown that normal subjects deceived into believing that they have latent homosexual tendencies may react by attributing comparable tendencies to others. Disordered social comparison, which is perhaps best seen as a special class of disordered cognitive restructuring, occurs where the Self-protective attributions "projected" onto others take on a distinctly irrational and rule-breaking flavor—that is, where the attributions are devoid of consensual validity.

The most familiar, although not necessarily the most frequent, variety of disordered social comparison involves the excessive attribution of "bad" characteristics to others so that, by comparison, one's own characteristics stand out as admirable. The pronounced misanthropy and "injustice detection" of certain so-called "paranoid" individuals, which are often accompanied by excessive claims of personal moral virtue, provide an illustrative case in point; the person employs a distorted type of social comparison in propping up his Narcissistic position. There is a reverse version of the same process that often escapes attention, where the person exaggerates the "goodness" of others in order to highlight the completeness of his own "failure." Thus, a person driven to the depths of a Masochistic stance may come to the conclusion that he is the "greatest sinner the world has ever known" on the basis of having engaged in some mildly questionable or unethical behavior.

THE UNITY OF PERSONALITY DISORDER

It has been convenient in the immediately preceding discussion to deal separately with the several ways in which persons may manifest personality disorder. It should be clear, however, that the processes described are not mutually exclusive ones, nor are they even entirely distinguishable conceptually. To at least as great a degree as the normal person, the disordered person may be expected to use whatever resources he has at his disposal to enhance and maintain his security when it is threatened; we should expect to see him employ simultaneously and in various degrees and combinations all of the methods of incongruency reduction described here, and possibly others. Total mobilization is the typical response to serious threats to the Self. This total mobilization, moreover, tends also to be a unified one. The seriously threatened person does not suddenly relinquish his needs to maintain consistency among his feelings, cognitions, and behaviors. As a result, we continue to see strains toward consistency such that rule violations in, let us say, the behavioral domain tend to encourage corresponding rule violations in the cognitive and affective domains. Similarly, a Self-protective cognitive restructuring—perhaps one involving the intrusion of old personifications in the formation of current impressions of another person—would be expected to reflect itself in feelings and behavior directed toward that person. While a certain amount of "disorganization" is sometimes seen in the earliest phases of a disordered condition, a substantial degree of integration and order in the maintenance of a particular position is the much more typical picture; of course, much of this integration is achieved at the expense of rule violation.

Disordered Social Systems

Our attention to this point has been focused on the disordered person as an *individual* who breaks cultural rules in order to maintain an intact Self. We have emphasized throughout his frequent need for partners who can be induced or forced to provide Self-confirming social responses, and his recourse to rule-breaking in order to generate such responses, or a reasonable facsimile thereof. The partners, insofar as they are real persons, are themselves typically followers of the rules, and they cooperate in the disordered person's Plans only inadvertently or reluctantly. In short, with certain exceptions, we have tended to portray the disordered person as a kind of lone rebel. This is probably an accurate portrayal for the majority of cases, but evidence of "collaboration" is nevertheless observed with sufficient frequency to require some additional comment.

The negotiated maladjustment contract—an interpersonal agreement whose terms *call for* rule-breaking by at least one of the contractors—has already been described at some length. I wish here merely to call attention to the fact that the negotiated maladjustment contract represents, in effect, an agreement that one or more residual rules *will not apply* within the relationship, and that certain peculiar ad hoc norms will be substituted for them. For example, one of the more common forms of negotiated maladjustment involves an agreement to falsify jointly some aspect of reality by denying its existence or distorting its meaning. We saw an example of this type of shared rule-suppression in the preceding chapter, where the parents of a young man negotiated an agreement to interpret his 13-month, mute withdrawal as anger at the nurses. This process is often described as *masking* (Spiegel, 1957) in the technical literature. The concept of *disordered social system* applies generally to any situation in which two or more persons develop a relationship governed by substitutive norms that stand in opposition to the residual rules of their culture.

DISTURBED FAMILIES AS DISORDERED SOCIAL SYSTEMS

Brief mention was made earlier of the phenomenon of rule-breaking caused by ignorance of the rules. At first blush, it may seem somewhat incredible that a person—even an unintelligent one—could fail to learn these basic lessons of acculturation; educational opportunities in this area are, after all, extremely insistent and pervasive. The evidence indicates, however, that it is *not* exceptionally rare for a person to be born into a family whose own "residual rules" in respect to various matters bear but little resemblance to those obtaining in the "outside world." A child growing up in a family of this kind will have conceptions of the real and the decent that are different from those of the larger culture, and as he moves out into the larger culture, his "autistic" ways will shortly be noted and will generate punitive and rejecting responses from others. Ignorant of the reasons for this harsh treatment, such a person becomes increasingly frightened, perplexed, and confused. His attempts to achieve cognitive clarity, limited as they are by his peculiar modes of thought, only increase his estrangement from the reality of others. Not infrequently, a sequence of events of this sort results in the person's incarceration in a mental hospital, typically with a diagnosis of schizophrenia.

The process whereby a disturbed family socializes a child in terms of a peculiar system of residual rules is described by Lidz and his colleagues (Lidz, Cornelison, Terry, and Fleck, 1958) as "the transmission of irrationality," and by Laing (1965) as "mystification." The tendency for such processes to be implicated in the development of at least certain types of so-called schizophrenic reactions is underscored in the flat assertion made by Laing that, *"we have never yet seen a preschizophrenic who was not in a highly mystified state before his or her manifest psychotic breakdown"* (p. 360; Laing's italics). The bizarre lengths to which the reinterpretation of reality may be taken in these families is well illustrated in a case reported by Lidz et al. (1958). It involves a set of identical twin boys, both of whom became schizophrenic in young manhood. Among the many peculiarities of cognition and behavior exhibited by these twins, they both thought that "constipation meant disagreeing with mother." The source of this odd definition of constipation is found in one of the many bizarre maternal practices of their singularly devoted (but disordered) mother: "Whenever one of [the twins] would argue with her, she would say they were constipated and needed an enema; both boys were then placed prone on the bathroom floor naked while the mother, in her undergarments, inserted the nozzle in each boy, fostering a contest to see which could hold out longer—the loser having to dash down to the basement lavatory" (p. 309).

The substitution within smaller social systems of idiosyncratic rules for the residual rules operating in the larger culture probably in most instances serves definite motivational purposes. Thus, the substitute rules sometimes adopted in disturbed families seem to be fabricated in response to the Self-protective needs of one or both of the parents. The disordered cognitive restructurings of these threatened parents become accepted within the family as rules relating to the nature of reality, as in the case of the "skewed" families briefly described in the preceding chapter (page 212). The mother of the twins alluded to above organized her own life and that of her family around the idea that she was the beloved mother, protector, and apologist of boys of incredible "genius," a self-image whose maintenance required very elaborate tinkering with cultural definitions of reality. In this fashion, then, the Self-protective cognitive restructuring of parents may be visited upon children in the form of a distorted appreciation of the residual rules of the culture outside of the family. The child, who may be "well adjusted" *within* the family, is a behavioral anomaly outside of it.

The person who persistently breaks residual rules primarily because of his ignorance of them is disordered in a fundamentally different way from the person who, knowing the rules, nevertheless is driven to reject them as a source of control over his public behavior. Unfortunately, however, the response of society—including all too frequently that segment of it representing the mental health professions—is usually undifferentiated in this respect. As a result, the confused, "innocent" rule-breaker, who may be as yet uncommitted to a particular stance toward the world, is quite literally forced into one by the punitive rejection of his extra-familial environment. In time he becomes markedly committed to a position within the narrow range left open to him—that is, within the Hostile-Submissive quadrant—and in due course his behavior becomes indistinguishable from that of persons whose Selves were originally shaped in this direction. The "last stop" in the sequence is the mental hospital, where, after a few years of residence, the behavior of all of the inmates is pretty much the same; this uniform "adaptation" may be described as quiet Hostile-Submission.

The powerful and extraordinarily uniform behavioral effects of mental hospitalization raise an interesting set of questions that are directly related to our immediate concern. Let us have a closer look at this type of institution.

LARGER DISORDERED SOCIAL SYSTEMS

The disturbed family is only one of several varieties of social systems in which substitutive norms in opposition to the norms of the larger culture are likely to develop. In general, *any* component social system that is cut off from intimate contact with its surrounding culture may evolve a network of deviant norms. Extreme, sustained cultural isolation is characteristic of those social systems meriting designation as *total institutions.* A total institution, according to Goffman (1962), is "a place of residence and work where a large number of like-situated individuals, cut off from the larger society for an appreciable period of time, together lead an enclosed, formally administered round of life" (p. xiii). Two highly typical specimens of such total institutions are prisons and —ironically—mental hospitals. In the case of prisons, it is well known that the social norms tending to evolve in them are often inimical to those of the larger society, and that a thorough socialization into the prison culture is apt to make one ill fitted to life outside of it. These observations have come to be accepted as truisms, even among prison officials. Of course, an appreciable stay in prison does not usually produce a *disordered* person, but only a more confirmed criminal; prison norms do not in the main replace society's *residual* rules, but rather its codified ones relating to acceptable modes of property acquisition and to the grosser aspects of interpersonal conduct. Criminality, while widely condemned, is rarely regarded as an unintelligible, irrational way of life; and a training program that increases commitment to and expertise in criminal activities does not thereby enhance the likelihood of residual rule-breaking. But what would you say of a training program that increased commitment to and expertise in the role of "mental patient"? I have little doubt that mental hospitals often produce this result.

The term "often" in the preceding sentence is meant to be taken quite literally. I believe that the result referred to is a common and frequent consequence of mental hospitalization, but it is by no means universal. There are numerous mental hospitals—especially among those remaining closely integrated within their supporting communities—that do a very good job of meeting their obligations to their patients and to society. Moreover, the number of truly effective institutional facilities for the care of disordered persons has increased dramatically in recent years as a result of changing viewpoints on the nature of the problem. We may hope that these changes, which are largely in the direction of the interpersonal perspective advocated here, will continue. As of the moment, however, we have a very long way to go. A visit to the "back wards" (often euphemistically known as "continued treatment," as opposed to "acute" or "admission," wards) of almost any state mental hospital will rapidly correct any undue complacency the reader may harbor on this score. The *deviation-amplifying* mental hospital, like the deviation-amplifying prison, is still very much with us. When we recognize that approximately half of all of the hospital beds in the United States are occupied by disturbed persons, the full impact of our past failures strikes us with telling force.

We cannot attempt here to catalogue and discuss all of the many ways in which the culture of the old-style, "unreformed" (but regrettably still modal) mental hospital encourages a continuation, if not an augmentation, of the disorders of a substantial proportion of its patients. That task has been competently discharged by a number of investigators, among them Goffman (1962), Belknap (1956), Caudill (1958), Dunham and Weinberg (1960), and Scheff (1966), and even by such knowledgeable popular writers as Mary Jane Ward (1955) and Ken Kesey (1962). It may suffice to note what is in many ways the most striking characteristic of such places—one to which brief allusion was made above. It is the monolithic homogenization of experience afforded the inmates, an experience embodying a peculiar and disabling system of reward and cost contingencies. The evidence suggests that acquired behavioral adaptation to the generalized payoff matrix of the typical inmate of one of these institutions would have for anyone the consequence of insuring that he would be disordered by the standards of the outside culture. The homogenized experience results, in time, in homogenized human products; most of the long-termers are (or at any rate feel) incapable of living outside of the microculture of the hospital, *despite* their no longer showing evidence of the type of disordered behavior for which they were originally incarcerated. Continuous occupation of a norm-sanctioned interpersonal position of degradation produces, finally, corresponding and highly destructive changes in the Self. Goffman (1962) comments on this process as follows:

> Persons who become mental-hospital patients vary widely in the kind and degree of illness that a psychiatrist would impute to them, and in the attributes by which laymen would describe them. But once started on the way, they are confronted by some importantly similar circumstances and respond to these in some importantly similar ways. Since these similarities do not come from mental illness, they would seem to occur in spite of it. It is thus a tribute to the power of social forces that the uniform status of mental patient cannot only assure an aggregate of persons a common fate and eventually, because of this, a common character, but that this social reworking can be done upon what is perhaps the most obstinate diversity of human material that can be brought together by society. (p. 129)

In summary, the present section has attempted to show that, while most personality disorder may be construed as a primary, unmediated violation of the residual rules of society, *some* instances of disorder are best seen as an adaptation to peculiar norms interposed between the individual and the rules of the larger culture in which he lives. That we should find conditions of this sort in mental hospitals is one of the more poignant tragedies of our era.

REFERENCES

ADAMS, H. B. "Mental illness" or interpersonal behavior? *American Psychologist*, 1964, **19**, 191–97.

ARTISS, K. L. (Ed.). *The symptom as communication in schizophrenia.* New York: Grune & Stratton, 1959.

BECKER, H. S. *Outsiders.* New York: Free Press, 1963.

BELKNAP, I. *Human problems of a state mental hospital.* New York: McGraw-Hill, 1956.

BRAGINSKY, B. M., and BRAGINSKY, D. D. Schizophrenic patients in the psychiatric interview: An experimental study of their effectiveness at manipulation. *Journal of Consulting Psychology*, 1967, **31**, 543–47.

BRAGINSKY, B. M., GROSSE, M., and RING, K. Controlling outcomes through impression-management: An experimental study of the manipulative tactics of mental patients. *Journal of Consulting Psychology*, 1966, **30**, 295–300.

BRAGINSKY, B. M., HOLZBERG, J., FINISON, L., and RING, K. Correlates of the mental patient's acquisition of hospital information. *Journal of Personality*, 1967, **35**, 323–42.

BRAGINSKY, B. M., HOLZBERG, J., RIDLEY, D., and BRAGINSKY, D. D. Patient styles of adaptation to a mental hospital. *Journal of Personality*, 1968, **36**, 283–98.

BRAMEL, D. A. A dissonance theory approach to defensive projection. *Journal of Abnormal and Social Psychology*, 1962, **64**, 121–29.

CARSON, R. C. Issues in the teaching of clinical MMPI interpretation. In J. BUTCHER (Ed.), *MMPI: Research developments and clinical applications.* New York: McGraw-Hill, 1969. Pp. 41–53.

CAUDILL, W. *The psychiatric hospital as a small society.* Cambridge, Mass.: Harvard University Press, 1958.

DUNHAM, H. W., and WEINBERG, S. K. *The culture of the state mental hospital.* Detroit: Wayne State University Press, 1960.

EYSENCK, H. J. The outcome problem in psychotherapy: A reply. *Psychotherapy*, 1964, **1**, 97–100.

FONTANA, A. F., and KLEIN, E. B. Self-presentation and the schizophrenic "deficit." *Journal of Consulting and Clinical Psychology*, 1968, **32**, 250–56.

FREUD, S. *The problem of anxiety.* New York: W. W. Norton, 1936.

GOFFMAN, E. *Asylums.* Chicago: Aldine Publishing Company, 1962.

HALEY, J. The art of being schizophrenic. *Voices*, 1965, **1**, 133–47.

HODGES, W. F. Effects of ego threat and threat of pain on state anxiety. *Journal of Personality and Social Psychology*, 1968, **8**, 364–72.

JOHNSON, D. T. Effects of interview stress on measures of state and trait anxiety. *Journal of Abnormal Psychology*, 1968, **73**, 245–51.

KELLEY, H. H. Attribution theory in social psychology. In D. LEVINE (Ed.), *Nebrasku symposium on motivation, 1967*. Lincoln, Neb.: University of Nebraska Press, 1967. Pp. 192–238.

KESEY, K. *One flew over the cuckoo's nest*. New York: Viking Press, 1962.

KIMBLE, G. A., and POSNICK, G. M. Anxiety? *Journal of Personality and Social Psychology*, 1967, **7**, 108–10.

LAFFAL, J., LENKOSKI, D., and AMEEN, L. Case report: "Opposite speech" in a schizophrenic patient. *Journal of Abnormal and Social Psychology*, 1956, **52**, 409–13.

LAING, R. D. Mystification, confusion, and conflict. In I. BOSZORMENYI-NAGY and J. L. FRAMO (Eds.), *Intensive family therapy*. New York: Harper & Row, 1965. Pp. 343–63.

LIDZ, T., CORNELISON, A., TERRY, D., and FLECK, S. Intrafamilial environment of the schizophrenic patient: VI. The transmission of irrationality. *A.M.A. Archives of Neurology & Psychiatry*, 1958, **79**, 305–16.

MAHER, B. A. *Principles of psychopathology*. New York: McGraw-Hill, 1966.

ROGERS, C. R. A theory of therapy, personality, and interpersonal relationships, as developed in the client-centered framework. In S. KOCH (Ed.), *Psychology: A study of a science*, Volume 3. New York: McGraw-Hill, 1959. Pp. 184–256.

SARBIN, T. R. On the futility of the proposition that some people should be labeled "mentally ill." *Journal of Consulting Psychology*, 1967, **31**, 447–53.

SCHEFF, T. J. *Being mentally ill*. Chicago: Aldine Publishing Company, 1966.

SCHOFIELD, W. *Psychotherapy: The purchase of friendship*. Englewood Cliffs, N.J.: Prentice-Hall, 1964.

SECORD, P. F., and BACKMAN, C. W. Personality theory and the problem of stability and change in individual behavior: An interpersonal approach. *Psychological Review*, 1961, **68**, 21–32.

SECORD, P. F., and BACKMAN, C. W. An interpersonal approach to personality. In B. A. MAHER (Ed.), *Progress in experimental personality research*, Volume 2. New York: Academic Press, 1965. Pp. 91–125.

SPIEGEL, J. P. The resolution of role conflict within the family. *Psychiatry*, 1957, **20**, 1–16.

SPIELBERGER, C. D. Theory and research on anxiety. In C. D. SPIELBERGER (Ed.), *Anxiety and behavior*. New York: Academic Press, 1966. Pp. 3–20.

STRUPP, H. H. The outcome problem in psychotherapy revisited. *Psychotherapy*, 1963, **1**, 1–13.

SZASZ, T. S. *The myth of mental illness*. New York: Hoeber-Harper, 1961.

SZASZ, T. S. *Law, liberty, and psychiatry*. New York: Macmillan, 1963.

WARD, MARY JANE. *The snake pit*. New York: New American Library, 1955.

WHITE, R. W. *The abnormal personality*. New York: Ronald, 1964.

CHAPTER 8

Psychotherapy: Disorder-Reducing Interpersonal Relationships

I approach the writing of this last chapter of the book with considerable trepidation. The various processes commonly included under the rubric of "psychotherapy" have been my major intellectual and professional preoccupation for more than a decade. However, despite my fairly intimate acquaintance with this field—and perhaps I should say *because* of it—I find the task of trying to communicate about it to a relatively neophyte audience very nearly overwhelming. I am not suggesting that I think there is anything arcane or mysterious about the process of inducing constructive personality change; on the contrary, my conviction is that it will turn out to be a quite straightforward matter. At this time, though, there is much that we do not know about it. Dispassionate and precise scientific inquiry is not easily achieved in an area in which questions about the fundamental nature of man are as deeply embedded in the texture of the problem as they are here.

At one time it seemed likely that the existing confusions in the field would be handled as they have been by those committed to a religious interpretation of human life—that is, by the creation of separate schools of thought based upon doctrinal, dogmatic authority. While the new wave of so-called "behavior therapy" [1] has shown some tendencies in this direction, as evidenced primarily by somewhat shrill and emotional attacks on opposing points of view (see, for example, Rachman and Eysenck, 1966; Wolpe, Salter, and Reyna, 1964), there are increasing signs that we have begun to emerge from the long night of psychotherapeutic dogma. Rogers (1963), himself the unwilling founder of one such sect, has commented on this as follows:

> I believe that the present variations in thought and practice mean that the day of systems, of schools of thought, of dogma, is over. Institutions and organizations which indoctrinate therapists in one point of view only are pure anachronisms in today's situation. I do not say this casually. I believe that psychoanalytic institutes—of whatever brand—with their cultish type of training, are on the way out. I would say exactly the same about university departments which expose their students only to training in client-centered [that is, Rogers' own framework] therapy, or in any other single approach to therapy. I know how hardy organizations are . . . but I believe their day of vital influence on thoughtful individuals is past. (p. 13)

[1] For readers who may be unfamiliar with this term, behavior therapy encompasses a number of procedures representing more or less direct applications of S-R learning theory to behavior retraining. The focus is on the modification of specific "responses" by the systematic manipulation of "stimuli." There are two general classes of behavior therapy, one based on association learning and the other on instrumental learning. The former is chiefly concerned with the extinction or counterconditioning of "anxiety responses" to particular cues. The latter attempts to alter specific overt behaviors by the use of "contingent reinforcement," the reinforcements used being typically of a rather crass nature—such as candy, cigarettes, electric shocks, explicit social approval, and so forth.

As these remarks suggest, there is at the present time no single, well-defined set of techniques utilized by psychotherapists in their efforts to help disturbed individuals. The abandonment of dogma has not been attended by a notable increase in firmly established knowledge. With exceptions, today's psychotherapist is a pragmatist of the first order; he uses whatever seems to him to "work." Good enough, but what are the techniques that work? Psychotherapists have many differing opinions, couched in many differing conceptual languages, concerning this question. Only rarely, however, can they point to any reliable evidence that they are correct. It has proven extraordinarily difficult to research the question of the efficacy of psychotherapeutic techniques with any degree of adequacy. Unqualified generalizations about the effectiveness or ineffectiveness of psychotherapy are therefore improper, although they have occasionally been made. We now know that there is an enormously complex array of contingencies that determine the outcome of any psychotherapeutic endeavor. Simplistic answers to simplistically formulated questions have not been and are not likely to be helpful in this field.

Even the most astute investigator of the present era finds research in psychotherapy a frustratingly intricate venture. Among other sources of difficulty, the very nature of the research task is commonly misunderstood. As in the more general case of personality disorder, a certain mythology has evolved concerning psychotherapy and psychotherapy research. Kiesler (1966) has provided an excellent and penetrating analysis of this mythology, one that we hope will be taken seriously by future investigators. Three of the common myths identified by Kiesler have been especially troublesome. They are the myths that psychotherapy clients constitute a homogeneous class of persons, that psychotherapists provide their clients with a homogeneous type of experience, and that a majority of "neurotic" persons experience "spontaneous remissions" of their difficulties within a brief period after their onset, in the absence of any therapy. (Thus, it is sometimes held that a therapeutic procedure, in order to be judged "effective," must produce a rate of improvement in excess of the alleged 60–70 percent spontaneous remission rate.) The first two of these propositions are patently false. The third may be traced primarily to a certain irresponsible and wholly unwarranted interpretation placed on the disability claims records of an insurance company, a curious source for obtaining supposedly "objective" information on recovery from disability. However, vigorous promulgation in the professional literature of this exceedingly optimistic outlook on spontaneous recovery from disorder has resulted in its gaining a stubbornly persistent credence in some circles.[2]

Psychotherapy clients present an enormous diversity of problems to their therapists, who in turn perform a variety of procedures in their efforts to help. Granting that we cannot usually specify with assurance the critical therapeutic factor(s), are clients ever helped by their encounters with psychotherapists? The answer is definitely *yes*—sometimes. But it appears to be also true that a client can be affected *adversely* by his experience with a therapist. This is one of the difficulties of attempting to research therapeutic outcomes. If some of the clients get "better" and some get "worse," the net or average effect in relation to an untreated control group may be nil. Obviously the conclusion that the therapy had been "ineffective" in such a circumstance would be something of a distortion. The reference work here is that of Bergin (1966). Bergin reexamines the data of seven of the better, controlled studies of psychotherapeutic outcome and emerges with the rather startling (and sobering) conclusion that *in every case* some of the treated clients improved and some "deteriorated," in contrast to untreated controls. Bergin goes on to note that untreated controls frequently show modest improvement themselves, but that this can often be accounted for by their establishing other, quasi-therapeutic relationships (with clergymen, physicians, and so forth), rather than by "spontaneous remission." From a review of research on therapeutic factors in therapist-client relationships, he concludes—I believe correctly—that the therapist's warmth, empathy, adequacy of personal adjustment, and length of professional experience have been established as positive correlates of therapeutic efficacy. Finally, Bergin concludes that client-centered therapy and behavior therapy based on learning principles are to date the only types of procedures to have established definitely their claims to therapeutic

[2] For a thorough discussion of the logical status of the "evidence," see Cartwright (1955).

efficacy. While I cannot dispute this assertion, I suspect that other, less well-researched types of therapy also have a reasonable share of successes, and failures. In any case, even in respect to client-centered and behavior therapy, there are serious questions as to how these procedures produce their (often-) beneficial effects.[3]

In the article cited earlier, Rogers (1963), after alluding to some of the same sources of disarray mentioned here, suggested that the field of psychotherapy could accurately be characterized as being "in a mess." To that concise judgment I can only add my own strong assent. Rogers went on to say, however, that he was optimistic—that out of all of the current disillusionment, ferment, and experimentation with new methods there would develop a more adequate art and science of constructive personality change. I doubt that Rogers would disagree with a qualification I should like to insert: I do not think that a haphazard, strictly empirical approach of trying out new methods, independent of progress at the conceptual level in understanding personality, is likely to go very far. I am, in fact, appalled by the absence of thoughtful, conceptual content in some of the "new methods" I learn about through television and popular magazines. Substantial progress in understanding psychotherapeutic processes, and therefore in being able to use them with precision and predictability of outcome, will occur only to the extent that we make substantial progress in the larger problem of understanding personality. The two are really quite inseparable and should be seen as interdependent enterprises.

It is unlikely at this point that the reader will have any serious doubts as to the general directions in which I think the study of personality, and therefore of psychotherapy, should proceed. My intent in the present chapter is to try to indicate in broad outline the major implications for psychotherapy of the interpersonal conceptions of personality we have discussed, and to assess in a

[3] For a discussion of the perplexities involved in accounting for the effects of behavior therapies, see Breger and McGaugh (1965, 1966); more recently Lang (1968) reveals unanticipated confusions in what had been thought to be a simple, straightforward procedure—the "desensitization" of focalized anxiety. Similarly, Gendlin et al. (1968) note serious problems recently encountered with the client-centered conception of the therapy process.

general way the adequacy of these conceptions in the light of relevant empirical knowledge concerning therapeutically induced behavior change. I shall try not to be dogmatic!

Dyadic Relationship Therapy As the Focus

The term *psychotherapy* is not denotative in nature. It refers to a hodgepodge of techniques and procedures having in common only the goal of altering behavior in a constructive, more personally effective direction. We shall limit our concern to dyadic psychotherapy (one client and one therapist) in keeping with the interpersonal unit of analysis employed throughout the book, although much of our discussion will have relevance for various group psychotherapeutic approaches. We shall also limit our concern to therapeutic processes in which the therapist-client relationship, per se, is the purported or suspected vehicle for producing changes in the client's personality and behavior. We are unconcerned with so-called *action* and *machine* therapies (London, 1964; Goldstein, Heller, and Sechrest, 1966; Lang, 1968), where the therapist as a person is either absent or of no unique consequence. Impersonal therapies of this type have a definite and promising place in the therapeutic armamentarium, especially in the initiation of therapy with disordered persons who lack interpersonal interests or skills, as in childhood autism (Lovaas, 1968). They are, however, outside of the scope encompassed by our framework.

I do not wish to exclude the entire field of behavior therapy, as I understand the category limits of that term. Many of the principles espoused by the behavior therapists, such as their emphasis on client *behavior* and their insistence that therapeutic change is mediated by new *learning*, are entirely compatible with the systematic ideas presented here. In their zeal to extrapolate from the incompletely understood behavior of albino rats and pigeons to the behavior of persons, however, the behavior therapists have often demonstrated an almost comical capacity for selective inattention. In its operational aspects much of behavior therapy, whether of the association learning (Wolpe, 1958; Lang, 1968) or operant-instrumental (Krasner, 1962a; Goldiamond and Dyrud,

1968) variety, is a reciprocally contingent interpersonal process that can be readily analyzed in terms of the present conceptual framework. In other words, a good deal of behavior therapy is probably not as mechanical as its practitioners often suggest, and a goodly number of behavior therapists are something other than "social reinforcement machines"—as even Krasner (1962a), who coined the term, seems completely aware. A recent comment by Hunt and Dyrud (1968) places behavior therapy in proper perspective:

> If behavior therapy is to realize its full potential, is to become not only an effective treatment procedure in a practical sense but is also to contribute to the more precise understanding of normal and pathological behavior and its functional dependencies, it must become more sophisticated and analytic about its own activities. Otherwise, it will remain just one more empirical approach that sometimes works. The level of behavior theory currently incorporated in behavior therapy is, all too often, simplistic and far below the level of the best now available. (p. 145)

The conception of psychotherapy employed in this chapter is both broader and narrower in particular respects than many other current conceptions of the field. We shall view it essentially as a two-person professional relationship in which one of the members uses the *relationship* in a planned attempt to alter the disordered behavior of the other. In keeping with the recent, superbly articulated thesis of Goldstein, Heller, and Sechrest (1966), psychotherapy is seen here as a special aspect of the psychology of behavior change in which social influence processes provide the dominant change-producing vehicle.

THE CENTRALITY OF THE RELATIONSHIP IN PSYCHOTHERAPY

While our framework would seem to require that a pre-eminent status be accorded the therapist-client relationship, its signal importance in psychotherapy can be supported on other, independent grounds. Most cogent, perhaps, is the fact of a near-universal consensus on this point. With the single exception of the most radically mechanistic behaviorist formulations, there is to my knowledge no formal theory of process in psychotherapy which does not recognize one or more aspects of the client's and therapist's personal relationship as the *sine qua non* of therapy. Despite their marked differences in other respects, nearly all psychotherapists are in fundamental agreement that whatever they accomplish therapeutically they accomplish through and by means of the technical, cognitive, and emotional resources they bring to bear in their relationships with their clients. Bordin (1959) makes the point thus:

> The key to the influence of psychotherapy on the patient is in his relationship with the therapist. Wherever psychotherapy is accepted as a significant enterprise, this statement is so widely subscribed to as to become trite. Virtually all efforts to theorize about psychotherapy are intended to describe and explain what attributes of the interactions between the therapist and the patient will account for whatever behavior change results. (p. 235)

Accumulating empirical evidence supports this testimonial consensus. It has been found repeatedly that the ingredients of an effective therapeutic relationship are determined, in part, by the personal characteristics brought to the relationship by *both* the client and the therapist. In certain studies, moreover, it has been shown that the *interaction* of client and therapist characteristics was as important in determining therapeutic outcome as the characteristics of the members of either group considered separately (Cartwright and Lerner, 1963; Hiler, 1958; McNair, Lorr, and Callahan, 1963; Mendelsohn and Geller, 1965; Rogers et al., 1967; Sapolsky, 1965). In other words, the effect upon outcome of certain characteristics of the client or the therapist appears to be contingent on particular characteristics of the *other* member of the therapeutic dyad. In one series of studies, reviewed by Carson (1967), an effect of this kind involving a reliably measurable (but as yet conceptually obscure) personality variable of psychotherapists appears sufficiently promising that it may justify pretherapy attempts to match therapists to different "types" of clients. In short, the empirical evidence is strongly in accord with therapists' impressions and opinions concerning the crucial significance of the therapist-client relationship in determining therapeutic efficacy.

POWER AND INFLUENCE OF THE THERAPIST

The absence of controversy regarding the importance of the therapeutic relationship is not matched by a similar unanimity concerning the precise factors in the relationship that operate to produce or to impede therapeutic progress. The notion of a therapeutic relationship means different things to different therapists, depending upon the manner in which they conceptualize the process of therapeusis. For example, therapists with a Freudian or psychoanalytic orientation (Menninger, 1958) tend to view the critical relationship factors in terms of transference and countertransference—the "inappropriate" intrusion of remnants of past relationships into the current one—while those with a client-centered viewpoint are likely to emphasize aspects of the relationship that encourage the client's exquisite "experiencing" of immediate feelings (Gendlin, 1964).

One thing seems clear: therapeutic change in clients occurs as a result of the influence generated by the therapist within the relationship. The therapist functions basically as a teacher, and—despite occasional disclaimers from therapists who like to see themselves as permissive and noncontrolling—he guides the client toward implicitly or explicitly predetermined goals. Not too long ago a statement sucn as this would have been regarded as heretical. The traditional view of the therapist's role could be compared to that of a horticulturalist. The therapist, according to this view, merely created the atmospheric conditions essential to the unfolding of the client's heretofore blocked but wholly self-determined personhood. The therapist, qua therapist, was an amoral person without values, and he assumed no responsibility for guiding the direction in which therapy proceeded. In some ways it was a comforting position; one did not have to get involved in the messy business of values, or—horror of horrors—act in an "authoritarian" way toward one's clients. But it was also realistically an impossible position to maintain. Rogers, as strong an advocate of self-determination as anyone in this field, admitted several years ago (Rogers & Skinner, 1956) that as a therapist he was deeply involved in interpersonal influence, an admission whose accuracy was subsequently demonstrated (Truax, 1966). The behavior therapists (such as Krasner, 1962a) have been particularly insistent in asserting, quite correctly, that it would be impossible for a therapist *not* to influence and control the client's behavior, and it therefore behooves therapists to be thoughtful and deliberate in the use of their influence. Numerous other writers, including Ellis (1962), Frank (1961), and Haley (1963), have recommended that the therapist give explicit attention to methods of actively guiding and directing the client's behavior. No doubt the emerging view of the therapist as a steering and controlling change-agent raises some serious ethical issues for the profession (Krasner, 1962b; London, 1964), but these were there all the time anyway; their frank exposure can only lead to a mitigation of whatever "brainwashing" dangers may attend the psychotherapeutic enterprise.

It would appear, then, that the therapist's influence over the client is one of the crucial components of the therapy relationship, and by implication is one of the more important determinants of the outcome of therapy—including presumably those instances where the therapy produces a negative or deteriorating outcome. The same general conclusion is reached by Goldstein, Heller, and Sechrest (1966), who devote an entire section of their book to an examination of possible methods of increasing the therapist's attractiveness to the client, thereby increasing the potency of the therapist's influence. Quite clearly, we are dealing here with aspects of *power* and *dependency,* concepts elaborated at length in Chapter 5. The therapist's ability to maintain the therapeutic relationship will be a function of his capacity to deliver supra-CL_{alt} outcomes to the client; and his effectiveness within the relationship will be determined in large part by his ability to vary outcomes above the client's CL_{alt}. This is a general statement intended to formulate the problem of therapeutic influence in terms of our own conceptual framework. We shall look at some of its implications later.

The Psychotherapeutic Task

As Ford and Urban (1963) have demonstrated at length, any systematically developed set of therapeutic procedures presupposes a certain model or theory of personality disorder and a related group of conceptions as to how personality may be changed, the latter being—if you will—a type of circumscribed learning theory. It would be well for us to be explicit about these matters here. The present section is therefore devoted to a focused review of conceptions developed earlier, with the aim of bringing them to bear on a conception of the psychotherapeutic task. We begin with the object of psychotherapeutic efforts, the disordered person.

THE PSYCHOTHERAPY CANDIDATE

Persons engage the services of psychotherapists for various reasons, not all of them meeting our definition of personality disorder. Uncomplicated anxiety is one such condition. I have no doubt that psychotherapists can be extremely helpful in such circumstances. Indeed, if the anxiety has an identifiable external focus, and if the therapist is acquainted with certain simple "desensitizing" techniques devised by the behavior therapists (such as Wolpe, 1958), there is every reason to look forward to a very prompt alleviation of the difficulty. These techniques have had quite dramatic success in resolving such minor problems as snake phobias (Lang, Lazovik, and Reynolds, 1965) and fears of public speaking (Paul, 1966) in college students. However, the coed who is "unrealistically" afraid of snakes, or the young man who is anxious about making speeches, hardly qualify as disordered persons. Accordingly, we shall not be concerned with this level of problem.

Assertions have been made, chiefly by Wolpe (1968), that these simple, mechanical techniques also produce recovery in "complex neurotic states," although the treatment takes longer. However, the data in support of this assertion have been subsantially less rigorously developed than in the cases mentioned above. Moreover, as Breger and McGaugh (1965, 1966) have pointed out, the procedures actually carried out in uncontrolled clinical trials of this so-called "reciprocal inhibition" (of anxiety) therapy typically go far beyond the idealized, theory-specific descriptions of them—so much so that they strongly resemble commonly used techniques in conventional psychotherapy. Thus, Wolpe (1968) has recently described the apparently successful treatment of a "shiftless," sexually promiscuous, suicidal [4] woman partly in the following terms:

> A behavioristic analysis of the case revealed interpersonal fear of disapproval that inhibited almost any kind of assertiveness and thus made her largely incapable of withstanding the demands of others or of making known her own. The therapist strongly urged her to express her legitimate demands; and soon grasping the reasonableness of this, she made efforts to comply. . . . [Her] treatment was a combination of sustained encouragement of self-expression and desensitization of [anxieties concerning rejection and ridicule]. (p. 136)

Published examples of this type of behavior therapy are replete with instances of such "extra," theoretically nonspecific procedures as "encouragement," "instigation," and "behavioristic analysis" (that is, interviewing the client about his life problems). I consider it extremely likely that the tendency of behavior therapists to focus on definite life problems has a marked therapeutic advantage over methods encouraging the client to wallow in undirected "free association," but this type of focusing is certainly not the exclusive province of behavior therapy. The point is that the effective treat-

[4] It is noteworthy that this woman had "attempted suicide many times" during the course of her previous lengthy but unsuccessful psychoanalysis and had made "several further attempts" in the first few weeks of the current therapy. In the matter of suicide, of course, once is enough if that is what one is really after. Multiple episodes of such behavior must be interpreted as attempts at analogical interpersonal communication. Wolpe gives no indication that he understood the message. Whether he did or not, I think it likely that imperviousness to significant communications is one of the dangers of a too-exclusive preoccupation with the impersonal, technical procedures of behavior therapy.

ment of "complex neurotic states" probably *requires* a type of therapeutic influence *not* accounted for within a strict interpretation of reciprocal inhibition theory, but nevertheless found in the repertoires of effective therapists of many differing theoretical persuasions.

To return to our effort to describe the kind of clientele in whom we are primarily interested—persons having complex neurotic states or, more generally, disordered persons—we shall conceptualize them in terms of the processes discussed in the preceding chapter. In the abstract, then, our typical psychotherapy candidate is a person who obtrusively breaks residual rules in his social behavior in order to reduce or avoid anxiety that is consequent to an actual or threatened mismatch between his Self and his current interpersonal experience. He presents himself, or is presented, to the therapist for the purpose of effecting relatively permanent changes in his unadaptive social behavior.

Now, a relatively permanent change in behavior implies the necessity of new learning. How shall this new learning be conceived and implemented? Before proceeding directly to this critical question, let us try to formulate the situation of the disordered person in behavior theory terms. The traditional way of doing so is to speak of "habits" and stimulus-response connections. You will recall from Chapter 3, however, that considerable doubt was expressed concerning the adequacy of the S-R approach to complex human behavior. In its stead, a more cognitively oriented theory involving the concepts of Image and Plan was advanced. Thus, the issue for us becomes one of describing the disordered person in terms of his Image and his Plans and the relations obtaining among them.

The immediate cause of the disordered person's maladaptive behavior is to be found in the nature of the Plans he executes; in effect, his Plans are rule-breaking ones. That much is self-evident, if not tautological. It is also only a small part of the problem. Recall that the function of a Plan is to exploit the Image, including realization of the "values" contained therein. Seen from this perspective, the disordered person's rule-breaking Plans are only an expression or manifestation of some peculiarity in his Image. The relationship is perhaps most clear and direct in those instances where the disordered behavior merely reflects the unfortunate acquisition of an eccentric set of residual rules—that is, an eccentric Image of what is real and decent—as described in Chapter 7. Plans constructed on the basis of such an Image would necessarily produce rule-breaking behavior. However, a condition of this sort is not characteristic of the typical psychotherapy candidate. We will forego any specific discussion of therapy in these cases, concentrating instead on the more common and somewhat more complicated (although often less "severe") disorders in which the rule-breaker has had extensive exposure to the rules. We assume that the Image of the latter type of rule-breaker for the most part contains an adequate representation of the residual rules of his culture. What, then, is wrong with it? Clearly, we should expect to find the locus of the difficulty in those aspects of the person's Image that relate to his Self.

We have portrayed the disordered person in general terms as someone whose Self is highly constricted and markedly intolerant of experience that fails to make a precise criterial match with its own narrow category limits. The Plans of the disordered person are mobilized to an extraordinary extent to protect and confirm his Image of Self and of Self-in-relation-to-others. These rule-breaking Plans would be unnecessary, and therefore disposable, if the Image could be rendered less demanding. The latter must therefore be seen as the ultimate therapeutic aim. How shall it be accomplished?

PSYCHOTHERAPEUTIC STRATEGY

The broad or strategical aspects of the psychotherapeutic task are perhaps now reasonably clear. The role of the therapist is to provide his client with experiences that result in an expansion and loosening of the client's Image of Self. Success in this venture would free the client from his slavish devotion to the maintenance of a constricted Selfhood, and from his need to manufacture crucial evidence in its support. The Self of the successfully treated client would be of sufficient extension to accommodate incoming information of virtually any type, making it possible for the client to formulate and execute Self-relevant Plans wholly on the basis of their likely contribution to personal "values" other than Self-protection. His range of choices in any situation would be to that degree expanded, and he would be free to act in accordance with an Image of the world relatively undistorted by considerations of personal security. It is perhaps not surprising that this view of the successfully treated client is markedly concordant with Sullivan's conceptions of an "adequate orientation in living" (page 45) and psychological adulthood ("late adolescence"—page 47), and with Rogers' (1959) conception of the "fully functioning person."

Knowing the goal provides a direction, a target. It suggests in a general way what needs to be done. The therapist must cause the client's Image to be changed, particularly that aspect of it constituting the client's fundamental conceptions of himself in relation to the world. The focus of the effort is therefore a cognitive, or at least quasi-cognitive, structure. In a sense the client needs to be provided with a different and more adequate set of *beliefs* about himself and his life. Now, we are touching here on a very venerable concept in psychotherapy, that of *insight.* The concept of insight in psychotherapy goes back to the earliest formulations of the therapeutic process in Freudian psychoanalysis, where it was used in reference to "making the unconscious conscious." It was held that an analysis was successful only to the extent that the client gained "insight" into his unconscious conflicts and their effects on his behavior. Many other systems of psychotherapy have embodied somewhat similar conceptions with varying degrees of prominence. In recent years, however, the notion that insight is of prime importance in producing therapeutic change has fallen into disrepute. Thus, Hobbs (1962) has suggested that insight is an effect rather than a cause of therapeutic success, and certain psychoanalysts (Alexander and French, 1946) maintain that analytic successes are achieved through "corrective emotional experiences" rather than through insight. The behavior therapists, of course, are quite disparaging of the concept, a fact that has prompted one commentator (London, 1964) to refer to their program as an "epitaph for insight." Can it be that our analysis has led us into a blind alley, one already thoroughly explored and abandoned as therapeutically sterile by numerous, theoretically diverse investigators? I do not think so.

Hobbs (1962) mentions that he first became disenchanted about the efficacy of insight on the basis of an observation familiar to many psychotherapists—namely, the failure of a client's behavior to change, as it was theoretically supposed to do, following the occurrence of "a significant insight." I would suppose from the context that the type of "insight" to which Hobbs refers involves the client's achievement of a cognitive linkage between some current aspect of his life and some item of personal history whose relationship to the current circumstances had heretofore been unappreciated, or even "repressed." This is the usual or standard meaning of the term, and classical psychodynamic theories of personality do indeed make the assumption that more adaptive, constructive behavior will follow from the client's genuine or "emotional" insight into the presumed historical sources of his maladaptive behavior. In other words, the client will alter his behavior when he fully appreciates its origins in past relationships, independent of its current payoff value for him. Stated thus baldly, and in the light of the analysis developed here, the theory seems naïve. It *is,* and the conception of insight embodied within it richly deserves its contemporary demise as an important element of therapeusis. However, there may be other types of cognitive learning of greater import. In the same paper in which he devalues the insight concept, Hobbs advances the idea that one of the essential "sources of gain" in psychotherapy is the opportunity afforded the client to adopt or invent a more adequate "personal cosmology." This personal cosmology is the cognitive structure whereby the individual imposes order on his world and his relationship to it. In a word, it is his Image.

"Insight," in the more extended sense of an altered perspective on oneself and one's environment, continues to be a prime goal of many revised versions of older therapies and of most newer, modern ones. The cognitive aspects of a "corrective emotional experience" constitute insight of this sort, as does the "re-construing" of self-relevant experience that is sought in the cognitively oriented therapy procedures advocated by George Kelly (1955). The centrality of this notion to a wide variety of contemporary conceptions of the therapeutic process, excluding perhaps only those based on a strict S-R interpretation, could be readily demonstrated. I shall forego such a *tour de force* in the interest of keeping to the main point of differentiation I want to make concerning varieties of "insight." It is hardly surprising that a client does not change his behavior in relation to, say, his boss merely because he becomes capable of appreciating the ramifications and vicissitudes of his purported childhood "castration anxiety." It would be very surprising indeed if his behavior did not change following an alteration of his Image of Self-in-relation-to-boss. The former would by no means automatically produce the latter; and the latter could be accomplished without benefit of the former. The singular importance of Image modification—especially Self-Image modification—in psychotherapy stems, I think, from its provision of a vehicle whereby what is learned in the contemporary psychotherapy relationship can be transferred or generalized to contemporary and future relationships *outside* of therapy. We shall give greater attention to this point in a later section.

In summary, the strategic task of the psychotherapist is to change his client's Self-in-relation-to-world Image, rendering it more encompassing, permeable, and flexible. An Image is changed through the provision of experience that is both new *and* assimilable in terms of existing, accessible cognitive categories. Cognitive categories, especially perhaps those relating to the Self, cannot be bludgeoned into change; they tend to repel experiences that do not "fit" them. This is the great paradox of the therapist's role: he must alter category boundaries within the Image through the use of inputs that initially conform in some measure to those boundaries, and he must avoid giving further confirmation to critical, disorder-producing cognitive structures without driving the client below CL_{alt}. It is, to say the least, a delicate operation.

Basic Psychotherapeutic Processes

Having set the stage via a model description of the psychotherapy client and what needs to be accomplished in relation to him, we may now proceed to a consideration of how the desired changes are to be brought about. Obviously, this is not the place to present a comprehensive manual or handbook of psychotherapy techniques—even if it were within the author's range of competence to do so. Rather, the intent is to describe in general terms the conditions the therapist will seek to create and the tactical procedures available to him for achieving his goal of alleviating personal disorder. The term "conditions" of therapy is here used to refer to certain basic essentials in the relationship without which it is unlikely that any therapy will occur, or even that the relationship will persist.

BASIC INGREDIENTS: TRUST AND CONFIDENCE

Successful psychotherapy almost invariably involves the client in a series of painful episodes and confrontations. This is true empirically, and it is also a logical derivation from theory. The therapist's task involves nothing less than the alteration of the client's Image of Self; it follows that at varying points in the interaction he will be called upon to disconfirm the current Self of the client and to disrupt the latter's Self-relevant Plans, leading to the eruption of more or less severe anxiety. To put it another way, the interaction matrix of the therapist and his client contains certain cells involving highly noncorrespondent outcomes, where the cost component to the client may be very substantial and where the therapist's reward is equally substantial because of his professional commitment to behave in ways that promise to benefit the client in the long run.

The existence of these highly noncorrespondent cells in the therapeutic relationship matrix, deriving in part from the therapist's professional responsibility, means that the relationship will be basically mixed-motive in nature. That is, there will be strains toward "cooperation" *and* "competition" in respect to outcome distribution between client and therapist even though both will usually be working toward the same goals in the long run. As has been noted in Chapter 6, this is a circumstance favoring the development of contractual regulations. The therapeutic contract is usually an implicit one, but, as Menninger (1958) has pointed out, it is a basic and essential component of a therapeutic relationship. The terms of the contract call for the therapist (the high-power person) to utilize his interpersonal skills wholly for the benefit of the client, typically in return for a suitable financial consideration; he is *not* to use or exploit the client for the purpose of gaining security or other forms of personal satisfaction. The client, on the other hand, agrees to present himself for therapy on some regular basis, to pay his fees, and to remain "loyal" to the relationship through difficult periods until such time as there is a mutual agreement that goals have been attained.

The therapeutic contract is not a perfect guarantee. The stresses of a deep interpersonal involvement are sometimes sufficient to cause the contract to be broken, usually—but regrettably not always—by the client. The client's role is an especially difficult one, because in due course he will be required to undergo a series of very low-outcome experiences. There is always the inherent danger, then, that the client will be driven below CL_{alt} to the extent of escaping from the relationship, despite his contractual obligations. Such disruption is an all too common event in beginning therapeutic relationships where, because of excessive haste, misjudgment, or inexperience, the therapist may overload the client with intolerable early costs relative to actual or anticipated rewards. Thus, most therapists take great care to supplement the formal terms of the therapeutic contract by seeing to it that the client receives suitable additional compensation, beyond the promise of future benefit, in regard to his total outcome experience. In other words, the therapist strives to enhance the intrinsic value of the relationship to the client.

The relationship-enhancement process is often described in terms of "building a relationship" with the client. Necessarily, it involves the delivery of a high proportion of rewards relative to costs, and it has the intended consequence of making the therapist an important and valued person in the client's life. Now, it should be clear that it will generally not be to the therapist's advantage to utilize the client's need to have his Self confirmed as a principal source for the fabrication and delivery of relationship-enhancing rewards. To do so would be to work at cross purposes with the ultimate goals of therapy. The therapist needs to have other resources available for dispensing an adequate level of compensatory rewards to the client, resources that do not have the effect of confirming a defective Self. By and large, this requirement is met through the provision of a basically respectful, warm, interested, and discerning atmosphere. The atmosphere remains largely constant, and is therefore noncontingent ("unconditional") in regard to the client's behavior.[5] While it is *generally* rewarding for most clients, it does not *specifically* reward or confirm any particular stance the client may take. It goes without saying that the therapist must be personally equipped to generate such an atmosphere.

There is one further resource available to the therapist for generalized relationship-enhancement—for maintaining the client's dependency upon him through difficult periods. This is the prestige and purported expertise that are attributed to him as a member of a respected profession. The very substantial power accruing to the therapist from this source alone has been thoroughly analyzed by Frank (1961), who notes that societies have always created specialized roles of great influence and prestige for the performance of "healing" functions. The characteristics normatively attributed to persons functioning within this role are such that they tend to inspire faith in the client in respect to the practitioner's good will and "curative" powers. Faith in the therapist's as yet undemonstrated therapeutic powers, when combined with his demonstrable power to affect the client's outcomes, tend together to produce a state of high motivation in the client to maintain his coalition with this "powerful agency of control" (Thibaut, 1964).

In summary, it may be suggested that the client's trust and confidence are basic to the therapeutic process. The client's "faith" and the therapist's "attractiveness" as a source of generalized rewards, buttressed as they are by recognized contractual obliga-

[5] With certain clients—those preferring to occupy positions in the outer ranges of the Hostile-Submissive quadrant—excessive displays of respect and warmth in the early phases of therapy are likely to be unduly threatening and are therefore to be avoided. These clients present a special problem to the therapist because they forcefully repudiate the very intimacy the therapist seeks to create in order to carry out his therapeutic task. My own approach to these clients emphasizes full disclosure and utter, scrupulous honesty in respect to my goals, intentions, and feelings about the relationship. A certain element of firmness seems often to be helpful. With diligence, many of these clients can be brought at least to the point of trusting the therapist, and therapy may proceed from there.

tions, are what sustain the relationship through crises that would otherwise result in the client's abrupt departure. With these factors operative, the delivery of an occasional strongly negative outcome to the client—in a general context of markedly positive ones—does not rupture the relationship. On the contrary, it tends to enhance the therapist's power in the dyad by maintaining a broad range of outcome experience for the client, and by increasing the subjective value of his positive outcomes through its retarding effect on his CL (see page 129).

THE CRUCIAL THERAPEUTIC TACTIC

We have portrayed the disordered person as someone who breaks rules in his relationships in order to maintain certain Self-confirming positions. Can he be expected to behave in the same manner with his therapist? Yes indeed, often very forcefully and dramatically. The concept of *transference* in psychotherapy is as venerable as that of *insight* and, like it, derives originally from Freudian psychoanalysis. Early in his career as a psychotherapist, Freud noted that his clients frequently developed during analysis "irrational" behaviors directed toward him as a person, such as professing their love for him. The psychoanalytic position is that these irrational "transference" behaviors represent remnants of intrapsychic childhood conflicts "acted out" toward the therapist (acting *in loco parentis*) in the course of analysis. In fact, the cornerstone of psychoanalytic therapy is said to be the analysis and resolution of this "transference neurosis." While one may reasonably doubt the accuracy of the attributed childhood source of these "transference reactions," I shall argue that skillful and effective handling of the referent client behaviors would have to be one of the cornerstones of *any* workable approach to psychotherapy.

I doubt that there exists an experienced therapist of any theoretical persuasion who has not been impressed by the strength of the temptations provided by his clients to deviate from his established therapeutic plan—temptations to react "personally" and according to the impulse of the moment. The operations performed by the client in order to achieve this state of affairs are called transference reactions in psychoanalytic terminology, and the "impulsive" response of the therapist, should it occur, is called *counter-transference.* (In a somewhat similar vein, Sullivan attributes the emergence of this type of "irrational" behavior to the intrusion of historically determined "parataxic distortions.") We may reformulate the process in our own terms by referring to the client's activity in this area as an attempt at the "evocation of congruent responses," and to the therapist's "error" as one involving the provision of a complementary response. As Menninger (1958) points out, in engaging in this type of behavior, the client attempts to abrogate the "rules" of the therapeutic contract (and often residual rules as well) by demanding of the therapist a type of response outside of the limits of those originally called for. If the therapist persistently supplies the demanded response (or a reasonable facsimile of it), he will in most cases be failing the client as a therapist, and may to that degree become a contract violator himself.

Assuming that the therapist's task is to *change* the client, and not merely to mollify or "support" him, these considerations lead to the identification of a cardinal therapeutic tactic: The therapist must avoid the adoption of an interpersonal position complementary to and confirmatory of the critical Self-protective position to which the client will almost invariably attempt to move in the course of the therapeutic interaction. In other words, the therapist must be one person in the client's life—and he will frequently be the *only* one in a sustained relationship—who does not yield to the client's pressure to supply confirmatory information (digital or analogic) to the latter's crippled Self. If the therapist significantly fails in this task, he will fail in his therapy, and indeed may *increase* the severity of the client's problems.

There is wide agreement on this point. Halpern (1965), in a brief paper addressed directly to the issue, puts it quite unequivocally: *"For psychotherapy to succeed the therapist must avoid becoming unwittingly ensnared in the disturbance-perpetuating maneuvers of his patient"* (p. 177, Halpern's italics). Beier (1966), writing from an eclectic position, suggests that, "one can see the therapeutic process as one in which the therapist refuses to reinforce the patient's present state of adjustment by refusing to make the response the patient forcefully evokes in him" (p. 13). Menninger (1958) and Tarachow (1963), representing the psychoanalytic point of view, present a similar argument. Tarachow speaks of the therapist's imposing a *therapeutic barrier* between himself and the client such that the client's personal demands on the therapist are not even regarded as being *real:* "The therapeutic task can be imposed only by means of a disappointment and by transformation of a real into an *as if* relationship. We force thinking in place of reality. . . ." (p. 14). In other words, the analyst does not *respond* to the client's demand, but only *uses* it to instigate reflection on what is going on in the relationship.

The therapeutic necessity of invoking what we have here called the crucial tactic of therapy—that of nonconfirmation of the client's constricted Self—seems quite straightforward and clear. How to manage it is considerably less clear. We have already had occasion to note that the disordered person, driven by powerful forces, is likely to have acquired a very high degree of expertise in moving others into the positions he needs them to be in, and he is often quite prepared, if necessary, to go to very extreme lengths in the exercise of power (manipulation of the other's outcomes) in order to achieve his goals. Consider the following instructive illustration, provided by Halpern (1965):

> A male anxiety neurotic, in his early thirties, defines himself as a passive, bewildered, helpless [Docile-Dependent] little boy—precisely the way his parents defined him. In one session the patient announced that he was going to put into action a scheme on his job that was consciously designed to win him plaudits and a promotion but which the therapist could easily see would get him into deep trouble and, at the very least, result in his being fired. The therapist felt tremendous pressure to point out to the patient the self-defeating nature of what he was doing and to explore, probably with profit, the patient's need to harm himself. But the therapist was also aware that bringing this to the patient's attention would be a way of reassuring this particular patient that he really is a helpless, bewildered little boy who needs someone to tell him what is and what is not appropriate

> behavior. So the therapist said nothing and waited as the patient, in session after session, increased his pressure to win the therapist's intervention. Finally, the day before the patient was to spring his scheme, the patient said, "You know, the more I think about my plan, the more I feel it will probably lead to nothing but trouble." This moment represented the essence of change. When he could not get the therapist to reaffirm that he is incapable of making his own decisions, he had to make some shift toward viewing himself as having mature judgment and the power to use it. (p. 177)

Halpern's example nicely illustrates a common dilemma faced by the psychotherapist. He wants to help, he wants to be "good" to his client, he wants to rescue him from various disasters, minor and major. But he finds with a regularity far too impressive to be accidental that these wishes paradoxically array themselves *against* his ultimate therapeutic goals. Sometimes he gives in, sometimes he does not, and sometimes he finds a means of compromise. My own experience as a supervisor of journeyman therapists is that the management of this type of problem is the greatest stumbling block in the education of new therapists. In general, they either lean too far in the direction of giving in, or they become inappropriately resistant and hostile because of their clients' so-called "manipulative" tendencies. Balanced judgment is difficult to teach in this area, and it is even more difficult to learn. Again, psychotherapy is an encounter in which at least one of the participants—the client—can usually be counted on to be an expert; at its best, the other participant is on approximately equal terms.

CHANGING THE IMAGE

The therapist's systematic demurring on opportunities to enact behavior complementary to the Self-protective behavior of the client is a powerful instrument of therapeusis. Instead of strongly confirming the disorder-maintaining Image of Self proffered by the client, the prestigeful therapist produces a class of responses at the very most ambiguous in this respect. Beier (1966) refers to this class of therapeutic responses as "asocial" ones; it is an apt term, for it conveys the sense of impunitive nonresponsiveness that is contained in the most skillfully fashioned and delivered of these therapeutic interventions. The therapist is neither complementary nor anticomplementary—he merely maintains contact. Silence and inactivity can perhaps be viewed as the prototypic asocial response in psychotherapy, but all of the training programs inspired by the various theoretical positions in this field liberally supply their trainees with a host of other imaginative asocial tactics. Haley (1958) has written amusingly of the various asocial "ploys" used by psychoanalysts. It is my impression that much of the ritualistic paraphernalia of behavior therapy also serves this function.

The asocial responses of the therapist tend to abort the disorder-maintaining Plans of the client and produce feedback to the client that persistently fails of making a good match with his Image of Self. Under such circumstances, the client typically becomes increasingly anxious, and he executes search-and-solve Plans of an increasingly desperate character in order to induce the therapist into a more favorable position. The client in this state is highly vulnerable to therapeutic change. The category boundaries of his Image of Self have been weakened through repeated failures to obtain confirmatory feedback. He is anxious and uncomfortable, and he is seeking a way out of his dilemma. His unaided attempts to do so by reaffirmation of his original Self have become somewhat gross and transparent in comparison with his earlier, more suave and well-practiced security operations. In short, he is a man with a problem, often one that is—at least superficially—substantially different from the one for which therapy was purportedly initiated in the first place. As we have seen, this is what psychoanalysts, with perhaps some hyperbole, call the "transference neurosis." In any case, with his Plans disorganized and his Image of Self in a somewhat disheveled state, the client badly needs some new directions in which to move in the therapeutic relationship. It is the therapist's task to provide these.

The limitations of "instruction." One possible approach the therapist might use is simply to tell the client what is wrong with his Image and to suggest quite directly the various revisions needed in it in order to permit the client to lead a more effective life. I suspect that this is one of the most commonly employed techniques in the entire psychotherapeutic realm. In certain systems of therapy—for example, the "Rational-Emotive" position advocated by Ellis (1962)—it is regarded as the fundamental therapeutic tool. By and large, however, therapists use such "instructional" techniques only in an adjunctive and supportive way, relying on other methods to carry the major burden of change-inducement. There is a very good reason for this reluctance to rely too heavily on what would seem to be the most direct and straightforward approach. It is often, by itself, entirely ineffective. Somehow the message fails to penetrate, and the client continues to behave as though his Image had remained unaltered except in respect to his new awareness that the therapist likes him to mouth certain phrases in the course of their interactions. The crucial Image categories remain closed or inaccessible to the informational content of the therapist's direct attempts to induce cognitive restructuring.

The frequent failure of the instructional approach can be explained in several ways. In the first place, the import of the message might be obliterated or distorted at the point of reception through the operation of selective inattention. At a still more central level it may suffer various secondary distortions as it is cognitively "processed," because of pre-emption by nonveridical—but highly accessible—categories. Even if we assume adequate transmission and decoding of the message, however, there is no reason to suppose that it will produce, in itself, an Image change of sufficient magnitude to support the performance of new behavior patterns. Images and Plans—the cognitive maps or templates by which behavior is guided—are not altered that easily. Repetition and rehearsal at the cognitive level *and* in the actual performance of the new behavior seem frequently necessary in order to "stamp in" the newer components of the Image. Why this should be the case is far from clear and is a matter of considerable controversy; we note here only that the observation is pragmatically accurate. One does not "learn" to drive an automobile with any degree of finesse on the basis of instruction alone, although good instruction will be of significant help, especially at the outset of the learning process.

Automobile driving, involving as it does a rather substantial component of highly specific motor skill, is actually not very à propos as an example. The kinds of behavior change sought by the psychotherapist are much more complex in nature, and, in comparison with the problem of operating an automobile, they must be adaptable to a much more varied and unpredictable situational context. A more relevant example in many ways is the problem confronting an individual who has just undergone an abrupt and significant "status passage" involving a relatively sudden augmentation of the contents of the Self and a dramatic alteration in the character of his relationships with other persons. Getting married or going off to college are illustrative, if somewhat routine, instances of this sort of transition. The individual may seem completely prepared and knowledgeable at the cognitive level in terms of having a firm "fix" on who and what he is, and on what to expect from his interaction partners. Nevertheless, until he has had some concrete "practice" in the enactment of his new role(s), he will usually be anxious, awkward, and inexpert in his performance; not infrequently, "inappropriate" remnants of overlearned behavior from the past will intrude themselves. The situation facing the psychotherapy client is analogous, with the important exceptions that the Image changes required are more drastic in nature, and will be more strongly resisted.

It was suggested above that the task of the psychotherapist could be construed as involving an alteration in the client's "beliefs" about himself and his relationship to the world. And yet the conclusion we seem to be coming to here is that the therapist's powers of cognitive persuasion have limited effect unless he can get the client to "practice" new behaviors. There is no fundamental incompatibility between these positions. One of the more efficient ways to induce changes in beliefs (and "attitudes") is to induce changes in behavior. In other words, if a person can be induced to behave in a way that is "discrepant" from his beliefs, those beliefs tend to change in the direction of the discrepant behavior. This phenomenon is very dependable, having been replicated in numerous experiments by diverse investigators. The magnitude of the effect is contingent on many variables, including the degree of improvisation involved in the new behavior. (The greater the improvisation, in general, the greater the effect.) Its interpretation is the subject of an ongoing theoretical controversy. Investigators committed to a "cognitive dissonance" explanation believe the effect is greatest when the subject has least "justification" for engaging in the discrepant behavior, while those committed to an "incentive" explanation believe it is greatest when the subject derives maximum "reward" from his performance. Both groups of investigators can adduce compelling empirical evidence in support of their positions, and it seems likely that both groups are correct but are looking at slightly different aspects of the phenomenon. The nature of the resolution that will evolve from the current very active research in this area cannot be foreseen with certainty, and we cannot take the time here to analyze the available evidence in any detail. Interested readers can find excellent discussions of the problem in Jones and Gerard (1967, Chapter 12) and in Feldman (1966). While we may expect a more differentiated conclusion to be possible in due course, we content ourselves here by reiterating the now quite unassailable generalization that a change in behavior tends to produce corresponding changes in the relevant belief system of the behaving person. It seems to me that this fact is of enormous significance in the psychotherapeutic enterprise.

It would thus appear that the therapist need not rely exclusively on *direct* modes of Image alteration (instruction) in his attempts to establish new forms of interpersonal behavior. Indeed, there may be distinct advantages to his *not* doing so. If he can get the client to *behave* in other than his usual ways, he can thereby encourage needed practice at the skill level in the construction of new Plans, and—more important—he may be able to *indirectly* effect positive changes in the client's Self-relevant Image. This method of change-induction can be rendered quite subtle and unobtrusive, minimizing threat and the consequent mobilization of Self-defensive behaviors. Moreover, if the client can be induced "voluntarily" to produce desired new behavior, it would seem likely that any Self-relevant information embedded in that behavior would be more readily assimilated within appropriate Image categories than would similar information deriving entirely from "external" sources. Let us now extend our analysis to a brief and very general consideration of tactics available to the therapist for getting new behavior initiated.

The induction of new behavior. As we have seen, if the client's Plans are disrupted by the therapist's asocial behavior, he will be searching for a way out of his dilemma. Sometimes, I have no doubt, psychotherapy clients in these circumstances hit upon favorable solutions virtually unaided by the therapist; they cast about trying out various behaviors and cognitive restructurings and, on occasion, come up with a combination that "works" much better than what they had going for them before. However, we may surmise that in most instances the therapist's active guidance will add at least some increment of effectiveness to the procedure. The planned induction of specifically tailored Self-corrective behaviors may be regarded as one of the more important of the therapist's tasks.

The most direct method available to the therapist for getting the client to "try on" new behaviors is that of prescription. The therapist simply tells the client to behave in given situations *as though* some set of conditions other than those represented in the client's Image were the case. The "fixed role therapy" of George Kelly (1955) and the "psychodrama" techniques of Moreno (1946) are illustrative applications. Rigorous research on the therapeutic effectiveness of such techniques, as is too often true with many other promising innovations, is completely lacking at this time. Therapists who have used techniques of this kind tend to be enthusiastic about them, and it would seem probable on theoretical grounds alone that at least some of the enthusiasm is justified. However, there is one potentially disadvantageous factor in prescribed role-play therapy, and that is its obviously contrived format. If the dissonance theorists are even partly correct—and they almost certainly are—the fact that the behavior is *prescribed* by the therapist provides a ready means for the client to "reduce dissonance" in ways other than changing his Image of Self; he can tell himself that he did it only to please the therapist, for example.

Our analysis of interpersonal transactions, detailed in Chapter 5, suggests the possibility of a more subtle class of techniques for the initiation of new, Self-expanding behaviors. Let it be said at the outset that the therapeutic efficacy of techniques based on this model are also completely lacking in rigorous empirical confirmation at this time. It is my intent here only to call attention to the potential application of the model in therapeutic work. I am referring to the possibility that the therapist might induce new behavior by suitable manipulation of the client's costs and rewards in the course of the therapeutic transaction. By varying his own stance toward the client in deliberate, planned ways, making full and sensitive use of the prompts and "reinforcements" available to him, he may succeed in inducing the client to sample repeatedly portions of the matrix that he previously neglected or avoided. The use of complementarity and possibly other sources of outcome control in the systematic way indicated here would have the immediate effect of steering the client toward new varieties of interpersonal experience, and it should thereby have the ultimate effect of expanding and rendering more malleable the limits of his Image of Self. It is not unlikely that many experienced therapists have learned "intuitively" to conduct their therapy somewhat along these lines. The advantages of a systematic, deliberate application seem obvious, however, and on this issue I find myself in the camp of the behavior therapists.

The personality of the therapist. If the effectiveness of the therapist is dependent in part on his ability to move the client at will through various portions of the interaction matrix, it follows that the success of therapy will in turn depend in part on the therapist's capacity to adopt stances complementary to those with which the client needs to have experience. The most *generally* effective therapist should be one who can move comfortably to virtually any position in the matrix, a characteristic that is tantamount to maximum personal adjustment. Therapists having security-imposed restraints of one kind or another on their free movement in the matrix will suffer a corresponding reduction in the proportion of clients they are likely to be successful in treating. The client who "needs" for therapeutic reasons a lot of experience with the Docile position is unlikely to get what he needs if his therapist is incapable of assuming a Managerial stance. I suspect that this sort of matching factor underlies at least some of the empirical findings showing a considerable amount of the variance in therapeutic success to be attributable to *combinations* of therapist and client characteristics, as alluded to above. Unfortunately, the particular client-therapist variables investigated in these studies do not readily lend themselves to precise translation into our terms, and so detailed evaluation of this hypothesis will have to be left to future research.[6] The other side of the coin, if this analysis is correct, represents a positive danger to the client's remaining resources for effective living. That is, if the client's disordered stance preference should happen to coincide with (be complementary to) an inordinately strong position preference in the therapist, there is the possibility that the relationship will produce a further augmentation of the client's difficulties. It goes without saying, of course, that therapists should not engage their clients in disorder-maintaining interpersonal "games," although I think this occasionally happens. When it does happen, it is apt to manifest itself in a therapeutic relationship of interminable duration (Stieper and Wiener, 1959). As in any relationship, the therapist's *power* to affect the client's behavior will be partly determined by his own security requirements.

The "Transfer" of Therapeutic Learning

Psychotherapy can be justified as an enterprise only to the extent that the client's everyday behavior *in relationship with persons*

[6] Sapolsky's (1965) study comes closest to providing relevant information on the point at issue. Using the FIRO techniques developed by Schutz (1958), he found that patient-doctor "interpersonal need compatibility" was positively related to therapeutic outcome. In the FIRO system, interpersonal compatibility is measured on the basis of the degree of "fit" among three postulated interpersonal needs: Inclusion, Control, and Affection. The Control dimension is quite similar to our Dominance-Submission one, and our Hate-Love dimension appears in some ways to be an amalgamation of Inclusion and Affection. It may be, then, that *some* degree of complementarity in the preferred stances of client and therapist is therapeutically favorable.

other than the therapist undergoes changes in the direction of reduced residual rule violation. It will be of little benefit to the client or to his family and associates if he continues to be self-defeating and ineffective in his life generally, regardless of how fine or rewarding his relationship with the therapist may become. To put it another way, the learning that occurs in the psychotherapy relationship must "generalize" to other relationships if the procedure is to be regarded as even moderately successful. Clinical experience and other sources of evidence suggest that such generalization cannot be routinely assumed. It sometimes happens that psychotherapy clients undergo marked, positive changes in their relationships with their therapists without showing corresponding changes in other areas, such as their family or work relations. It would seem desirable, therefore, for therapists to take these contingencies into account in their therapeutic planning, and to try to incorporate into that planning measures designed to encourage wide application of therapeutic results. Generally speaking, there are two possible approaches to this problem, one of them centering in the therapeutic interaction itself and the other relying on auxiliary steps that can be taken outside of the therapy relationship. Each of these will be considered in turn.

IMAGE DEDIFFERENTIATION

The question of the transfer of therapeutic learning to other relationships has been seriously neglected in the psychotherapy literature. Quite evidently, the traditional assumption has been that the process will occur inevitably and automatically, and that the therapist need not concern himself with the problem. There is as a consequence a disproportionately greater gap in our knowledge in this specific area than is the case for psychotherapy generally. With unusual perspicacity, Goldstein, Heller, and Sechrest (1966, Chapter 5) have clearly delineated this gap and have attempted to fill it in as best they could with available conceptual tools and empirical findings from areas of research peripheral to psychotherapy. The effort is a laudable one, and they derive from it a number of worthwhile suggestions that should be tried in therapeutic practice. For example, the use of multiple therapists might deter excessive specificity of therapeutic learning. Unfortunately, however, the authors chose to formulate the problem—and their solutions to it—basically within a mechanical, stimulus-response framework. It happens that phenomena relating to the "transfer" of behavior to new situations have provided S-R theory with some of its most embarrassing perplexities.

If the problem of transfer from the psychotherapy to other relationships is formulated in the conceptual terms used here, it becomes largely a matter of the nature and permeability of category boundaries in the Image. The "generalization" aspects of the therapeutic task, then, must be concerned with breaking down or rendering more permeable various of the boundaries separating "therapy-related" from "nontherapy-related" Image categories. To the extent that the client compartmentalizes as unique the Image components relating to his experience with the therapist, his behavior in extratherapeutic relationships will remain unaffected by changes wrought in those Image components. The "you" in certain critical aspects of his I-You Image of Self must be undifferentiated with respect to "therapist" versus "other persons."

This suggests various tactics the therapist may employ in the course of his interaction with the client in order to discourage the formation of such unwanted differentiations. He may, for example, attempt systematically to disclaim any unique attributions the client makes concerning him as a person. As a rule, these disclaimers will be accurate ones, the therapist's understandable pleasure in being regarded as some special type of person notwithstanding. Seen from this perspective, it should be helpful for the client to know that the therapist is a *real* person who shares a great deal in common with every other member of the species. Jourard's (1964) recommendations regarding therapist "transparency" seem to be relevant to this point, as are the disarmingly frank therapist behaviors that ideally characterize the Kaiserian (Fierman, 1965) therapeutic "style." In some ways this may be related to therapist "expressiveness," a variable shown by Rice (1965) to be positively correlated with both therapist experience and therapeutic success.

There is at least one other widely used therapeutic tactic that we would expect to contribute to the breakdown of inappropriate Image differentiations of the type we are concerned with here. This is the tactic of constantly drawing attention to the parallels existing between events in the therapeutic relationship and events in the client's relationships with other significant persons in his life. Patterned behaviors, while often differing substantially in their manifest aspects, are in most instances very striking indeed in their cross-relationship redundancy, if sufficient attention is paid to them. In a certain sense, in fact, the therapy relationship can be seen as an allegorical synopsis of the client's current personality, with the exception that the therapist's responses are to an unusual degree based on knowledgeable planning. By repeatedly calling attention to the relationship-replication aspects of the client's behavior, the therapist is able to place the therapy relationship in a very broad context, and thereby to encourage the generalization of therapeutic learning.

It would be neither appropriate nor practicable to attempt here a comprehensive catalogue of Image dedifferentiation therapeutic tactics. The field is a broad one which offers many opportunities for therapeutic inventiveness on an ad hoc basis. The important thing is that the therapist recognize the problem of extratherapeutic transfer as a real one, for it is only then that he will remain alert to the opportunities available in the relationship to enhance the likelihood of its occurrence. One of the more positive features of the behavior therapy movement, with its penchant for detailed behavioral analysis, is that it has focused attention on this long-neglected area.

INTERVENTION IN OTHER CLIENT RELATIONSHIPS

If, as a result of therapy, the client begins to behave differently—that is, to occupy differing positions—in his everyday relationships with other persons, these other persons can normally be counted on to make appropriate adjustments in their own stances toward him. The complementary feedback thus generated serves as confirmation of the client's newly expanding Self and is a very significant factor in perpetuating and extending the client's gains. The "value" attaching to the more recently acquired components of the client's Image of Self is further enhanced by these confirmatory responses in others, and an ongoing process of Self-development is thereby initiated. I think it is quite true, as some have said, that most of "therapy" goes on *outside* of the therapy relationship; the therapist only prepares the way.

There is sometimes a fly in the ointment. Occasionally—actually rather more often than one likes to think—the psychotherapy client has become enmeshed in very complicated relationships with one or more other persons in his life, usually members of his family. These other persons may not find the changes in the client to their liking, because they have come to depend for one reason or another on his enacting his particular variety of disordered behavior. The heretofore unnoted existence of a negotiated maladjustment contract is, in fact, often first detected on the basis of the dire reaction of a family member to the client's "improvement." I have seen family members forcibly intervene to terminate an emergently successful therapy relationship on this basis, and I know that my own experience with this is by no means unique. In short, other persons in the client's system of extratherapy relationships, such as his parents or spouse, may have strong motives to subvert and counter any gains the client may make. They therefore sometimes put enormous pressure on the client in order to force him back into his old ways. We saw some examples of this sort of pressure in the illustrative materials presented in Chapter 6. It goes without saying that such counter-pressure, applied precisely at the critical juncture when the client is making his first attempts to assert a new Self, is something less than therapeutically favorable. The therapist in these circumstances is confronted with a choice; he can refrain from extending the boundaries of his efforts and continue to work exclusively with the client, hoping to provide enough support to enable the client to overcome the external resistance, or he can "wade in" and try to effect some changes in the "system" within which the client lives his everyday life. Traditionally, the former has been the recommended course, the recommendation often being supported by fairly elaborate but questionable "theoretical" considerations. Various contemporary developments, including the rapid advances being made in "family therapy" (Boszormenyi-Nagy and

Framo, 1965), indicate that the old tradition is breaking down. I, for one, am not sorry to see it go.

Some therapists believe that with certain types of personality disorder, such as "schizophrenic" behavior in adolescents, a *systemic* approach to therapy is the only feasible alternative to almost certain therapeutic failure. They tend to see the disordered behavior of the "primary patient" as being merely a manifestation of a grossly disturbed system of intrafamilial relationships. The client will not, cannot, change unless the system is changed, they assert —with considerable empirical justification. We cannot take the time to review the interesting work being done in this area, and I allude to it only to point up the fact that the client's life frequently includes several important payoff matrixes other than the one that is operative in the client-therapist relationship. If the therapist is genuinely committed to helping his client, he may have no alternative but to wade in and try to alter the payoff characteristics of those other matrixes.

What can the therapist do outside of the relationship if he finds that his attempts to change the client's Image of Self are being systematically thwarted by the power resources of other persons in the client's life? We find ourselves here in another of those grey areas where reliable knowledge is almost wholly lacking. In some instances he might encourage any moves the client makes in the direction of separation or divorce, but a solution of this kind is often not very feasible. As is commonly done with the parents of child guidance clinic clients, he might try to arrange a circumscribed type of therapy for the other person(s) with one of his professional colleagues. Alternatively he might perform this service himself. At appropriate times he might convert his one-to-one relationship with the client into a "family therapy" or "marital counseling" format, inviting the other persons to collaborate in the hope of effecting some change in relevant aspects of *their* Images. He might exploit his professional prestige to instruct, persuade, or cajole the other persons involved into terminating at least certain of their more overt destructive actions toward the client. We have no way of knowing which of these procedures, or other comparable ones, are likely to be most helpful in given circumstances. It therefore becomes a matter of the therapist's best judgment. In a situation such as the one described, however, it seems to me that he does *not* have the option of doing nothing.

REFERENCES

ALEXANDER, F., and FRENCH, T. M. *Psychoanalytic therapy*. New York: Ronald, 1946.

BEIER, E. G. *The silent language of psychotherapy*. Chicago: Aldine Publishing Company, 1966.

BERGIN, A. E. Some implications of psychotherapy research for therapeutic practice. *Journal of Abnormal Psychology*, 1966, **71,** 235–46.

BORDIN, E. S. Inside the therapeutic hour. In E. A. RUBINSTEIN and M. B. PARLOFF (Eds.), *Research in psychotherapy*. Washington: American Psychological Association, 1959. Pp. 235–46.

BOSZORMENYI-NAGY, I., and FRAMO, J. L. (Eds.), *Intensive family therapy*. New York: Harper & Row, 1965.

BREGER, L., and MCGAUGH, J. L. Critique and reformulation of "learning theory" approaches to psychotherapy and neurosis. *Psychological Bulletin*, 1965, **63,** 338–58.

BREGER, L., and MCGAUGH, J. L. Learning theory and behavior therapy: A reply to Rachman and Eysenck. *Psychological Bulletin*, 1966, **65,** 170–73.

CARSON, R. C. A and B therapist "types": A possible critical variable in psychotherapy. *Journal of Nervous and Mental Disease*, 1967, **144,** 47–54.

CARTWRIGHT, D. S. Effectiveness of psychotherapy: A critique of the spontaneous remission argument. *Journal of Counseling Psychology*, 1955, **2,** 290–96.

CARTWRIGHT, R. D., and LERNER, B. Empathy, need to change, and improvement with psychotherapy. *Journal of Consulting Psychology*, 1963, **27,** 137–44.

ELLIS, A. *Reason and emotion in psychotherapy*. New York: Lyle Stuart, 1962.

FELDMAN, S. (Ed.). *Cognitive consistency*. New York: Academic Press, 1966.

FIERMAN, L. B. (Ed.). *Effective psychotherapy: The contribution of Hellmuth Kaiser*. New York: Free Press, 1965.

FORD, D. H., and URBAN, H. B. *Systems of psychotherapy*. New York: Wiley, 1963.

FRANK, J. D. *Persuasion and healing.* Baltimore: Johns Hopkins Press, 1961.

GENDLIN, E. T. A theory of personality change. In P. WORCHEL and D. BYRNE (Eds.), *Personality change.* New York: Wiley, 1964. Pp. 100–48.

GENDLIN, E. T., BEEBE, J., CASSENS, J., KLEIN, M., and OBERLANDER, M. Focusing ability in psychotherapy, personality, and creativity. In J. M. SHLIEN (Ed.), *Research in psychotherapy, Vol. III.* Washington: American Psychological Association, 1968. Pp. 217–38.

GOLDIAMOND, I., and DYRUD, J. E. Some applications and implications of behavioral analysis for psychotherapy. In J. M. SHLIEN (Ed.), *Research in psychotherapy, Vol. III.* Washington: American Psychological Association, 1968. Pp. 54–89.

GOLDSTEIN, A. P., HELLER, K., and SECHREST, L. B. *Psychotherapy and the psychology of behavior change.* New York: Wiley, 1966.

HALEY, J. The art of psychoanalysis. *ETC.*, 1958, **15,** 190–200.

HALEY, J. *Strategies of psychotherapy.* New York: Grune & Stratton, 1963.

HALPERN, H. M. An essential ingredient in successful psychotherapy. *Psychotherapy*, 1965, **2,** 177–80.

HILER, E. W. An analysis of patient-therapist compatibility. *Journal of Consulting Psychology*, 1958, **22,** 341–47.

HOBBS, N. Sources of gain in psychotherapy. *American Psychologist*, 1962, **17,** 741–47.

HUNT, H. F., and DYRUD, J. E. Commentary: Perspective in behavior therapy. In J. M. SHLIEN (Ed.), *Research in psychotherapy, Vol. III.* Washington: American Psychological Association, 1968. Pp. 140–52.

JONES, E. E., and GERARD, H. B. *Foundations of social psychology.* New York: Wiley, 1967.

JOURARD, S. M. *The transparent self.* Princeton, N.J.: Van Nostrand, 1964.

KELLY, G. A. *The psychology of personal constructs.* 2 vols. New York: W. W. Norton, 1955.

KIESLER, D. J. Some myths of psychotherapy research and the search for a paradigm. *Psychological Bulletin*, 1966, **65,** 110–36.

KRASNER, L. The therapist as a social reinforcement machine. In H. H. STRUPP and L. LUBORSKY (Eds.), *Research in psychotherapy, Vol. II.* Washington: American Psychological Association, 1962(a). Pp. 61–94.

KRASNER, L. Behavior control and social responsibility. *American Psychologist*, 1962(b), **17,** 199–204.

LANG, P. J. Fear reduction and fear behavior: Problems in treating a construct. In J. M. SHLIEN (Ed.), *Research in psychotherapy, Vol. III.* Washington: American Psychological Association, 1968. Pp. 90–102.

LANG, P. J., LAZOVIK, A. D., and REYNOLDS, D. J. Desensitization, suggestibility and pseudo-therapy. *Journal of Abnormal Psychology*, 1965, **70,** 395–402.

LONDON, P. *The modes and morals of psychotherapy.* New York: Holt, Rinehart & Winston, 1964.

LOVAAS, O. I. Some studies on the treatment of childhood schizophrenia. In J. M. SHLIEN (Ed.), *Research in psychotherapy, Vol. III.* Washington: American Psychological Association, 1968. Pp. 103–21.

McNAIR, D. M., LORR, M., and CALLAHAN, D. M. Patient and therapist influences on quitting psychotherapy. *Journal of Consulting Psychology*, 1963, **27,** 10–17.

MENDELSOHN, G. A., and GELLER, M. H. Structure of client attitudes toward counseling and their relation to client-counselor similarity. *Journal of Consulting Psychology*, 1965, **29,** 63–72.

MENNINGER, K. *Theory of psychoanalytic technique.* New York: Basic Books, 1958.

MORENO, J. L. *Psychodrama.* Boston: Beacon Press, 1946.

PAUL, G. L. *Insight versus desensitization.* Stanford: Stanford University Press, 1966.

RACHMAN, S., and EYSENCK, H. J. Reply to a "critique and reformulation" of behavior therapy. *Psychological Bulletin*, 1966, **65,** 165–69.

RICE, LAURA N. Therapist's style of participation and case outcome. *Journal of Consulting Psychology*, 1965, **29,** 155–60.

ROGERS, C. R. A theory of therapy, personality, and interpersonal relationships, as developed in the client-centered framework. In S. KOCH (Ed.), *Psychology: A study of a science,* Vol. 3. New York: McGraw-Hill, 1959. Pp. 184–256.

ROGERS, C. R. Psychotherapy today or where do we go from here? *American Journal of Psychotherapy*, 1963, **17,** 5–16.

ROGERS, C. R., GENDLIN, E. T., KIESLER, D. J. and TRUAX, C. B. (Eds.). *The therapeutic relationship and its impact: A study of psychotherapy with schizophrenics.* Madison, Wis.: University of Wisconsin Press, 1967.

ROGERS, C. R., and SKINNER, B. F. Some issues concerning the control of human behavior: A symposium. *Science*, 1956, **124**, 1057–66.

SAPOLSKY, A. Relationship between patient-doctor compatibility, mutual perception, and outcome of treatment. *Journal of Abnormal Psychology*, 1965, **70**, 70–76.

SCHUTZ, W. C. *Firo: A three-dimensional theory of interpersonal behavior*. New York: Holt, Rinehart & Winston, 1958.

STIEPER, D. R., and WIENER, D. N. The problem of interminability in out-patient psychotherapy. *Journal of Consulting Psychology*, 1959, **23**, 237–42.

TARACHOW, S. *An introduction to psychotherapy*. New York: International Universities Press, 1963.

THIBAUT, J. The motivational effects of social dependence on a powerful agency of control. In W. W. COOPER, H. J. LEAVITT, and M. W. SHELLY (Eds.), *New perspectives in organization research*. New York: Wiley, 1964. Pp. 87–96.

TRUAX, C. B. Reinforcement and nonreinforcement in Rogerian psychotherapy. *Journal of Abnormal Psychology*, 1966, **71**, 1–9.

WOLPE, J. *Psychotherapy by reciprocal inhibition*. Stanford: Stanford University Press, 1958.

WOLPE, J. Behavior therapy in complex neurotic states. In J. M. SHLIEN (Ed.), *Research in psychotherapy, Vol. III*. Washington: American Psychological Association, 1968. Pp. 130–39.

WOLPE, J., SALTER, A., and REYNA, L. J. (Eds.), *The conditioning therapies*. New York: Holt, Rinehart & Winston, 1964.

Name Index

Subject Index